Principles of a Free Society

By

Nathanael Smith

Senior Research Fellow
The Locke Institute
and
Department of Economics
George Mason University

Email address: nathan_smith@ksg03.harvard.edu

The Locke Institute © 2010

First published in the United States in 2010 by
The Locke Institute
5188 Dungannon Road
Fairfax, Virginia 22030
www.thelockeinstitute.org

The mission of The Locke Institute is to promote the principles of limited government, individual liberty, private property, and the rule of law.

ISBN 978-0-615-42034-9

Printed and bound in the United States by
Fairfax Printing
E-mail: printers@cox.net

CONTENTS

Acknowledgements

Since this book began in a series of scintillating personal debates, the first people to thank are my interlocutors in those arguments, of whom the chief were my father, Steven Douglas Smith, sister, Rachel Smith, mother, Merina Smith, and friends Nathan Powell and Thomas Reasoner. Next and most importantly, I owe a debt of gratitude to Charles Rowley, my co-author of one academic article and the book *Economic Contractions in the United States: A Failure of Government*, published in 2009, and the Locke Institute. Though Dr. Rowley is not one to shrink from controversy, I must nonetheless credit his courage in publishing this rather dangerous little volume. I was pleasantly surprised to discover that he agreed with me on more points than I expected, though not on all. I would like to thank Nick Schulz, formerly editor of *Tech Central Station*, who published some of these ideas at that online magazine a few years ago; Tom Palmer, whose courses on the history of liberty at the Cato Institute were an invaluable introduction to the history of (classical) liberal thought; and Lant Pritchett, my old professor at Harvard and a fellow enthusiast for migration as a means to economic development. Lastly, I am grateful to Seth Vitrano-Wilson, a friend of many years, for his close reading and encouraging and thoughtful comments. (I took most of his advice, though not his suggestion to drop Chapter 6.)

About The Author

Nathanael Smith

Nathanael Smith, 32, was raised mostly in the vicinity of Boulder, Colorado, received a Bachelor's in History and Economics from Notre Dame in 2001, then earned a Masters of Public Administration in International Development at the Kennedy School of Government at Harvard in 2003. In spite of that, after three years at the World Bank and one at the Cato Institute, he felt he needed to learn more, and is now a PhD candidate at George Mason University, with a specialization in the fields of public choice and international development. He is a Senior Research Fellow at The Locke Institute, while also working full time for the InterMedia Survey Institute in Washington, D.C. He has traveled extensively and worked (paid or unpaid) in Russia, Tajikistan, Azerbaijan, and Malawi, as well as the United States, and is fluent in Russian. A romance in Russia beginning in 2002 led to a brief, unhappy marriage in 2005-06, which, however, had one happy side-effect: an introduction to the Russian Orthodox Church. Raised as a Mormon, Nathanael was baptized as an Orthodox Christian in 2006, and is now a member of the parish of St. John the Baptist Russian Orthodox Cathedral in Washington, D.C. He is the author of several reports for the World Bank, many articles at the online magazine *Tech Central Station*, the blog freethinker.typepad.com, a book, with Ritva Reinikka, on "Public Expenditure Tracking Surveys in Education" published by UNESCO in 2003 (available online) and (with Dr. Rowley) *Economic Contractions in the United States: A Failure of Government* (also available through the Locke Institute).

Dedication

The book is dedicated to all those who, in a country that pays lip service to the idea that "all men are created equal," are denied the right to work, or threatened with deportation and separation from their families, for no other reason than their place of birth, though all they ask is to be left in peace as they seek to support themselves and their families through honest labor. In the hope that the violence may cease.

Introduction: Epistemology, or how to read this book

This treatise is for the most part a fairly conventional defense of the principles of a free society, similar to what any conservative or libertarian intellectual might have written. But it contains one surprise: open borders.

I write as a rationalist and as a spokesman for tradition. Do you think that these aims are inconsistent? But the rationalist project of building human knowledge on indubitable propositions like "I think, therefore I am" is too big to accomplish in a single human lifespan, and we need to be able to rely on others, and to accept what is "handed down," or in Latin *traditus*, whence the word "tradition," to make progress. Even within a rationalist's own mind, it is impossible to hold an extended chain of reasoning in its full entirety, and complex ideas must be thought through in pieces, accepting at each stage what is "handed down" from the last. By the same token, anyone who seriously studies tradition will find that it is full of disagreements, tensions, conflicts and contradictions, and that his own intuition, experience, and reason must reconcile or arbitrate among them. A good rationalist must be a traditionalist and vice versa. To speak for tradition is not to be in favor of the *status quo*. The very word "*radical*," in Latin radicalis, means "of or having roots."

My exposition is light on facts and figures and emphasizes argument and what might be called *analytical history*, a search for the large trends and patterns in history, and for the historical origins of contemporary concepts and institutions. I anticipate that some readers may be bewildered by my seeming inconsistency in making subtle and laborious arguments for some uncontroversial claims, then taking definite stands on hotly debated issues, without offering any defense, as if I am unaware that there has been any dispute about them. There is method in this madness. My goal here is to *communicate* a position,[1] not rigor-

---

[1] The word "position" here is a placeholder for a more precise word that has, unfortunately, become politically incorrect: *ideology*. An ideology or "study in ideas" (from Greek) is any systematic effort to think through the most important facts and values pertaining to man and society. Unfortunately, in recent years some pundits and writers, who found it distasteful to engage the Bush administration on the plane of argument, have developed a habit of calling themselves "the reality-based community," contrasting themselves with the "ideology" of the Bush administration, as if it were possible to perceive reality without the intermediation of ideas. The word *ideology* needs to be rehabilitated, but in the meantime, I will avoid the word.

ously to prove it from indubitable foundations. I will have succeeded if readers *understand* that position, even if they are unwilling (for the moment) to accept it. I have not tried to muster compelling arguments where I think a mere assertion will be adequately understood. On the other hand, many seemingly obvious terms and propositions, which are accepted habitually and uncritically, are more complex than they appear, and/or are related to each other in non-obvious ways, and must be unpacked and interpreted, or in some cases reinterpreted and dissociated from certain errors, before they can find their proper place in the principles of a free society. Arguing for truisms may seem silly, yet it can lead to exciting discoveries. For example, the concept of a *state* requires the concept of *violence* of which it is characteristic of the state to claim to be the sole legitimate practitioner, and that in turn requires the concept of *natural rights*, else what is the violence violating? I trust that each reader will take my method into account, and not to drop the book at the first claim with which they disagree, and which I fail to prove, but rather bear with me, and try to assimilate the argument as a whole, before forming a judgment.

Some parts of this essay could have been written better by a trained lawyer, which I am not. My training, instead, is in economics. Now, there are many "economic imperialists" who have "colonized" the turf of other fields by studying a new subject-matter using the peculiar economics paradigm of methodological individualism and constrained maximization. I am not one of those. My point of departure is a concept in which some lawyers believe but which most economists will find strange: *natural law* or *natural rights*. I have been led to appreciate the validity of this concept by studying economics *and seeing the limitations* of its approach to understanding human nature and behavior. One cannot think clearly and constructively about the way economies work without making assumptions, explicit or tacit, about morality and governance, and one cannot think clearly and constructively about morality and governance without thinking about natural rights. There will be occasions, however, when the economist's mental toolkit will come in handy.

To attempt to acknowledge all the thinkers to whom I am indebted for the ideas offered here would require more pages than I would want to impose on the reader, but there is one thinker in particular whom I have emulated. John Locke's thought articulated the ideals of the order that emerged from the 1688 Glorious Revolution in England, then went on to inspire the 1776 Revolution in America—the famous words that open the Declaration of Independence were channeling Locke—and thus laid the foundations for the great liberal polities that have been the model, bastion, and champion of liberty for the past three centuries. He served as a bridge across the turbulent waters of Cartesian skepticism, by which the natural law tradition of the High Middle Ages passed into English common sense and thence to the world. That said, Locke's practical bent and deference to common sense sometimes led him to neglect lines of inquiry that became important later. This book seeks to complement Locke's *Second Treatise of Government*, to follow the radical tradition of Locke, while yet speaking to the present day.

1

Habeas Corpus

A human being is mind and body. The body has a particular *telos*, or peculiar flourishing, of which we have some natural understanding. Thus, we see the difference between a healthy body and a body wounded, injured, decrepit, or sick, though it would probably be impossible mathematically to define the difference in microphysical terms. To flourish, the body must have food, water and air; must not be subjected to cold or heat too extreme or for too long; must not be pierced by sharp objects or crushed by heavy blows; must not be exposed to certain substances, certain types of radiation, certain intensities of sound; must be allowed a certain degree of movement and a certain amount of sleep; should not spend too much time in water or darkness; and so forth. Each body is naturally subject to one human mind. To be subject to that mind is part of the body's *telos*. The means by which the body can be subjected to the power of other human minds—it can be beaten, wounded, dragged in chains, and so on—trespass against or violate the body's *telos*. The body should belong to its natural possessor.

I will call this the *habeas corpus* principle. In doing so, I am taking some liberties with a venerable phrase from the English common law, yet faithfully capturing, I think, both its strict semantic sense and its highest historical significance. *Habere* means (in Latin) "to have," *corpus* is "body," and *habeas* is the second-person subjunctive of *habere*, giving the phrase an intentional or normative connotation. "You should have the body" is one way to translate the phrase. A writ of *habeas corpus*, in the common law, is a petition against wrongful detention of an individual. Dating back to England's Magna Carta of 1215, and later reinforced by the Habeas Corpus Acts in 17th-century England, the legal principle of *habeas corpus*, which prohibits arbitrary detention, has long been central to English liberty, and by extension to American liberty. The "you" in *habeas corpus* refers, in a legal context, not to the individual, but to a magistrate whom the sovereign has ordered to "produce the body" to stand trial. But since, for the subject, what this meant was that he could not be arrested without being charged of a particular crime, nor imprisoned indefinitely without being tried for that crime, the effect of *habeas corpus* was that that English subjects "had [their own] bodies." It was in this institutional context that John Locke formulated the principle of self-ownership, that people own themselves. They "have the body," *habeunt corpus*.

Violence

Violence may be defined as any violation of the *habeas corpus* principle, when person A trespasses on the body of person B. A crudely spatial notion of violence, as an action trespassing on the physical space occupied by someone else's body, is sufficient to capture most of the actions that are usually and properly considered violent: blows, stabs, pistol shots, seizure and abduction, etc. But the concept of violence must be extended beyond these simple cases, as is clear if we consider Edgar Allen Poe's short story "The Cask of Amontillado." In this story, a secret enemy of one *Fortunato* lures him into a hollow place and builds a wall of masonry behind him, trapping him. There is no trespass on the physical space occupied by *Fortunato's* body, yet he is deprived of liberty and, in due course, of life, by the deliberate action of another. It would be absurd to define violence too narrowly to include this situation.

We must recognize, then, that the spatial needs of the body extend beyond the space that it physically occupies at any given time. *Habeas corpus* implies some degree of freedom of movement, but how much? A prison cell is too little. But we cannot grant to every man a right complete freedom to go wherever his legs will carry him, if for no other reason than that the sustenance of modern human populations requires the practice of agriculture, and crops must not be trampled underfoot. To the question, "how much freedom of movement does a person have a right to?" the answer "more than a prison cell but less than the whole face of the earth" is a start, but is obviously insufficiently specific.

We may invoke the concept of *telos* again as a placeholder for further discussion in **Chapter 4**. The body cannot, without violence, be spatially confined by the action of another so as to deny it the ability to flourish. This is vague, but I can propose at least one regime which is not consistent with the principle, namely, a certain kind of libertarian utopia in which all land is privately held. In this hypothetical society, a person's neighbors might box him in, denying him the right to leave his land in any direction; or a person might sell his land and not have the right to exist anywhere. I claim that such a society would violate the *habeas corpus* principle. A person "has the body" by natural right; has a right for that body to exist in some *place* as it necessarily must; has a right to enough freedom of movement to fulfill the body's needs; and is deprived of these rights if he can be excluded from all bits of land, or compelled to remain in a piece of land arbitrarily small and perhaps inadequate to sustain human life. A regime of private property rights in land cannot justly be made so comprehensive that the basic rights of *habeas corpus* are violated.

Coercion

Coercion is a broader concept than violence because it includes both violence and the effective use of *threats* of violence to induce (or prevent) certain actions. These threats may never be carried out because the threat successfully induces (or prevents) the desired (or forbidden) action. The Internal Revenue Service is a coercive, but not a violent, institution. If the state has a monopoly of legitimate violence, the state also has a monopoly of legitimate coercion, since only the state can legitimately threaten violence.

War, peace, and civil society

If *habeas corpus* defines (by inversion) violence, it also defines *war*, which is a social situation (*social* = involving the interaction of persons) in which violence is endemic. If war is a social situation, it is convenient to define *peace*, too, as a social situation, specifically one in which violence is *not* endemic. Should we define peace as a social situation in which *coercion*, too, is not endemic? No, that is going too far: even the world's freest societies rely at least to some extent on the threat of violence to maintain order. When people live together peacefully they may be called a "city," and the phrase "civil society" from the Latin word *civis* or "citizen," may be introduced as a synonym for peace (or peaceful coexistence).

Rights

From the natural facts about the body that are affirmed in the *habeas corpus* principle—natural facts which, however, transcend mere physical description—we can derive the idea of "natural rights" or "natural liberty." I do not think a free society is possible without some concept of rights. Yet from a certain modern point of view, rights may seem to be ontologically odd. Certainly one would not expect to be able to offer a micro-physical description of what a right is.[2]

Our natural and humane reaction to all violations of *habeas corpus*, i.e., to all unprovoked violence, is a place to begin in understanding rights. We react to the violent death, or to the maiming or beating, of innocent people, with a horror and disgust that is qualitatively different from our reaction to events that may plausibly be equally damaging from a utilitarian point of view, e.g., the destruction of a crop by a hailstorm, or the wrecking of an expensive piece of machinery through an accident. This reflects our perception that *rights have been violated* in the former but not the latter cases.

Rights are practically important because rights considerations override utilitarian considerations. If I believe that there is a 20% chance that Person A, whose pyromaniac tendencies are getting worse every day, will burn down the city, I cannot decide, on the basis of a cost-benefit analysis, to kill him. Yet we probably cannot say that rights should *never* be violated, because there are situations in which we have no choice but to do so. To illustrate, suppose I am the engineer of a coal train whose brakes have malfunctioned. There is a fork in the

---

[2]The utilitarian philosopher Jeremy Bentham dismissed natural rights as 'nonsense on stilts.' The phrase would be a more apt description of utilitarianism, with its whimsical notion of 'utility' as a pseudo-mathematical summary of pleasure and pain. Since Bentham's time, economists have thought rigorously about utility. They still find the concept useful. But the new, refined concept of utility, justified by the method of 'revealed preference,' possesses only ordinal, not cardinal, significance, and is not interpersonally comparable, which makes Bentham's motto, "the greatest happiness of the greatest number," meaningless. The chief desideratum in modern utility theory, 'Pareto-optimality'—a situation in which no one can be made better off without making someone else worse off—represents a partial return to the idea of rights, since it in effect places absolute value on each individual's enjoyment of a certain degree of welfare and rejects utilitarian redistribution among persons. However, the concept of Pareto-optimality leaves entirely unanswered the question of who should have which rights (or, which Pareto-optimal distribution should be chosen). One way to escape this agnosticism is to return to Locke's expedient of being attentive to our moral intuitions.

A partial rehabilitation of Benthamite utilitarianism is helpful here, so that we can appeal to utilitarianism later in the argument without seeming inconsistent. While 'revealed preference' cannot reveal, or even give any meaning to, the relative strength of utility among different individuals, humans are similar enough to one another that some intuitive judgments can be made. It seems clear, for example, that a loaf of bread gives more utility to a starving beggar than to a feasting prince. But it is a mistake to think that utilitarianism is somehow more rigorous or scientific than natural rights theory.

track. If I do nothing, the train will remain on Track A, to which fifty people are helplessly tied. I cannot stop the train, but I can switch it onto Track B, where only one person is tied up. It is possible to argue that I must never kill *by a positive action* and so ought passively to let fifty be killed, rather than actively to kill one. But it seems more plausible that I should switch the train onto Track B, that is, that I should choose the course of action which results in lesser violation of rights. This improbable scenario is more important than it seems, because it can be generalized to include the problem of the state, which characteristically violates some rights to protect others. Rights trump utilitarian considerations, but may conflict with each other.

There is no right to sustenance

One seeming ramification of the *habeas corpus* principle must be stated clearly in order to be decisively rejected. It is as follows: in order for a person to "have the body," he must provide for the body's needs. He must first of all have food, and probably also shelter, clothing and/or medical care. His right to his own body implies a right to these necessary means of sustaining it. Therefore, *habeas corpus* requires a welfare state.

The reply to this is that rights are defined not solely or principally *vis-a-vis* the state, but *vis-a-vis* all of one's fellow men. The state has an obligation not to detain me, or to beat or maim or kill me, without just cause; and all my fellow men have the same obligation. They have this obligation *not because the state imposes it on them, but by natural law.* That is to say, a person would do wrong to murder me, imprison me, or do any unprovoked violence to me, even in the absence of an effectual government, or even if the government declared murder or random violence or abduction to be legal. When it comes to respecting natural rights, the state and its agents have no special obligations, but merely the same obligations that all men have towards their fellow men. Because rights are ontologically prior to the state, we can discuss rights while postponing (until Chapter 3) the difficult task of defining what the state is, and/or of justifying a claim to special obligations or powers for the state. But the absence of a distinction between man and state means that if a person has a natural right to sustenance *from the state*, he must have the same right to sustenance *from all his fellow men.*

One reason this conclusion is unacceptable is that "ought implies can." One cannot be obligated to do something one is incapable of doing. We have seen that there are special cases in which a person cannot avoid killing another person, and this creates a problem for the theory of rights. But it is not a special case but the usual, even the universal case that a person cannot provide sustenance for all his fellow men, that is, that if all his fellow men had a right to sustenance from him, he could not avoid violating this right. Indeed, it is not clear that even modern states, with their vast resources, are capable of securing the sustenance even of all their own citizens, and if sustenance were a natural right, each state's (like each individual's) obligation to provide sustenance could not be limited to its own citizens, but would apply towards all mankind. Of course, we may have a low opinion of a person who refuses to give of his superfluity to feed a starving neighbor, but "feed the hungry" cannot be formulated as a rigid principle for human conduct like "do not kill."

Negative and positive rights

To the above argument against a right to sustenance, I will add a subtler but more fundamental argument against the right to sustenance, and in general against what may be called "positive" rights. It relates to the way the rights of others limit the scope of a person's permissible actions.

Every right of A is a limitation on the liberties of B. For example, A's right not to be punched in the face implies that B's liberty, to wave his fist in the air stops at A's nose. But this limitation is infinitesimally small relative to the set of all possible actions available to B. B can wave his fists in 99.9% of the air without hitting A's nose. In this sense, respecting the *negative* rights of others is typically consistent with (the retention of almost all of) one's own freedom.

But if A has a *positive* right to sustenance from B, B's actions are limited in a much more comprehensive way. Even if B is capable of providing sustenance for himself and A, there may be only one, or only a few, ways he can conduct himself so as to accomplish this end. Certainly, the set of actions that will achieve it is an infinitesimally small subset of the whole set of actions available to B. In this sense, negative rights, such as the right *not to* be punched, are consistent with freedom, while positive rights, such as the right *to* sustenance, are not.

Rights and liberties

Anthony de Jasay, in *Before Resorting to Politics*, makes a useful distinction between *rights and liberties*. Liberties exist, as it were, in the gap between where A's rights end and B's begin. Because A has a right not to be punched in the face, B must not wave his fists in the air where A's nose is. If B waves his fists elsewhere, he may violate no one else's rights, but it does not follow that B has a right, himself, to wave his fists around in any particular place. At most, if shadow-boxing is a form of healthful exercise, B may have a right (as part of *habeas corpus*) to do it *somewhere*. What B has is a liberty to wave his fists in 99.9% of the air. Because it is not a right, others may be able to take it away without wronging B. If B is shadow-boxing on a footbridge, A may, by passing over the footbridge, oblige him to stop, that is, take away (briefly) B's liberty to shadow-box there. If B had a *right* to shadow-box on the footbridge—for example, because he built the footbridge himself on his own land for that purpose—A has an obligation not to prevent his doing so. The distinction between rights and liberties will become important when we explore the problem of streets in **Chapter 4**.

Negative rights impose obligations on others and curtail their liberties. Positive rights, if their existence is conceded, eat up the domain of liberty entirely.

Contract: relinquishing rights

In some cases, natural rights can be voluntarily relinquished by an individual if he sees some advantage from doing so. If someone walks up to me on the street and begins punching me, that is a violation of my rights. But if I engage in boxing as a sport, my rights (and those of my opponent) are not violated, because we have voluntarily given up, for the duration of the match and vis-à-vis one other person, the right not to be punched. To that extent the right not to be punched is *alienable*; but not all rights are.

Usury, slavery, and the limits of contract

Slavery usually comes about by capture, conquest, or birth into a servile station, and slavery that originates in any of these ways is clearly contrary to natural rights. But slavery can occur by consent, too. If A is starving, and B offers him food in return for his agreeing to be B's slave, A might rationally consent to the arrangement. Also, if A plans a large entrepreneurial venture, of the success of which he is highly confident, but which cannot raise sufficient capital to finance, he might, if permitted, use *himself* as collateral, borrowing from B with the promise to become B's slave if his venture fails and he is unable to repay.

It is generally held in democracies today that a certain basic liberty is *inalienable*, so that people cannot sell themselves into slavery. Why this is right may be seen if we divide the individual self into time-slices of arbitrarily small length, in which case the question of what contracts should be regarded as valid turns into the question of what rights *present selves* should have over *future selves*. To prohibit slavery based on ex ante consent is to say that the rights of present over future selves should not be absolute and unlimited. Bankruptcy laws and laws against usury, too, are means of protecting the rights of future selves against present ones.

In the Middle Ages, there was a greater acceptance of voluntary servitude, and even in the early history of the English colonies in North America, indentured servitude, whereby someone contracted to do several years of forced labor in payment of a debt, was common. On the other hand, the Medievals prohibited "usury," by which they meant any kind of interest. We know now that the prohibition of interest is an erroneous policy based on economic ignorance: there is no reason the rate of interest on loans should always be zero. On the other hand, contemporary American laws and policies have gone too far in the other direction, permitting and even—through subsidized student loans and the mortgage-interest tax deduction—encouraging people to become heavily indebted. Excessive indebtedness encouraged by government policy was a major cause of the 2008 financial crisis and subsequent economic meltdown.

Children

That children do not enjoy the full rights of *habeas corpus* is embedded in customs and evident to reason. They lack the physical strength, the knowledge and experience, the discipline and self-control to exercise full natural rights properly. Parents routinely use coercion and even mild forms of violence—spanking, or restraining force—against recalcitrant children, and could not do without it. So, occasionally, do certain non-parents, such as teachers or baby-sitters, though typically with explicit or tacit permission from the parents. This societal authorization of parental coercion sometimes has terrible consequences in the beating or sexual exploitation of children by parents, and these horrors may symbolize the normal human condition under tyranny where arbitrary power is decoupled from benevolent instinct. But parents can usually be trusted with this authority because of their strong ties of natural affection to their children, as well as the anticipation of reciprocity later in life, ensure that they usually govern their children for the latters' benefit, while their intimate knowledge of their children makes them able to discern fairly effectively what the welfare of their children demands.

Paternalism is when government tries, or claims, to coerce adult citizens for their own good, as parents coerce children. Such paternalism is a travesty because governments possess neither the natural affection for, nor the intimate knowledge of, their citizens that parents have for their children, and so cannot be trusted to coerce citizens for their own benefit. Moreover, whereas the economic dependency of children on their parents gives their subordination partly the character of an exchange, the state (except in special cases like petro-states) is necessarily economically dependent on its citizens, making the analogy to parental authority especially inapt.

Conclusion

Habeas corpus is first of all an ethical, and only secondarily a political and legal principle. Madison wrote in *Federalist Papers No. 51* that "if men were angels, no government would be necessary." Certainly, if they were virtuous enough, people could live and work and trade together in civil society while respecting *habeas corpus*, that is, respecting one another's natural rights, in the absence of any government, that is, any agency presuming a special right to use violence. This is the condition which John Locke called a "state of nature." But men are not angels, and it is implausible that all people in general would respect each other's rights if they were not subject to the threat of violence as punishment for failing to do so.

2

Freedom of Conscience

As we distinguish between body and mind, so we may distinguish between *habeas corpus* and freedom of conscience, which together comprise the essence of freedom. In the United States, it is more common to speak of "freedom of speech" and "freedom of religion" than of freedom of conscience. But freedom of speech and freedom of religion are special cases of freedom of conscience. We may illustrate this by showing how the proper scope of the freedoms of religion and speech can only be understood in light of the more fundamental principle.

Speech, religion, and conscience

Freedom of speech does not entitle a man, with impunity, to shout "fire" in a crowded theater, to state in the presence of a professional killer that the death of one's business partner will result in a large transfer of cash to the assassin, to publish under his own name a poem written by someone else, to shout through a megaphone at night in a quiet suburban street, to lie under oath in court, or even to claim on behalf of a commercial product certain useful features which it does not in fact possess. What, then, does it entitle a man to do? It entitles him to speak his mind. It is not literally *speech* that is free, but rather, the truthful expression of one's opinions and views. This freedom is important because conscience typically compels a person truthfully to express his views. Freedom of speech is thus a special case, or an aspect, of freedom of conscience. Of course, in practice, freedom of speech must extend well beyond truthful self-expression in order to make truthful self-expression secure. We cannot, in practice, protect the right to truthful self-expression without also protecting the right to a good deal of manipulative and misleading speech, meaningless chit-chat, even to some extent slander and pornography. Yet, democracies can legislate against libel and pornography without impairing freedom, as long as these restrictions are circumspect enough that they do not impinge on conscientious free speech.

As for freedom of religion, the range of activities whose practice is protected under this principle (in the United States, for example) can be boundlessly diverse, and it is not unusual for a practice to be permitted for the sake of religion which would ordinarily be unlawful. Children may be exempted from classes or school activities, otherwise compulsory, that offend their religious scruples. Orthodox and Catholic churches may serve wine (in small quantities) to under-age persons for liturgical purposes. Amish people, out of respect for their pacifist religious scruples, are exempted from military conscription. But the principle of religious freedom by no means implies that just any activity is permitted, provided it is religious. If a group of priests decided to hold a Mass in a baseball stadium as a pretext for seeing the game without buying tickets, the fact that their activity was religious would not make it permissible. And in the case of school prayer, the activity is prohibited *because* it is religious. To see why these norms are not inconsistent one must recognize that freedom of religion, too, is a special case or aspect of freedom of conscience. Conscience requires Catholic and Orthodox Christians to serve bread and wine at liturgy to adults and children alike. To perform a Mass at a baseball game is a religious activity, but an optional one, not required by conscience (the Mass could be performed at least as conscientiously in a church). As for school prayer, it is disallowed because it may offend the conscience of a student who does not believe in God, or who does not believe in worshipping God with these particular people, or in this particular way.

Right, wrong, or indifferent: conscience and action

Conscience is the sum of a person's faculties to perceive right and wrong. To simplify somewhat, conscience divides possible actions into three classes: (a) obligatory or right, (b) forbidden or wrong, and (c) optional or indifferent. A person must do all right actions, must not do any wrong actions, and may or may not do optional actions, according to preference. To have freedom of conscience is be permitted to act in accordance with conscience, that is, not to be coerced to refrain from any right actions or to commit any wrong actions. Coercion within the domain of morally optional actions does not violate freedom of conscience. It is also not a violation of freedom of conscience when conscience and coercion are on the same side, that is, when one is forced to do what one believes is right, or to refrain from doing what one believes is wrong. It may be a violation of freedom of conscience to tax a man even a single penny to support a war he believes is unjust. It is not a violation of a man's freedom of conscience, though it is a violation of the *habeas corpus* principle, to conscript him against his will to fight and die in a war which he supports, though he would prefer to leave the fighting to others.

Conscience and contracts

Conscience affects the validity of contracts because one cannot bind oneself, *morally*, to do an immoral act. To *promise* to do something has the effect of reclassifying an optional or indifferent action as a right or obligatory action. Had I not promised to do x, x would be optional, but I promised, therefore I must do x. A promise to do a right action is laudable but in a sense irrelevant: I promised to do y, but I was morally bound to do y in any case. But if I promise to do wrong action z, my promise, which was itself a wrong action, does not make z a right action. Conscience demands, not that I fulfill, but that I repent of my promise. (I am speaking, of course, of the morality, not of the legality of contracts. The law may sometimes require a man to fulfill a contract which he has come to believe is wrong. But in such a case, he may have a duty to disobey the law and take the consequences)

Freedom of conscience, habeas corpus, and civil society

Conscience is fallible, or, if you prefer, we sometimes misunderstand it. Hardly any generalization can be made about what conscience may or may not tell a man to do. As a result, the pure principle of freedom of conscience may conflict with the *habeas corpus* principle. For example, someone's conscience might require him (or he might *think* it requires him) to wage *jihad* against the infidel. In that case (assuming the population includes infidels or potential infidels) the would-be jihadist's freedom of conscience must be curtailed if civil society is to exist at all. Whether civil society is consistent with freedom of conscience, and therefore, whether civil society is possible at all, depends on the moral beliefs of the people. For freedom of conscience is also a prerequisite for civil society. Assuming that each person obeys his conscience, people can only live together peaceably under the rule of law if what the law requires of each person is consistent with what his conscience requires of him.

Of course, if a population is sufficiently cowardly and indifferent to the demands of conscience, it may be possible for a state to compel the population to engage in wrong actions or refrain from right ones without provoking resistance and war. But the state itself must often rely on conscience, for example to make its soldiers keep fighting in its defense in the face of probable or certain death, to make its citizens obey the laws and officials fulfill their duties despite the inevitable imperfections of systems of monitoring and punishment, or to make ministers and generals submit to the Crown when they have an opportunity to seize it. Inasmuch as a population lets the state deprive them of freedom of conscience, the state must be feeble, corrupt, and unstable, the population morally degraded, contemptible, and destitute of humanity and genius.

A necessary ambiguity

To revisit the point we just made, is it really a violation of freedom of conscience if a jihadist is forbidden to wage war on the infidel? In general, does freedom of conscience consist in being allowed to do what *one thinks* is right, or what *really* is right?

Let freedom of conscience in Sense A be a situation in which a person is free to do what *he thinks* is right. Let freedom of conscience in Sense B mean that a person is free to do what *really* is right. Clearly these are different things. Ought we not to coin different words for them, and maintain a firm distinction between the two?

A striking historical example of a case where freedom of conscience in senses A and B conflicted was a dilemma faced by the early British Raj, which had to decide how to deal with the indigenous Indian institution of *suttee*, the practice of burning widows alive. Indians believed that *suttee* was right, whereas in reality it is wrong. By prohibiting *suttee*, the British Raj deprived its subjects of freedom of conscience in Sense A—it prohibited them from doing what *they thought* was right—while establishing freedom of conscience in Sense B—it gave them the freedom to do what *really was* right, specifically, the freedom for widows to do the right thing by continuing to live.

As odd as it may sound, and in spite of the *suttee* example, I think we must continue to use the phrase "freedom of conscience" ambiguously, leaving it unclear, most of the time, whether freedom of conscience in Sense A or Sense B is meant. Ultimately, freedom of conscience in Sense B is more desirable, for we want people above all to be allowed to what really is right, not anything they might mistakenly believe is right. But because the moral attitudes of the citizens of a country are often, or usually, more sound than those of the government, the best way for a government *really* to establish freedom of conscience in Sense B is for it to *aim* to establish freedom of conscience in Sense A. If it aims to establish freedom of conscience only in Sense B, it may end up compelling its subjects to commit its own moral errors. Freedom of conscience in Sense A is also, in most cases, desirable in itself, because sometimes the most effective way for people to recognize their own moral errors is to act on them and see the consequences, and to do the wrong thing may be less corrupting than to do the right thing for the wrong reason.

To this it may be objected that coercion is an important, probably an indispensable means of instilling virtue in children. But a parent usually does not coerce a child to do *what the child thinks is wrong*, but rather what the child dimly believes is right or at least regards as morally indifferent but is tempted not to do out of laziness or selfishness. Also, the coercion is almost always accompanied by persuasion, and cannot achieve its aim (the improvement of the child's character) unless the persuasion succeeds.

Is freedom of conscience reducible to habeas corpus?

The principle of Ockham's razor, of not multiplying entities unnecessarily, implies that we ought, if we can, to reduce the principle of freedom of conscience to that of *habeas corpus*. Can we? No, for two reasons. First, *habeas corpus* is alienable, as the example of boxing for sport shows, while freedom of conscience is *inalienable*, since any contract to do (what one believes is) wrong is invalid. Second, while *habeas corpus* involves only *negative* rights, such as the right not to be punched, freedom of conscience involves *positive* rights, such as the right to criticize the King. If I am forbidden to criticize the King, that is a very small reduction in the range of permissible actions available to me; but if the King needs criticizing, it is a reduction I cannot conscientiously submit to.

3

State and Social Contract

—Steal a little and they throw you in jail; steal a lot and they make you king. – Bob Dylan, "Sweetheart Like You"

The Dylan epigram of this chapter is a terse summary of much of the political history of mankind, as well as of the political philosophy of Thomas Hobbes, who, in preparing the ground for his peculiar version of social contract theory, argued that

> Covenants entered into by fear... are obligatory. For example, if I Covenant to pay a ransom, or service for my life, to an enemy; I am bound by it. For it is a Contract, wherein one receives the benefit of life; the other is to receive money, or service for it... If I be forced to redeem myself from a thief by promising him money, I am bound to pay it. (Hobbes, *Leviathan*)

If this argument is acceptable, just government can originate when any conqueror's offer of servitude or death is accepted by an abject people, an implication which Hobbes later explicitly accepts. But if there are natural rights, Hobbes' argument is not acceptable, because what the thief traded for the ransom—his victim's life—was not (justly) his to trade.

It is easy to see how *unjust* government might emerge, and conquerors from Alexander the Great to Napoleon to Hitler furnish historical examples. The harder question is: Is *just* government possible, and if so, how? Is it possible to establish government while respecting *habeas corpus* and freedom of conscience? Is there an alternative to the sad cynicism of Dylan or the ruthless maxims of Hobbes? Yes, there is, and it is to be found in *social contract theory* as articulated, most famously, by John Locke.

The social contract: Delegating the right of retribution

Legitimate violence, which the state claims to monopolize, originates in the principle of retribution. According to the principle of retribution, persons who suffer injury are entitled to proportional retaliation[3] against the perpetrator of the injury. If all the individuals in a population consent to transfer their right of retribution to a single agency, agreeing to give up private revenge, a state with a monopoly of legitimate violence is established by social contract. But though the idea of revenge, retribution, or retaliation is familiar enough, people today may be reluctant to concede that retribution is a valid motive for action. If it is not, this justification for legitimate violence fails.

I think there are three main reasons for this reluctance to accept the validity of retribution. First, the citizens of a state must typically relinquish the rights of private revenge, after which the impulse of private revenge becomes illegal and a source of disorder and crime. Second, Jesus Christ taught an ethic which transcended retribution: "You have heard that it was said: 'An eye for an eye, and a tooth for a tooth.'... But I say unto you... do good to those who hate you, and pray for those who despitefully use you." (Matthew 5: 38, 44) Third, from a utilitarian perspective, revenge *per se* is indefensible, as it typically cannot mitigate the harms from crime—murder victims cannot be revived, rape cannot be reversed—but only adds to them by imposing fresh harms on the perpetrators.

We may reject the principle of retribution but justify the punishment of criminals on other grounds, such as *rehabilitation* or moral reformation, *deterrence* of crimes by others who are induced to fear punishment, or *prevention* of further crimes by those whose criminal propensities have already been displayed in criminal acts. But while rehabilitation, deterrence, and prevention may be secondary objectives of punishment, they cannot be accepted as the sole or primary motives for punishment, because only retribution can make punishment *just*.

To see why this is the case, observe that punishment for purposes of rehabilitation, deterrence, and prevention might, in special cases, quite reasonably be applied *against the innocent*. A person who has committed no crimes but has serious character flaws might be no less appropriate a subject of government-imposed moral reformation, i.e., rehabilitation, than a convicted criminal. Preventive incarceration might be applied *before* any crime is committed, to persons whose demographic profile and/or material and emotional state makes crime likely, in order to lower crime rates for the public good. And if A committed a

---

[3] In asserting that retaliation must be proportional I am following the Biblical (Old Testament) principle of "an eye for an eye, a tooth for a tooth" (Exodus 21:24). Locke, however, seems not to accept the principle of proportionality, endorsing unlimited punishment for any crime.

murder but the public is incorrigibly convinced that the culprit is B, it might be a more effective prevention measure to punish B than A.

Even if punishment is restricted to the guilty, deterrence, prevention, or rehabilitation might motivate punishment out of all proportion to the crime— executing pickpockets, for example. While others motives may legitimately affect penal policies within the framework defined by retribution, we must accept retribution as the indispensable justification for punishment, without which no punishment at all is just, in order to justify punishing only the criminal, and in a properly limited way.

As for the other objections to retribution, to use Jesus's teaching as a justification for rejecting retribution as a motive for punishment by the state is to risk inconsistency, since Jesus also taught, in the same sermon, "turn the other cheek" and "do not resist the wicked man," teachings apparently inconsistent with any kind of state, a position few wish to adopt. (We will revisit Jesus's teachings about the state in **Chapter 10**.)

And if the prohibition of private revenge in civil society is interpreted as delegation of these rights to the state, the prior existence of a right to revenge injuries is presupposed. We assert, then, that a right of retribution exists in natural law. The connotations of the word "justice" provide semantic evidence in favor of this conclusion. Clearly, (a) to refer to the act of avenging an injury as "justice" is an appropriate and even the most typical use of that word; and (b) justice is regarded as a good thing.

If the right of retribution is accepted, the transfer of this right to a state is not especially problematic. The right to defend or avenge an injured person is not limited to the injured person him- or herself, but may justly be carried out on his behalf by another. It may also be voluntarily waived by the injured person. So it is consistent with justice and natural rights for a group of people generically to waive the right to avenge injuries against themselves, but at the same time to authorize another agency, the state, to exercise this right on their behalf. If everyone in a given population agrees to this social contract, a state with a monopoly of legitimate violence (and coercion) has been justly established.

The historicity of the social contract

I used to wonder how citizens of the Soviet Union reconciled in their minds the facts that, although their official ideology held that property is theft, they still owned things and used money. Later, I realized that a similar revolutionary hypocrisy exists in America. Americans like to quote approvingly the *credo* from the Declaration of Independence that "governments... derive their just powers from the consent of the governed," as if that legitimized our revolution and explained our form of government. Yet in fact, neither the government nor any representative thereof has ever asked me, or anyone I know, whether we wish to be ruled by the federal government in Washington, D.C. or not. When did consent of the governed occur?

If citizens of the United States never explicitly agreed to be subject to the federal government in Washington, D.C., did they do so tacitly? This might be plausible under Hobbes' theory, according to which contracts extorted by fear are valid, for citizens actually do find themselves under a threat of punishment if they violate the law, and do typically respond by obeying most laws most of the time, including those laws they would otherwise prefer not to obey. But if people have natural rights, the state's power cannot be justified by the fact that people submit to its rule from fear.

That government *could* justly be established through a social contract would seem to have limited relevance, unless such a social contract has actually occurred, *in history*. Has it? One famous event that seems on the surface to be an instance of state formation through social contract, on closer inspection, is not. Even when it was first established, the U.S. Constitution was formed through an agreement among *states* rather than individuals. Most of the states had originated in royal charters, thus deriving their authority from a non-consensual source, and of course, slavery was practiced in most of them at the time the Constitution was signed, further invalidating their claim to enjoy consent of the governed. Massachusetts' origins may (arguably) be traced to the Mayflower Compact, possibly the purest example that history affords of the establishment of a state through an explicit social contract. But even the Mayflower Compact was signed, on November 11, 1620, by only forty-one of more than a hundred passengers on the *Mayflower*.

What may cause us to *under*estimate the historicity of the social contract is that John Locke and Thomas Jefferson both insisted on combining the social contract doctrine with an emphasis on *equality*. Equality may be a desirable feature of a social contract. It is not a necessary one. A stylized account of the origins of feudalism is that peasants sought the protection of knights against Norse invaders, and offered labor services on the knights' lands in return. This is a social contract, albeit an unequal one. That the term *feudalism* is derived from the Latin *foedus*, meaning a compact, covenant or agreement is a semantic reminder that the feudal order of medieval society was based, in principle, on social contracts, mostly of a vertical rather than a horizontal character. It is striking etymological evidence for the generality of the notion of consensual government that *feudalism* and *federalism* are derived from the same Latin word.

Even today, the House of Lords is a fading vestige of the feudal origins of English constitutionalism.

To argue that much of the political order of modern European civilization, and its overseas offshoots in North America and Australia, has its origins in a feudal social contract which was later reorganized on an egalitarian basis, is too large a task to undertake here. In any case, it would seem strange that half-forgotten historical events in the early Middle Ages could be an important factor in the legitimacy of a modern government. And this leads us to the most serious problem with social contract theories of government: the problem of *succeeding generations.* Even if the Mayflower Compact was a binding social contract for those who signed it, there were children on the Mayflower too young validly to consent, and soon there were children who could not have consented to the Compact because they were not born when it was signed.

A social contract can be written so as to make it extendable to persons who were not signatories of the original contract. Persons A, B, and C might undertake mutual obligations x, y, and z to one another *and* to any others who agree to these mutual obligations. If D then agrees to the obligations, no fresh consent from A, B, and C is needed to make D a full member, for the original social contract already covered this contingency. This suggests one way of solving the problem of succeeding generations: children born into polities thus governed will be regarded as exempt from the positive laws enacted by the polity (not from natural law) until such time as they are old enough validly to consent to the obligations of membership in it, receiving in return the rights associated with this membership. No society seems to have attempted this kind of political arrangement, however.

Of social orders based on the principle of adult consent, history may provide one example in the Christian monastic orders, which, though not polities in the sense of claiming a monopoly of legitimate violence, provide a comprehensive framework for the life of their members, and which have endured for centuries by recruiting adult members willing to submit to their rules. But the fact that one of the rules of the monastic orders is *celibacy* underlines the difficulty of the problem of succeeding generations. Monks only avoid the problem of incorporating children into the social contract by not having them.

So while the concept of a social contract is by no means destitute of historicity, it is doubtful whether any polity in the history of the world, and in particular whether any modern polity, can truly claim to "derive its... powers from the consent of the governed." And an examination of *free-rider problems* casts doubt on whether any government ever could.

Public goods and the free rider problem

Many or most of the core functions performed by governments are often characterized, rightly or wrongly, as the provision of *public goods*. Economists define *public goods* as goods which are "non-rival" and "non-excludable." National defense is the paradigm case. It is non-rival, because no one's enjoyment of freedom from foreign invasion impedes anyone else's enjoyment of it. It is non-excludable, because if foreign invasion is prevented, every citizen benefits from its absence, even if some citizens refused to pay. Even this example can be challenged. For one thing, if part of the population prefers the foreign invader to the national government, national defense is not a good at all for them.[4]

Which other categories of goods are public, and hence have a claim on public subsidies, is controversial. The prevention of contagious diseases is a public good but "public health" in general is probably not. Roads are often called public goods, but traffic jams prove that roads can be rival goods, and toll roads, that they can be excludable. Education's claim to be a public good is tenuous: it has large private returns, while the existence of social returns to education in excess of private returns is difficult to establish. Even in the case of a *bona fide* public good, public provision does not solve all the problems. For one thing, *how much* of the good should the government supply or subsidize? Also, the government may not be very efficient in supplying it. Some public goods might more effectively supplied if they are left to the voluntary sector.

In theory, a government could get the public's consent through a unanimous public goods auction.[5] The abstract concept of an ideal public goods auction provides a basis, in principle, for conceiving the conditions in which individuals *would rationally consent* to pay for the public goods provided by the government *if* they could be required to purchase the public good individually rather than having an opportunity to free-ride. In this case, coercion could be

---

[4] When national "defense" budgets finance wars overseas that a substantial part of the population opposes, the argument for national defense as a public good becomes still more tenuous.

[5] This would work as follows. First, the government sets a price for each citizen of the public goods it provides. Then it makes a credible once-for-all offer to provide them only if every citizen consents to pay. If the benefits from the public good exceed the costs of providing it, there will be some set of prices such that (a) every citizen would rationally (and self-interestedly) consent to pay the price specified and (b) the total payments would be sufficient to finance the provision of the public good. But this public-goods auction would only work if (a) the government could credibly commit never to renew or renegotiate the offer if it were rejected, and (b) all citizens were rational.

Pareto-optimal, beneficial to everyone. We can call this justification for public goods provision a social contract by "presumed consent." A government that implemented this public goods policy would violate the rights of its subjects without, on balance, harming them.

Is this a legitimate move? Since we said earlier that "rights trump utility," and since the coercive financing of public goods is still a violation of rights even when the policy is Pareto-superior to the alternative, it may seem that we are compelled to reject the argument at once. But of course, not only utility but *rights* are at stake when citizens are coerced to support national defense, rather than letting the free-rider problem expose the country to a foreign conquest which would surely result in violations of natural rights on a large scale. This brings us back to the train tracks problem from **Chapter 1**, with the state in the role of the driver of the train, pulling the lever of coercive taxation to steer away from the track of foreign invasion.

What makes the problem more urgent is that the argument can be generalized from national defense to the ordinary enforcement of laws by the police. The jailing of criminals, too, at least in its removal, if not in its incarceration aspect, is a "non-rival" and "non-excludable" good, which would be under-supplied if it were paid for on a subscription basis.

Is it lawful to violate rights to protect rights?

The legitimacy of government, then, appears to depend on the principle that it is acceptable to violate rights in order to protect rights; yet this principle is clearly very dangerous. Any member of the *Cheka* or the *Gestapo* could claim that all his acts of torture and murder were means to prevent "imperialist aggression"— that is, that he is violating rights to protect rights. If we want to curtail this dangerous principle, how can we do so?

First, a vague but plausible idea that there are different "orders" of rights may be introduced. We may assert that the violation of "lower-order" rights for the protection of "higher-order" rights may be acceptable, but that violations of rights of the same order as the rights to be protected thereby cannot be tolerated. This offers a possible solution to the national defense problem, because the rights to life and liberty which foreign invaders would violate are of a higher order than the property rights which are violated if the authorities tax citizens to pay for national defense. It does not solve the train-tracks problem, since the rights at stake—life—are the same on both sides.

Second, we may borrow from the Catholic tradition of natural law what has been called "the doctrine of double effect." According to this notion, the *intended* effect of an action may be distinguished from the *foreseen side effects* of an action. In the train tracks problem, the intention is to save the fifty people on Track A by diverting the train; the side effect is to kill the one person on Track B; since this is only a foreseen side effect, the person who does it is not guilty of killing a human being.

Ramifications

We have been only partially successful in developing a theory of government consistent with respect for natural rights. We have shown how a just government could, in principle, derive a monopoly of legitimate coercion within a specified population from the consent of each member of the population to transfer his natural right of retribution to the state. But no historic government seems to satisfy the social contractarian standard, and any attempt to establish one that does seems likely to encounter insuperable free-rider problems. We will be able to improve on this somewhat in Chapter 4, after we have studied property rights. The expedients by which we have suggested the free-rider problem might be solved—"presumed consent," and the occasional permissibility of violating rights to protect rights—open the door to tyranny.

"Government by consent of the governed" turns out to be, after all, not a practical plan, but an unattainable ideal. Yet real governments may be nearer to, or further from, that ideal. The burden of government coercion may be larger or smaller; the degree of consent by citizens, greater or less. And we can make some generalizations about what features of governments position them closer to, or further from, the consensual ideal.

Redistribution (bad)

Any policy whose objective is redistribution is *prima facie* inconsistent with a social contract based on "presumed consent." It cannot be claimed that a person *would rationally consent* to a policy which deprives them by force of some of their property to benefit others. After all, if they want to give some of their property to others, they can always donate it without waiting to be coerced.

Progressive taxation (acceptable)

However, there is no reason that the state cannot justly "price discriminate" in its provision of public goods, charging much to the rich and little or nothing to the poor, as long as the rich are not charged more than the public goods are worth to them (although measuring the value of public goods to any individual person is a serious problem). To the extent that the state generates "surplus value," it has some scope to be particularly generous to some without being unjust to others.

Social safety nets (bad)

In **Chapter 1**, we rejected the idea that a man has a natural right to sustenance from his fellow men. Now that we have developed a concept of the state, we may ask, is it the case in general, or might it be in particular cases, that citizens of a state are entitled to sustenance from the state?

The problem with incorporating a right to sustenance into the social contract is that the state's coercive powers are transferred from individuals, and natural law only permits violence in response to violence, in self-defense or for retribution. Individuals do not have the right to use violence to take sustenance from others, so they cannot transfer to the state the right to do this on their behalf. Nor can the welfare state be justified as the use of coercion to provide public goods, because a welfare check is not a public good.[6]

The idea that the state must provide subsistence to its citizens has been a tenet of leftist ideology since the French Revolution, when an uprising of the peasants was driven by actual hunger resulting from an overall scarcity of food. Today, a revolution in agricultural productivity has made it trivially easy for advanced states to avert general famine. Instead, the subsistence good that people are demanding that the state supply is *health care*.

Public debts and deficits (bad)

The existence of a public debt implies that some of a state's revenues are transferred to the holders of government bonds. Short-term public debt is morally unproblematic, because in the short run there is little change in the composition of the citizenry, so that the same citizens who must pay the debt benefited from the borrowing, that is, from having in the recent past paid lower taxes or

---

[6] Hochman and Rogers (1969) argue for the possibility of "Pareto-optimal redistribution," but it is not clear that they appreciate how special the form of the utility function has to be (not to mention homogeneous across persons) for the claim that such redistribution needs to be done coercively and cannot be mediated through private charity. I consider it implausible that any significant degree of coercive redistribution is either strictly or approximately Pareto-optimal, and will assume so here, but the argument can be carried on elsewhere if there is interest in it.

enjoyed more public spending than could otherwise have been afforded. (If the money was spent in a wasteful or harmful way, that is a different kind of problem.) Long-term public debt imposes burdens on new generations which did not consent to it because they were not born. In the best case, public debt is incurred to pay for publicly-owned durable goods, like the interstate highway system,[7] which continue to benefit the later generations that help pay for them. Even then, future generations might have a different opinion about whether the project was worth it.

A new generation which inherits a huge sovereign debt from its parents might rationally refuse to pay it. Of course, some members of that generation will inherit government bonds and so benefit from the debt, but that does nothing to mitigate or justify the burden placed on those who do not inherit bonds but only the obligation to pay for them. A state apparatus which compels, by force, the new generation to pay the debts incurred by its parents may be guilty of injustice. In short, public debt tends to undermine the legitimacy of the social contract.

Does this imply that the United States, for example, ought to pass a constitutional amendment requiring a balanced budget? While that might help protect the social contract in the long run, most macroeconomists think it is useful for the government to run deficits in times of recession or depression. If this is true, a balanced budget amendment would have to be carefully designed in order to protect future generations from inheriting excessive debt without paying a high price in the form of a lower quality of macroeconomic management. In principle, though, budgetary principles of intergenerational justice hardly conflict with the use of short-term deficits as a tool of macroeconomic management.

The current long-run deficit trajectory of the US government, for example, is a threat to the intergenerational social contract, without having any plausible justification as a means of managing the macroeconomy. Future generations will be under legal compulsion but will have little or no moral obligation to pay the bills for excess government spending by today's irresponsible politicians.

Federalism / voting-with-the-feet (good)

If there are many similar jurisdictions and individuals enjoy free mobility among

---

[7] I have not called the interstate highway system a "public good" because it does not seem to meet the criteria. Highways are excludable, and sometimes rival.

them, the consensual nature of the government is enhanced. Individuals have the option of "voting with the feet," and in moving to a new jurisdiction, or even to a lesser extent in staying in the one they were born in when they had the option of moving, they indicate a certain degree of consent to the government they live under, and they are likely to be conscious of this. Governments that provide an attractive mix of public goods will attract new citizens, while ineffectual or oppressive governments will lose them.

The American tradition of federalism, wherein state and city governments exist side by side in a setting of internal freedom of migration, is an important part of America's heritage of freedom and makes America's claim that its constitution embodies "government by consent of the governed" much less spurious than it would be otherwise.

The world was a freer place in the decades before 1914 than it is today, because there was more freedom of migration, and millions voted-with-the-feet to live under the free institutions of the United States rather than those of, for example, Wilhelmine Germany, or Tsarist Russia, though those polities, too, were freer than their Nazi or Soviet successors.

Tolerance of individual secession (good)

The state may, with some justification, insist that the wealthy and prosperous citizens whose property rights it protects would rationally consent to pay for its services rather than lose them, even if they would prefer to free-ride. But there are others who choose ways of life that really do minimize their need for the state, and whose claims that they would prefer not to be subject to it, even at the cost of forfeiting its benefits, are compelling. In ancient times, hermits and monastics fled into deserts and wild places to escape a society they saw as hopelessly corrupt. Similarly, in our times, the Amish endure great sacrifices of personal freedom and modern technological convenience in order to maintain a way of life that does not entangle them in what they see as the moral compromises of the surrounding society, in particular its violent propensities.

Of course, it is not possible for the Amish to avoid benefiting from the protection which the US military provides to the entire North American continent. But the Amish credibly signal, by their way of life, that they do not merely wish to free-ride on the American social contract, but really desire not to be the beneficiaries of anyone's violence.

A consensual government should tolerate or accommodate this kind of nonviolent individual or group secession. How best to do so depends on particulars, such as why the group wants to secede, and what its way of life is. If it is convenient for the government to classify such persons as citizens, and if they have no objection to being so classified, it might be appropriate to formalize their membership of the community in this way while exempting them from conscription, compulsory education, specific regulations and taxes, and so on. But to the extent that persons or groups make good-faith efforts to minimize free-riding, the state should be ready to accept the existence of effective non-members in its midst.

Elections (good but no panacea, and useless without strong protection of rights)

Elections and equality are closely associated with consensual government in the contemporary mind, but are far less essential to it than is usually supposed. First, let us review elections. Unlike the mythical social contract, elections are dramatic events, where real voters make real decisions, and where real politicians are elected into or rejected from office. Democratic accountability shapes every aspect of governance in the wealthy democracies of the West, as politicians are constantly husbanding their public support with a view to winning re-election. So it is understandable that consensual governance has come to be identified almost exclusively with regular conduct of free and fair democratic elections.

But this identification will not do. The problem with elections is that there is really no good, general reason why a minority should submit to the will of a majority. Two arguments are sometimes made. Both cannot be valid, and the fact that both are made proves that neither is valid. On the one hand, it is sometimes said that by voting, one agrees to accept the outcome of the election, even if the candidate one opposes should win. On the other hand, it is said that by *not* voting, one forfeits one's chance to change the outcome and therefore one's right to object to whatever the outcome might be.

If only one of these arguments were made, it might be valid. Social conventions can define how consent is expressed. There is no inherit metaphysical connection between signing a piece of paper and consenting to transfer a piece of property, but convention has established that connection. Similarly, society could legitimately establish a principle *either* that the act of voting *or* (maybe) that the act of not voting was a signal of consent to accept the outcome of an election (perhaps with a write-in and/or "against all" option for those unable conscientiously to endorse any available candidate), provided that the other choice was clearly understood *not* to imply consent. Since society has not exempted either voters for defeated candidates, or non-voters, from duties associated with the presumption of consent, it can make no claims that elected leaders enjoy consent of the governed on the basis of voting behavior. Even those who vote for the winning candidate do not thereby bind themselves to obey that candidate once in office.

Elections are a decision-making rule for a polity already constituted. As such, they exhibit a striking contrast to market capitalism, in that they are (in all contemporary democracies) far more egalitarian—one person, one vote— but also a striking *similarity* to market capitalism, in that they institutionalize *competition* in the political sphere. Political "entrepreneurs" have an incentive to develop innovative new packages of policies and increase their "market share" of the electorate. Consequently, electoral democracy galvanizes civil society and unleashes energies that can make democracy a dangerous form of government in the absence of a strong institutional and cultural framework for protecting natural rights.

Without freedom, democracy self-destructs: which is why viable democracy is a *symptom* of—not a synonym for—freedom in the contemporary world. The Nazi regime in Germany, the Soviet regime in Russia, the Fascist regime in Italy, among others, came to power after interludes of electoral competition. Elections exacerbated inter-ethnic tensions in Yugoslavia before its bloody breakup.[8] Properly tamed, political competition may help to keep rulers humble, disrupt corruption, make governance relatively transparent and honest, and/or prevent class stratification. But elections do not mitigate the need to presume consent to a social contract, at the expense of whatever humbug and rationalization such presumed consent involves.

It must also be borne in mind that the institutions of democracies like the United States are less comprehensively democratic than we tend to imagine. An independent judiciary, which is widely treated as an important *desideratum* for free societies, is an undemocratic institution. Judges must be appointed by someone, and in America there is no authority other than elected politicians to whom this task can be assigned; but judges are deliberately insulated from democratic accountability, and a long tradition of reliance on precedent in the common law gives the judiciary roots in traditions older than the U.S. constitution itself. The U.S. military, too, though scrupulously obedient to the civil authorities in terms of whom it fights against, has its own traditions of ritual and discipline, in which elected politicians interfere little, and usually at their peril. More recently, the deliberate insulation of the Federal Reserve System from po-

---

[8] http://en.wikipedia.org/wiki/Breakup_of_Yugoslavia. Also see chapter 7 of Spencer (1998).

litical influences bears witness to a justified lack of faith in elected leaders to conduct wise monetary policy.

Political equality (only indirectly relevant, and not essential)

It was argued above that equality is not a necessary condition of the social contract; so why is this principle such a widespread tenet of modern democracies? Does it have any connection with the consent of the governed? Yes, but weakly. One reason people may consent to a system of government, and their place in it, is that it is all they know. If everyone is politically equal, I see no one whose rights are different from my own, and it may not occur to me to wish I had a different station in life. Also, "all men are created equal" in that they enjoy the same natural rights of *habeas corpus* and freedom of conscience, if nothing else, and this rules out any class system that allows one class to violate the rights of another. But "one person, one vote" is in no way an essential condition of consensual government.

A social contract does not imply a territorial state

From the fact that a group of people has agreed to certain mutual obligations, including the delegation of their rights of self-defense and retribution to a new agency called a government, it does not follow that this government attaches to any particular geographical *territory*. The government's authority extends to a certain group of *persons*, namely, those whose assent to a social contract established that government and its powers. Territorial *limits* may be written into the social contract, if, for example, the contract stipulates that it shall have the right and duty to defend its citizens only when they are located within a certain geographical territory. But nothing in the argument so far explains why a government based on social contract should claim *exclusive* rights to a given territory.

Who guards the guards?

The Roman writer Juvenal complained that wives cannot be trusted, and it is no use guarding them, because guards cannot be trusted either, leading to the profound question: *who guards the guards?* Who polices the police? Who judges the judges? If we hire a new set of guards to guard the first set of guards, who guards *those* guards? Clearly the question points to an infinite regress. It is at least as great a problem for any social contract theory of the state, as it was for the marital relations of decadent Romans. Our fellow men, or some of them, are wicked and will violate our rights if they can; so we organize a state to protect us against them. But the state, too, may violate our rights, and who will protect us against it? Hobbes, the advocate of absolute and arbitrary government, offers an answer, that, if hardly appealing, is at least clear: no one guards the guards, the guards can do anything they like.[9] To find a better answer than Hobbes' will occupy us for the rest of this book.

---

[9] While some passages in Hobbes would support this blunt summary of his position, other passages do suggest that there are things a sovereign ought not to do, whether because of natural law or divine law (if Hobbes' talk about God can be taken seriously). Hobbes is so insistent, however, that in a state of nature/war, which according to him sovereigns are still in, every man has a right to everything, that his occasional gestures towards the possibility of moral restraint on the part of the sovereign may be taken as overridden. See Chapter 5.

4

Property Rights

We suggested earlier that the *habeas corpus* principle must include a certain degree of freedom of mobility. It is equally necessary to extend it to include some rights of use in objects external to the body. A person must eat. If another takes away everything available to him to eat, he will not "have the body" for long. To enjoy secure possession of one's body one must be able to establish rights over food, and analogously over other necessities like clothing and shelter, and means of production like land and tools, such that others cannot justly invade them, at least not in such a way as to deprive one of the use of them. In short, there must be *property rights*.

John Locke sought to define a fully-developed regime of property rights that was ontologically prior to the state. That is quixotic. Though every culture and nation recognizes property rights of some kind, there is not enough consensus about their nature and definition to provide the basis for sophisticated systems of property, unless people's innate notions and prejudice about property are shaped, guided and reinforced by the operations of a legal system. Locke's theory of the origin of just property rights—that they originate when a person "mixes his labor with" the free gifts of nature—is plausible. But specialization and trade quickly attenuate the link between labor and property, and *de facto* property rights initially established through force and fear must sometimes be accommodated later, as they have been mingled through exchange with legitimate rights rooted in labor. A fertile yet flawed marriage of Locke's deontological theory of property rights with a utilitarian theory of property rights that we may associate with the name of economist Ronald Coase underlies the property rights systems of the advanced modern states.

Property rights and legal systems

All of us, certainly in civilized societies but also to some extent in primitive ones, have some way of expressing the concepts of "mine" and "yours," identifying certain objects as possessed by certain persons. Theft, the taking of someone else's property, is a crime perhaps no less widely recognized than violence, the invasion of someone's body. Yet one's ownership of a hammer or a plot of land is not a simple natural fact in the sense that one's ownership of one's body is. Often there are plausible competing claims to ownership of an object. It becomes the task of the legal system to resolve the disputes that constantly arise over who owns what, and thus to define a distribution of objects among persons.

The legal system never defines the *entire* allocation of property. It only needs to, and can only afford to, decide property questions when conflicts emerge. For example, there is a TV in my house which I think was left there by a tenant when he moved out. I do not know whether the TV was abandoned, so that I can now claim it as my property, or whether it is still the property of the former tenant. In this case, there is no need for the legal system to intervene because, although there is an unresolved question, there is no dispute: my former tenant is not trying to claim his TV, and if he did come back to claim it, I would give it to him, since I do not really need the TV. If, however, my tenant tried to claim his TV back and I refused to give it to him on the grounds that he had abandoned it, it would be the type of question that courts need to be able to resolve. Since, in principle, the legal system should be able to resolve *any* property dispute that arises, and since its decisions should be consistent with each other, it should possess a latent ability to define a complete allocation of property among persons.

A complete allocation of property rights does not mean that every object is allocated to a unique person. Some objects—a remote Alaskan mountain; the ocean; a novel in the public domain—might belong to no one. People might also possess different rights in the same object. Thus, the landlord owns the house, that is, he is entitled to a stream of income from it and is alone entitled to bulldoze it and build another in its place; but the tenant has the right to live in it for the duration of the lease. Again, I own the books in my bookshelf, yet the publishers of those books have rights in the texts of those books which I do not have, which preclude my photocopying, reprinting, and selling those books myself.

Property rights in natural law: John Locke

Locke's argument for property rights begins with the principle of self-ownership, what we have called the *habeas corpus* principle, which he extends by saying that one's ownership of one's own labor extends to physical embodiments of one's own labor, that is, to what one produces. To this there is an obvious objection, namely that human beings cannot create anything *ex nihilo*,[10] but must use

---

[10] The Latin phrase *ex nihilo*, or 'from nothing,' is used as a theological phrase to describe the creative act of the Jewish God, who created the world out of nothing.

materials derived from the natural world. While human labor may rearrange matter into forms more useful for people, nothing (or hardly anything) is *merely* an embodiment of human labor, so the problem remains: even if it is granted that a person owns his labor, how does he establish ownership over the materials with which he works?

Locke addresses this problem, but his arguments (a) have an explicitly theological basis from which they cannot be detached, and (b) are not compelling in the light of later developments in the theory of value. Locke says, first, that the world was created by God and given to all mankind to satisfy his needs, and since it is no use to us unless we can "appropriate" bits of it from "the commons," it follows that we are entitled to do so.

Moreover, argues Locke, the value of things derives almost wholly from labor. The same acre of land deep in the wilds (when he was writing) of North America may be inherently similar, for example in the climate and the soil, to an acre of land in the midst of London, but it is not nearly as valuable. Locke claims that the difference is that more labor has been invested in the London plot of land. This is called the "labor theory of value," and although using it puts Locke in some good company—the economists Adam Smith, David Ricardo and Karl Marx all used some form of it—the theory is by now well known to be false.

This may easily be seen if we consider commodities, such as Saudi Arabian oil, which are cheap to bring to market but command high prices because of scarce (inelastic) supply and high demand. In the case of land, an acre in London would be worth more than an acre in Iowa even if it had somehow remained completely wild, because its location near a large center of population means that it has many profitable uses. If it were true that 99% of the value of land comes from the labor invested in it, it might be unproblematic to grant property rights in land to the laborer. If, on the contrary, land is scarce, either in general or in a particular place, so that uncultivated land is not a free good but has positive market value, the claims of the first-comer who appropriated it may seem to give him an unfair advantage.

One aspect of Locke's argument that seems odd today, although he put a great deal of emphasis on it, is that our God-given right to appropriate from the commons is only for purposes of *use*, not *waste*, so we can only justly appropriate what we are able to make use of (including trading it to others who can make use of it).

It will perhaps be objected to this, that if gathering the acorns, or other fruits of the earth, &c. makes a right to them, then any one may ingross as much as he will. To which I answer, Not so. The same law of nature, that does by this means give us property, does also bound that property too. God has given us all things richly, 1 Tim. vi. 12. is the voice of reason confirmed by inspiration. But how far has he given it us? To enjoy. As much as any one can make use of to any advantage of life before it spoils, so much he may by his Labour fix a property in: whatever is beyond this, is more than his share, and belongs to others. Nothing was made by God for man to spoil or destroy. (Locke, 1689, Chapter 5)

Locke's condemnation of waste here seems to contradict the "doctrine of sunk costs" taught by modern economists. For Locke, one may not "fix a property in" something in order to "spoil or destroy" it. For economists, by contrast, one should ignore the "sunk cost" of labor invested in a thing, considering only whether the benefit of using it in future is worth the cost. Don't clean your plate! If you have eaten all you want (and you know where your next meal is coming from), it is wasteful to make yourself uncomfortably full. The contradiction is illusory. Locke says that what a man cannot use *belongs to others*: that is, if you cannot eat all your dinner, you should (be ready to) give the rest to someone who can eat it. If no one wants it, it has no real value, and there is no waste in throwing it away. Locke's idea that waste is unjust will be important in our study of the problem of streets.

Property rights for efficient markets: Ronald Coase

The quintessential skill of the economist is to refute the untrained mind's impulse to call prices "unfair" and demand the introduction of price controls. Economists understand how prices reflect the way the invisible hand of the market equilibrates demand and supply, giving rise to optimal allocations without the help of government. Since the operation of markets depends on property rights that are well-defined, credible and alienable (tradable), economists can work backwards from market efficiency to make a utilitarian case for a property rights regime that satisfies these *desiderata*. But economists have no good answer to the question of who, in the initial distribution, should own what.

Ronald Coase is especially lucid about the need for firm property rights, on the one hand, and the indeterminacy of who should have them, on the other. In a famous 1960 paper called "The Problem of Social Cost," Coase deals with the problem of "externalities," as when a rancher's cattle stray into the fields of a neighboring farmer and destroy his crops. Coase argues that externalities are really a problem of ill-defined property rights, and that if *either* the rancher's right to let his cattle stray, *or* the farmer's right to be compensated for the damage done by the rancher's cattle, is firmly recognized by a court and made tradable, the market will achieve an efficient outcome. If it is more efficient to let the cattle stray, either the rancher will compensate the farmer (if the court decides in the farmer's favor) or the farmer will take the losses (if the court decides in the rancher's favor). If it is more efficient to cease cattle ranching on that particular plot of land, the rancher will do so voluntarily if the court rules against him, or the farmer will pay him to do so if the court rules in the rancher's favor. As long as property rights are defined, efficiency will be achieved.

Coase is indifferent to whether it is *just* for the farmer to be compensated for damages or not. He is only interested in efficiency, and for that, any distribution of property rights will serve, as long as they are well-defined, credible, and alienable. But how can the court make its decisions credible? How can it commit not to reverse itself? For if it cannot, actors will speculate about and plan for possible reversals, thereby destroying the efficiency of the property rights system.

The fertile yet awkward marriage of Locke and Coase

It should be understood that the names "Locke" and "Coase" are used here as labels for ways of thinking with long traditions in the common law behind them, traditions which in each case began well before these thinkers articulated (rather than invented) them. Much of the common law as regards property can be understood with the help of Locke's theory or Coase's theory or both.

There is a strange kind of practical symbiosis, and at the same time of tension, between Locke's and Coase's theories of property. Coase needs property rights to be credible. To achieve this, it is useful for there to be some *principle* about how property rights originate, though Coase does not care what that principle is. A principle of the origins of property can enable courts to be consistent and private actors to anticipate their actions, minimizing the inefficiency due to property rights that are ill-defined or lacking in credibility. Coase has no principles to offer, so he might as well borrow those of Locke. Meanwhile, Locke's case for property rights is less persuasive in light of the modern theory of value, and in modern conditions when the connection between labor and property has become extremely attenuated because of capitalism's ever-increasing division of labor. He might want to buttress it by borrowing the utilitarian argument of Coase.

Yet the philosophical differences between Locke and Coase are so large that it would be surprising if Locke's principles did not, in some cases, undermine Coase's and vice versa. Such differences might occur with respect to the justice of a government auctioning resource rents[11] to private firms (Coase would approve, Locke would object), or annulling well-established property rights whose origins are discovered not to have been just (Coase would object, Locke would—if consistent—approve). Still, Locke and Coase make a fertile if awkward marriage, a marriage which is more or less realized in the property rights systems of the United States and Great Britain.

Precedent

The common-law legal systems of the English-speaking nations place great emphasis on *precedent*. This emphasis can be readily defended in terms of either the Lockean or the Coasean theories of property rights, but in different ways. A Lockean regards property rights as *real*, having a basis in natural law. The task of the judge—and some of what is said here of judges may be cross-applied to legislators—is not to define but to *discover* the law. Precedent is to be respected, because the decisions of other judges are *evidence* of what the law is, somewhat as a scientist might appeal to the experimental findings of other scientists. For a Coasean, the arguments a judge employs are irrelevant; what matters is the judicial decision, which *creates* law. Respect for precedent is desirable (though it might sometimes be overridden if established rules imply exorbitant transactions costs that impede efficiency) because it makes court decisions predictable, which induces private agents to be productive rather than to engage in rent-seeking.

Organic metaphors in the social sciences are historically dangerous, yet one may be useful here in illuminating the transition from *discerning to creating* law, and from *natural* to *positive* property rights. In primitive, subsistence economies, the property rights of hunter-gatherers or small farmers, based on appropriation and labor, and held with a view to the direct satisfaction of basic human needs, may be described as *natural*. A judge who protects them is more likely to feel that he is merely *discerning* what is, if considered impartially, self-evidently right and just. The role of the judge himself is like that of a hunter-gatherer: he grabs hold of the obvious, he takes what he finds.

In an advanced economy with an elaborate division of labor, there may be few who own anything they have made themselves, and the allocation of property rights that emerges may seem quite artificial, and to avoid being arbitrary

---

[11] The term "rent" in economics refers to revenues in excess of costs enjoyed due to a natural or artificial (policy-related) scarcity. For example, if Saudi oil costs $5 per barrel to produce, while the world price of oil is determined by the $45 cost of producing oil somewhere else, the Saudis can sell for $45 per barrel and retain $40 per barrel in "rents."

only inasmuch as its structure is dictated by the needs of *efficiency*. A judge who decides the subtle cases resulting from contract, exchange and enterprise in such a system is likely to feel that he is exercising *discretion*. These rights may be best described as *positive* rights. Now the judge's role is more creative, and it calls for not only experience but also *forethought*, even an element of social engineering. The judge has become more like a rancher or farmer.

Yet there is, nonetheless, a continuum between the Lockean, natural law judge and the Coasean, positive law judge, just as there is between the hunter-gatherer and the rancher-farmer. Just as the domestication of plants seems to have been a side-effect of gathering them (and accidentally spilling them near the camp), so the great legal systems emerged as a side-effect of judges articulating principles in their efforts to resolve individual cases.

And just as the farmer's modern wheat and maize are genetically akin to the wild grasses his ancestors gathered, so a modern judge's utilitarian use of precedent continues to use old rules of first possession and appropriation from the commons, and of the rights of labor, that seemed self-evident to his judicial forerunners. A contemporary legal system whose decisions were not grounded in justice would be as unable to contribute to human flourishing as a farmer who planed his field with stones.

Law, the division of labor, and revenue collection

Adam Smith rightly noted that the greatest increase in the productive powers of labor derives from the division of labor, specialization and trade. Although technology has become more important since Adam Smith's time, the advance of technology almost always involves a heavy reliance on and a growing complexity of the division of labor. The growth of the division of labor involves increasing interdependence, and an increasing complexity, of property rights and contracts, at least some of which need to be enforced by courts. By serving as third-party enforcer for these contracts, the state plays an important, and in effect a *productive*, economic role. It helps to generate *surpluses*; and it does not seem unreasonable for the state to appropriate some of these to cover its associated expenses.

This justification for revenue collection is subtly different from, and I think stronger than, the argument offered, as a dubious expedient, in Chapter 3, that the state can "presume" the consent of its citizens to pay for basic public goods like security. Previously the state was charging people to protect their *natural* rights; now the suggestion is that the state may define, assign, and regulate *positive* rights, which grow out of natural rights but require judicial support, in such a way as to serve its revenue collection needs, while still leaving large surpluses for private actors who use its judicial services by taking advantage of the new possibilities of action created by positive law.

Corporate taxes are a good example of this phenomenon. Corporations are artificial persons, legal constructs, with their own bylaws or, so to speak, constitutions, with various useful commercial features, particularly *limited liability*, the rule that allows shareholders to incur downside risk equal to the value of the corporation, without putting their other private assets on the line. For the government to impose taxes on these artificial entities—corporate taxes—can be regarded as a fee for using this special form of business organization created by positive law, which firms consent to pay when they organize as corporations. Corporate taxes may be distortive and inefficient, but it would be somewhat odd to call them unjust.

If revenue collection is justified by the state's power of generating surpluses through the development and enforcement of positive contract law, a social-contractarian state may be more feasible than **Chapter 4** suggested. On the other hand, the whole idea of property rights makes the reconciliation of rights and freedom more problematic.

Negative and positive rights revisited

In **Chapter 1**, we studied the distinction between "negative" and "positive" rights, and found that they can be distinguished in that an individual's negative rights constrain the actions of his fellows in only a slight degree, ruling out only a very small part of the courses of action otherwise available to them, whereas positive rights rule out most of the courses of action available to an individual's fellows. A man who must not punch his neighbor in the face is free to wave his fists in 99.9% of the air; whereas a man who must provide for his neighbor, even if he can do it, is limited to a very few ways of conducting himself that are consistent with attaining this end.

But this method for distinguishing negative and positive rights breaks down when we introduce property rights. Of course, *my* property rights do not much limit the courses of action available to my fellow men: they can access 99.99% of the globe and more without trespassing on my land. But to be obligated to respect *everyone's* property rights is to have one's freedom of mobility restricted very significantly. Property rights do not fit comfortably into either the class of positive or of negative rights. It is part of the judicial art to ensure that they do not impinge on each other; but they greatly curtail the domain of liberties, the space between where A's rights end and B's begin.

Inequality and redistribution

It is often helpful to illustrate a theory by applying it to a practical problem, but property is so rich in practical problems that I would not know where to begin. Even if I were to devote much more space to the problems, it would be hard to make an adequate apology for the lack of comprehensiveness. Inheritance, insurance, debt and other financial instruments, trespass and nuisance, intellectual property, environmental law, and reputational capital are just a few of the thorny and important areas to which one might try to apply the Locke-Coase property theory developed above; but I will not do so.

One urgent question raised by a theory of property rights is that of *redistribution*. Is it right to take from "the rich"—by coercion, that is, for the ethics of soliciting voluntary charity is not controversial—and give to "the poor?" It is a tautology to say that the arguments of Locke and Coase in favor of property rights are arguments against redistribution. But it is not necessarily inconsistent to say that the arguments have some force, yet might to some extent be overridden by the consideration that the marginal utility of a dollar for the richest man may be safely assumed to be much less the marginal utility of that dollar for the poorest man, and therefore redistribution should be pursued for the sake of "the greatest happiness of the greatest number."

I will not, however, explore the ethics of rich-poor redistribution further because I do not think it has any serious advocates. There are, of course, government programs that tax some to finance transfers to others, and people who support them. But as these transfers occur almost entirely *within* rich or poor countries, they are irrelevant to the major rich-poor gap in today's world, which is *between* rich and poor countries. Of course, there is foreign aid, too; but it is fiscally trivial. Even within rich countries, transfers usually go to mostly non-poor seniors, farmers, and students.

There can be little doubt that the most effective means of raising the condition of the world's poor is by letting them migrate to rich countries. A serious advocate of rich-to-poor redistribution would, first of all, demand open borders, then he might want to supplement this policy with fiscal transfers, not of course to farmers or seniors or even the relatively poor in the West, but to the malnourished and illiterate of regions like South Asia and sub-Saharan Africa. I am not aware of anyone who argues this. (Jeffrey Sachs of Columbia University comes closest.) While it would be interesting to compare the arguments for and against a program of rich-to-poor redistribution along these lines, it seems to be worth postponing until there are people advocating it.

Instead, I proceed to apply the Locke-Coase theory of property to a question which was raised in **Chapter 1** but to which only a provisional answer was offered: the question of *freedom of movement* in natural law, beginning with the problem of *streets*.

Streets

A street is not a slab of pavement. It is not even a strip of land. It is a bundle of overlapping non-exclusive transit rights.

A street is not a slab of pavement because it would still be a street if it were unpaved. If (say) Grant Street used to be covered only with gravel or dirt, it was still Grant Street. If the city decides to replace the asphalt of Grant Street with charming cobblestones, it will still be Grant Street.

A street is not a strip of land because the land was there before it was a street and may still be there if it ceases to be a street. If Grant Street used to be a private hunting park, it was not a street. If Grant Street is abandoned and a forest grows on it and someone starts to use it as a hunting park, it will be the same land, but it will not be a street.

Grant Street consists of a bundle of transit rights, and it continues to exist as long as those transit rights exist, and is destroyed when they are destroyed, and changes to the material substance of the street matter only inasmuch as they affect these rights. Suppose Rogue Developer Dan puts a wall around Grant Street and starts building structures on it. If Dan does this without authorization, the rights of local residents to use Grant Street as a street still exist, though Dan is violating them, and we can still call Grant Street a street. We would complain that Dan has closed off access to a public street—thus bearing witness in our characterization that it is still a street. But suppose Dan gets the city government to endorse his takeover of Grant Street, and the citizens resign themselves to the usurpation and move out of their Grant Street homes. In this case, Grant Street has ceased to be a street.

Who owns Grant Street, then? The city? No, because the city cannot justly dispose of Grant Street in any way that it sees fit, by, say, selling the street to Developer Dan. It has to take into account the rights of Grant Street residents. We can solve the riddle by revisiting and extending the argument of Locke. The earth is originally common to all mankind, but we can appropriate it by mixing our labor with it. The residents of Grant Street have mixed their labor with Grant Street by walking or driving on it. Maybe they even turned it into a street physically by trampling down the natural vegetation that impeded movement.

A person who has transit rights—*natural* transit rights—in a street does not have the right to exclude others from the street, because their use of the street as a street does not preclude his. We can appropriate only to *use*, not to *waste*, and to exclude others from the street would be to waste it. He *may* justly object, however, if someone tries to grow crops or build houses in the street. He may have a right to object if someone tries to pave and drive cars on a street which he prefers to use as a pedestrian. This objection is weakened if a sidewalk is provided. If he and his neighbors were accustomed to play soccer in the street, the objection may be strengthened. Streets are not public, then, because the government declares them to be. Their public nature is a side-effect of the natural rights which comprise them.

This does *not* mean that everyone has an equal right to every street. And here the distinction between rights and liberties which we introduced in Chapter 1 pays off. Rights are derived from "mixing labor," that is, from use and from need. Only the users of Grant Street have a natural right to it and are injured if Developer Dan appropriates it. All others have a *liberty*—not a right—to use Grant Street, because the nature of the rightholders' stake in the street is such that it does not include the right to exclude others. The users of Grant Street might choose to convert it into a private hunting park. If all users of Grant Street, or more precisely all holders of transit rights in Grant Street, agree to this, it is just. Non-users cannot object on the grounds that they are being deprived of the liberty to use the street that they previously enjoyed. But as long as Grant Street is a street, it is public, because the use to which it is being put by those who have rights in it is not incompatible with others having access to it, and therefore gives them no just grounds to exclude others from it.

Now let us take off our Locke hats and put on our Coase hats. There is a trade-off between the use of land for streets and the use of land for other purposes, such as structures, farms, public gardens, etc. Let us suppose that, in City M, an inefficiently large amount of land is devoted to streets. How can the market reallocate land so that an efficient number of streets will exist? First, the transit rights of citizens in streets should be recognized and made alienable. Once this is done, developers will start bargaining with the owners of transit rights in streets, and some of the street land will be sold and repurposed, with owners either selling the property adjoining the streets or negotiating new ways of accessing their property.

This is not meant as a serious suggestion for how to deal with urban planning problems. It would be such a burden to the court system to recognize and enforce such complicated rights, and there would be such severe bargaining problems in the markets for them, that an attempt to implement the proposal might be useless or harmful. The hypothetical illuminates conceptually how an efficient allocation of land between streets and private uses is to be understood.

This theory of streets has a number of practical applications, the first of which is to avoid some bad consequences of another theory of streets, namely, that streets are "public property." Suppose streets belong to the public as represented by the government. It would seem to follow that the government could exclude individuals from the streets, thus imposing on them a form of arbitrary house arrest. No doubt there are elaborate legal arguments by which this ramification of the notion of streets as public property might be avoided even under a public-property view of streets. But if streets are bundles of overlapping non-exclusive transit rights, the objection to arbitrary denial of access of individuals to the streets is plain: no one has exclusive rights to the street, so no one can have transferred this right to the government. The theory also explains *why residential segregation is wrong*: since no one has exclusive rights to the streets, whites act unjustly in excluding blacks from "their" parts of town.

One startling ramification of this theory of streets is that it suggests that the automotive revolution may have been the occasion for large-scale injustice. Jane Jacobs and others have emphasized that streets are, or at least were, *communities*, places where people met face to face and got to know each other, forming what Robert Putnam calls "social capital," meaning that social ties have economic value. The introduction of cars tended to destroy streets' capacity to play this role, and was one reason for the urban blight that made the phrase "inner city," in the 1970s and 1980s, a byword for criminality and social disintegration. Greater attention to the natural rights of city dwellers, to their need for and habitual use of the community-building function of the street, might have avoided this disaster.

On the other hand, in an economy where cars are the dominant mode of transportation, the same principles of habitual use and need may give people a natural right to *drive cars* in the streets, provided that they do so responsibly and do not endanger others. Traffic control is clearly a legitimate government function, since reckless driving menaces others' natural right to life. The implication, then, is that the state cannot justly regulate traffic in any merely arbitrary manner, but must mediate the conflict between the right to use the street and the right to life in such a fashion as to minimize violations of these rights.

Although there is room for discretion in how to do this, *justice*, not simply the satisfaction of the arbitrary preferences of magistrates or voters, is at stake when the state decides to set the driving age at 16 or 18, or the minimum blood alcohol content at 0.05% or 0.08%. It might be just to deny driver's licenses to past drunk drivers, but unjust to deny them to sex offenders. And it is surely unjust to deny them to illegal immigrants *qua* illegal immigrants.

Libertarians should take comfort from this theory of streets, because it implies that in using the streets, they are not betraying their anti-government principles, but exercising their natural rights. Even if streets are paved by the government, the *pavement*, not the street itself, is the publicly provided good. If the government chose not to pave the streets, the streets would still exist, and probably at least some of them would be paved by private initiative, either philanthropic or commercial, though the modalities of paying for pavement are unclear.

Protestors can also welcome it, for it implies that they do not need the government's permission to protest in the street, at least as far as natural law is concerned. And while a certain power to regulate protests may be a side-effect of the state's traffic control and general police functions, the state cannot justly prohibit protests altogether. On the other hand, protestors may act unjustly if they unduly impede normal traffic.

Does this theory of streets imply that *toll roads* are unjust? Yes and no. If, when there are many ways to walk from A to B through land that is still in the commons, a private firm builds a paved road from A to B for automobiles, its claim to the road is the classic Lockean one—the members of the firm have mixed their labor with the land and thus appropriated it from the commons—and it can justly charge any price it likes for the right to use the road. If, on the other hand, there is only one way from A to B, which many people frequently use, and the state or a private firm takes it over and starts charging tolls, it is violating the rights of the road's habitual users.

If the state paves the road and charges a toll, *and all habitual users of the road consent ex ante to this policy*, the state acts justly—so would a private firm that did the same—and there may be room to apply the idea of "presumed consent" if coordination or hold-up or free-rider problems make it impossible to get universal consent to a plan which would be universally beneficial. I think there is a widespread feeling that toll roads are unfair, and that the reason for this feeling is an inarticulate awareness that the use of streets is a natural right and not a privilege granted by government. But the feeling is not always justified.

Congestion charges, too, may seem to be ruled out if the use of roads is a natural right, but this is not necessarily so. Locke's theory is that people can justly appropriate from the commons for use, not waste. Excluding people from a non-congested street is wasteful, therefore unjust. But the situation changes when a road is so heavily used that there are frequent traffic jams. In this case, for some users to appropriate and exclude anyone who did not pay a toll, so as to deter low-value users and mitigate traffic congestion, would not be wasteful. Reconciling the various rights of road users becomes complex at this point— how can all habitual users of the road be identified, and their consent asked, before the road becomes exclusive?—but congestion charges can be justly imposed in principle, and probably in practice without too serious a burden placed on the rights of users.

Economists tend to advocate congestion charges on efficiency grounds and find public resistance to this rational policy mystifying. I think the reason for the resistance is an inarticulate sense that congestion charges are unjust, a consideration to which economists are characteristically blind. But while a degree of uneasiness is justified, the public is probably mistaken if it feels that well-administered congestion charges on heavily-used roads are unjust.

Gated communities are another institution which would seem to violate the natural right to use the streets. Again, I think the public is uneasy about gated communities; that if asked why, the answer would be that gated communities are "exclusive" or "elitist," and that the only way to make sense of this—for people do not have the same sort of qualms about private health clubs or universities— is that people feel no one can justly exclude others from streets (such as those internal to a gated community).

Are gated communities unjust? It depends. If the streets are used only for transit, maybe that is so. But if a gated community fosters an environment where children can play and adults can socialize in the streets, there emerges a new way of using the streets that demands a certain degree of communal privacy for its realization; and in that case, a gated community might be justified in excluding outsiders from its streets.

Natural freedom of mobility

We saw in **Chapter 1** that the *habeas corpus* principle implies at least some kind of natural right to mobility, because it would be absurd to deny that a person who is trapped in a space inadequate to sustain life and left to die has been a victim of violence, i.e., has had his natural rights violated. We left open the question of *just how much* mobility a person has by natural right. We are now ready to revisit that question and give a more thorough and specific answer.

First, we can state what rights of mobility a person does *not* have. He does not have the right to trespass on private land, that is, on land that has been justly appropriated from the commons for private use by others. When land is private property a sort of inversion of *habeas corpus* occurs, by which a non-violent trespasser is regarded as an aggressor, while the owner who defends his land by force is (in natural law) regarded as acting in self-defense (though positive law may require him to delegate the defense of his land to the sheriff). It is as if his land is an extension of his body.

Even here there is a claim on the other side. If we take the case of agricultural land, while I clearly must not trample the wheat my neighbor has planted, it is less clear that I do him wrong if I stroll through his orchard, or walk through the furrows between his cornrows. Most modes of agriculture require that a field be penetrable to a farmer himself, e.g., by footpaths through his grain. Why should he be able to deny the use of these footpaths to strangers? In winter, when his fields are fallow, his claim to exclude me seems even weaker.

Probably the farmer's best argument for excluding strangers from his cornfields is that while they *might* not damage his crops, once strangers are in his field, monitoring them is not feasible and he is exposed to undue risk of theft or vandalism if trespassers are tolerated. One can imagine a society of people so morally enlightened, so universally inclined to refrain from theft and vandalism, that this argument would lose its plausibility. Then justice might demand even greater freedom of mobility than it does today.

In the case of streets, since no individual or group of individuals has exclusive rights to them, A acts unjustly if he tries to prevent B from entering a street by using (or threatening) force against his physical person. More generally, if Albert proposes to go from Beaverbrook to Castlerock through Deermeadow, Ellen acts unjustly if she tries to prevent this by force, unless she is the exclusive owner of Castlerock or of some relevant part of Deermeadow. Yet Ellen does not act unjustly if she *builds a wall* across Deermeadow to prevent Albert's using it, unless Albert was a habitual user of, with natural rights of transit in, Deermeadow. But nor does Albert act unjustly if he uses a ladder to get over Ellen's wall.

If Ellen has no real use for the wall (blocking Albert does not count), then Albert might even be justified in destroying Ellen's wall with dynamite. And because the cost of building physical barriers to movement is invariably far greater than the cost of evading or removing them, to restrict someone's mobility by this means is always impractical *unless the physical barrier serves as a threat of the use of force.* Suburban fences are effective, not because it is hard to get over them (except maybe for children) but because they are signals of the rights and intentions of a private owner. Likewise, the Great Wall of China, or Hadrian's Wall in Scotland, were somewhat effective only because they were manned by soldiers who would physically attack persons who attempted to cross them without authorization. The only case where physically containing a person is cost-effective is when the perimeter to be physically blocked is small, e.g., the four walls of a prison cell.

Without the special right to coerce trespassers that is associated only with private property, then, it is not just to limit a person's mobility. This is not to say that each person has natural access rights to all non-private land, but rather that each person has a *liberty* of movement extending to all non-private land. He cannot consider himself injured if a bit of the commons, or a public street, is appropriated on the other side of the world.

Rather, because no one can exclude him from the streets, or the commons, by force—and almost the entirety of the air and sea are at one with the streets and commons, since none of the uses to which they can be put, with a few exceptions like fish farms or private beaches, require exclusive possession—he enjoys a very wide freedom of movement, by default. While the phrase *natural freedom of mobility* aptly describes this situation, its connection to natural rights is indirect. A person does not enjoy natural rights to remote places he has never seen; rather, he carries his rights of *habeas corpus* with him wherever he goes, and only the claims of private property can stand in his way.

American citizens, within the territory of the United States, more or less enjoy just this kind of natural freedom of mobility. They cannot, without permission, enter the private property of others; but they can move through the streets from northern Alaska to Florida without encountering any interference. (I encountered one iniquitous exception to this rule at a checkpoint in Arizona.) As of 1900, a similar natural freedom of mobility existed on a global scale. Historian Harold James describes this lost world:

> Trade was largely unhindered, even in apparently protectionist states such as the German empire. Above all, people moved. They did not need passports. There were hardly any debates about citizenship. In a search for freedom, security, and prosperity—three values that are closely related—the peoples of Europe and Asia left their homes and took often uncomfortable journeys by rail and by ship, often as part of gigantic human treks. Between 1871 and 1915, 36 million people left Europe. In the countries of immigration, the inflows brought substantial economic growth. At the same time, the countries left behind experienced large productivity gains as surplus (low-productivity) populations were eliminated. Such flows eased the desperate poverty of, among others, Ireland and Norway. (James, 2002, Kindle Edition, locations 165-172)

If natural freedom of mobility is ultimately rooted in natural rights, then we cannot say that changes in preferences and technology have altered the national policy of most or all countries in the direction of closed borders, and leave it at that. The 19th century was right, and the 20th century was wrong, and people of conscience must do what they can to make the 21st century imitate the 19th.

Economists and natural rights

Adam Smith believed in natural rights, or as he called it, "natural liberty." He criticized the petty regulation of the British economy in his own day *both* on grounds of inefficiency *and* because it was contrary to natural liberty. Adam Smith's argument about the "invisible hand" of the market showed, what is not at all obvious, that a flourishing economy is consistent with natural liberty, i.e., that you do not need to use coercion to run the economy.

Laissez-faire, or "let it be," economics means that the government should "do nothing"—provided, of course, that everyone respects each other's natural rights, as they ought. Government only steps in when crimes are committed. The phrase *laissez-faire* only makes sense if you believe that there are natural rights, the state's protection of which is somehow *not* government interference in the economy, while a policy that infringes natural rights is. We can understand the phrase "*laissez-faire*" because we do believe in natural rights, at least a little bit.

Economics became utilitarian when the marginal utility theory of value proved to be superior to the labor theory of value in explaining the price system. Adam Smith followed Locke in identifying the value of things with the labor spent in obtaining them. In this, he was followed by David Ricardo, and the error of Smith and Locke finally bore disastrous fruit in Karl Marx's fallacious theory of exploitation (Marx thought all value came from labor, therefore whatever went to the capitalist was stolen).

Partly in reaction to this, in the last decades of the 19th century, economists of the late-19th century Marginal Revolution, such as Stanley Jevons, Alfred Marshall, Leon Walras and Carl Menger, explained (and justified) the price system by showing how competitive markets ensure that price equals marginal benefit equals marginal cost. Although water sustains life and diamonds are for mere decoration,[12] because water is so much more abundant than diamonds, *at*

---

[12] Or were when economists first began to puzzle over the puzzle of water and diamonds. Today, diamonds have industrial uses. Still, even today the high price of diamonds relative to water is a result of their scarcity and consequent high *marginal* utility, while water yields far higher total utility and is cheap only because it is abundant.

the margin diamonds contribute more to utility; and it makes no difference how laborious it was to mine the average diamond. It was left to Vilfredo Pareto to refine the concept of utility and give it a realistic basis in "revealed preference."

Yet when economists today derive the concept of utility from the revealed preferences of a consumer faced with various price vectors and budget constraints, they assume that (a) a person enjoys a huge array of choices, and (b) a person can act *non-strategically*, without asking anyone's permission or taking their interests into account. In other words, *the consumer's problem assumes a person who enjoys and is exercising his natural rights.* The consumer's problem cannot be sensibly applied to a slave or a prisoner.

Game theory *can* be applied to a slave or prisoner. Indeed, the "prisoner's dilemma" is a staple of game theory. But a full game-theoretic description of even a moderately-sized market would be hopelessly complex. Economists are able to shed light on markets by reducing them to optimization problems by *individuals*—individuals who do not have to take others into account, except at the margins. To have a sphere of autonomous decision-making where one does not need to take into account the interests of others is to have rights.

It is possible to insist on substituting for natural rights either (a) *positive* rights backed up by a tacit threat of legal action, or (b) *customary* rights which individuals respect because of tacit reputational mechanisms in the context of larger repeated games. Without denying that positive and customary rights are important, some rights-respecting behavior is difficult to explain in terms of either legal threats or customary rights. Also, law and custom are often seen by those who shape them (judges; parents) as efforts to *discern* and put into practice what is just and right, rather than arbitrarily to invent it.

Might-have-beens are cheap, but it seems likely that if economists had been more attentive to the claims of natural rights, they might have avoided a discreditable chapter in the history of the discipline. After the fall of Soviet communism, a large array of countries from Poland to Tajikistan found themselves in the position of having to replace the failing economic institutions of communism with the only system that seemed to work—market capitalism. It was a philosopher-king moment for Western economists, who were invited in as advisers at this critical time, and it ended badly. Most post-Soviet countries suffered an economic collapse as bad as or worse than the US Great Depression.

For the intellectual children of the Marginal Revolution and the Coase Theorem, the main thing was to let a price system emerge and allocate resources efficiently. Markets required firm and credible private property rights, but it did not much matter what belonged to whom. So (in Russia) prices were freed, unleashing inflation and hyperinflation, and privatization was implemented in a hurry; but the new property rights were not perceived as legitimate and were therefore politically vulnerable. The new owners, instead of developing the assets they had acquired, funneled capital abroad, and after 2000 a *de facto or de jure* renationalization began.

Before they were wiped out by inflation, Russians had a large "overhang" of rubles which they had saved during Soviet times because widespread shortages (due to controlled prices) meant there was little or nothing for them to spend their earnings on. An economist attentive to claims of natural rights might have recognized in the ruble overhang a set of rights derived from labor which could be translated into a new system of private property for the whole Russian economy.

In the absence of an effective system of monetary governance, prices and exchange rates would need to remain fixed by law in the short term, to preserve the value of these fragile tokens of the due rewards of accumulated labor, while they were converted, through the sale of industrial enterprises and agricultural land for rubles, into capital assets. By making a greater effort to be *just*, this reform program (somewhat similar to that pursued by China in the 1980s and 1990s) might also have achieved the *efficiency* that rapid price liberalization and arbitrary and chaotic privatization failed to achieve.

5

National Sovereignty

I n the first four chapters, we have been arming ourselves for battle, and now it is time to slay the dragon, which is called *sovereignty*. The word has some innocuous uses, which may be summed up in the word *jurisdiction*, but its full meaning is indelibly absolutist, and it is usually brought in when a state is doing something against the natural law. Indeed, it is often less an idea than, as it were, an anti-idea, a word shrouded in darkness, a thing people accept but prefer not to think about much, a place where thought stops. To say that so-and-so has sovereignty is to put reason to one side and defer to something absolute and inexplicable.

I shall try to show that Thomas Hobbes' *Leviathan* is a rare and precious book because he exposes the nature of sovereignty.[13] But to begin with we can get a glimpse of what sovereignty means if we consider the following word pairs.

(1) (a) MURDER, versus (b) EXECUTION
(2) (a) EXTORTION, versus (b) TAXATION
(3) (a) ABDUCTION, versus (b) ARREST

In each case, the actions are the same. Murder and execution refer to the killing of a human being. Extortion and taxation refer to the use of threats to take money. Abduction and arrest refer to the forcible detention of a person and removal to a place of secure physical confinement. But the first word in each pair is something *individuals* do, and is regarded as a *crime*, while the second is something *governments* do, and is regarded as *not a crime*. Apparently, we think that governments are *exempt from the moral law* to which individuals are subject.

No doubt the reader's impulse will be to leap up and defend the honor of governments, declaring, "But we authorize governments do these things for the common good!" Yes, that is the social contract theory which was the theme of **Chapter 3**, and to the extent that it is true, it makes a difference. In that case,

---

[13] The framers of the US constitution also thought carefully about sovereignty.

arrest and execution are part of a system of *just retribution* rather than merely abduction and murder; and taxation is like *billing for services rendered* rather than extortion. And when governments exceed their just powers, we do sometimes apply to them the vocabulary of crime usually reserved for individuals.

We might speak of the "judicial murder" of Socrates by the Athenians, but even that seems like a rhetorical flourish rather than a fact, and we should be less likely to (dare, or wish, to) say it if we were citizens of the Athenian democracy ourselves. More often, we grant this semantic absolution to any and every government, regardless of the degree of popular consent it enjoys, and regardless of whether it remains within the limits of its just powers. When we do, we accept, explicitly or tacitly, the idea of *sovereignty*.

Why power corrupts

In the beginning of his *Mere Christianity*, C.S. Lewis derives an argument for the reality of the moral law from the human practice of quarreling. "Everyone has heard people quarreling," writes Lewis. "Sometimes it sounds funny and sometimes is sounds merely unpleasant; but however it sounds, I believe we can learn something very important from the kinds of things they say. They say things like this: 'How'd you like it if anyone did the same to you?' – 'That's my seat, I was there first' – 'Leave him alone, he isn't doing you any harm' – 'Why should you shove in first?' – 'Give me a bit of your orange, I gave you a bit of mine' – 'Come on, you promised.'... The man who makes [remarks like these]... is appealing to some kind of standard of behavior which he expects the other man to know about," whence Lewis concludes that the moral law is real and we all know it.

But the examples also seem to show something else, namely that it is sometimes easier for *others* to see how the moral law applies in our own case, than for us to do so. Similarly, Adam Smith argued, in his *Theory of Moral Sentiments*, that our behavior should be such as to satisfy an "impartial spectator." For most of us, our capacity to apply the moral law to our own case depends heavily on observing the praise and blame which our behavior evokes in others.

Just as we can see ourselves better physically with the help of reflective surfaces, so our moral self-perception is usually (not always) enhanced as we see how our character and behavior is perceived by others. They are our mirrors. Also, the rewards and punishments which others will bestow or inflict on us often (not always) serve as a force inducing us to obey the moral law. It is often hard to distinguish even introspectively in our own case, let alone as a spectator, right actions done for right's sake from right actions done from fear of punishment, or hope of reward.

From these observations, we may infer the reason why, as Lord Acton said, "power corrupts, and absolute power corrupts absolutely." The more power a person has, the less he has to fear from the punishments that others can threaten, and the less he has to gain from the rewards that others can offer. At the same time, in view of the human propensity to be grateful for praise and angry at criticism, it becomes increasingly advantageous to praise him, and increasingly dangerous to blame or criticize him.

A person with great power may still be held to the moral law by reason and conscience, and in that case, power may enable him to do more good. But many behave morally only from fear of punishment or hope of reward, or they look for the praise and blame of others to guide him; and a person of this kind will see no need and/or will not know how to obey the moral law when power deprives him of fear and surrounds him with flatterers.

Throughout history, the great and powerful tend to disobey the moral law which ordinary people live by, and are not punished or even blamed for it, but on the contrary, praised and rewarded. Napoleon and Alexander "the Great" are murderers who were remembered as heroes. From this an opinion perennially arises, and becomes embedded in custom and language, that the powerful are exempt from the ordinary moral law.

This popular prejudice is the raw material for the idea of sovereignty. In many times and places, kings, pharaohs, and emperors have been regarded as divine or quasi-divine, and have been the subject of personality cults. This practice was greatly attenuated in Medieval Western Europe, where kings were *not* sovereign, but limited on all sides by feudal rights, custom, and the Church. Sovereignty made a comeback in the early modern period with the help of disinterested ideologists like the political philosopher Thomas Hobbes.

Leviathan as peace

Thomas Hobbes' *Leviathan*, a timely exposition of the concept of sovereignty that has never been surpassed, was published in 1651, shortly after the Peace of Westphalia laid the foundation of the modern European state system in 1648. Modern sovereignty is sometimes called "Westphalian sovereignty." The central principle of the Peace of Westphalia was *cuius regio, eius religio*, or "whose realm, his religion"—that is, the ruler gets to decide the faith of the realm.

Europe had resorted to this cynical maxim from exhaustion after bloody wars of religion had racked the continent for generations, following the 16th-century Reformation. The Westphalian principle would have been as unacceptable for a pious medieval layman as it is to a modern American democrat. For medieval man, the calendar was filled with fasts and feasts in honor of martyrs who had refused to accept the ancient version of *cuius regio, eius religio*, even at the cost of being tortured to death by (agents of) the pagan emperors of Rome. The thesis of *Leviathan* is that:

The finall Cause, End, or Designe of men, (who naturally love Liberty, and Dominion over others,) in the introduction of that restraint upon themselves (in which wee see them live in Common-wealths,) is the foresight of their own preservation, and of a more contented life thereby; that is to say, of getting themselves out of that miserable condition of Warre, which is necessarily consequent... to the naturall Passions of men, when there is no visible Power to keep them in awe...

The only way to erect such a Common Power, as may be able to defend them from the invasion of Forraigners, and the injuries of one another, and thereby to secure them in such sort, as that by their owne industrie, and by the fruites of the Earth, they may nourish themselves and live long contentedly; is, to conferre all their power and strength upon one man, or upon one Assembly of men, that may reduce all their Wills, by plurality of voices, unto one Will: which is as much as to say, to appoint one man, or Assembly of men, to beare their Person; and every one to owne, and acknowledge himself to be Author of whatsoever he that so beareth their Person, shall Act, or cause to be Acted, in those things which concerne the Common Peace and Safetie; and therein to submit their Wills, every one to his Will, and their Judgments, to his Judgment. This is more than Consent, or Concord; it is a reall Unitie of them all, in one and the same Person, made by Covenant of every man with every man... This done, the Multitude so united in one Person, is called a COMMON-WEALTH...

This is the Generation of that great LEVIATHAN, or rather (to speak more reverently) of that Mortall God, to which wee owe under the Immortall God, our peace and defence. (Hobbes, 1651, Kindle Edition, Locations 1830-50)

The first thing to note about this thesis is that it bestows absolute power on the sovereign, the extent of which becomes clearer as Hobbes draws out the ramifications of his thesis. Under no circumstances is revolution justified: "subjects cannot change the form of government" and "sovereign power cannot be forfeited." The sovereign can never be accused of injustice by his subjects because each of them is "by this Institution Author of the all the Actions and Judgments of the Soveraigne… and consequently he that complaineth of injury from his Soveraigne, complaineth of that whereof he himself is Author" (*Leviathan*, 1891).

The sovereign is the sole legislator, who determines the distribution of property—"the right of making rules, whereby the subject may every man know what is so his own, as no other subject can without injustice take it from him… is annexed to the Soveraigntie"—and the sole judge—"to [the sovereign] also belongeth the right of all judicature and decision of controversies"—makes peace and war, chooses all counselors, and enjoys the right "of rewarding, and punishing, and that… arbitrary."

But second, Hobbes' motive is not to flatter the sovereign, but to establish peace, at a time when England was emerging from civil war. Now, if we believe in natural law as articulated by Locke, we will see another way for people to live in peace with each other, other than total submission to a single sovereign: be just, observe the natural law. But what if, as is often the case, there is no consensus about what the natural law is (or whether it exists)? In that case, even an arbitrary law might be better than no law at all.

Game theory may elucidate. Consider the "Hawk-Dove" game, in which two players, A and B, can play an aggressive strategy, called Hawk, or a moderate strategy, called Dove. Each player gets a "payoff" depending on his own, and the other's, moves. If both play Hawk, a war ensues, and they each receive payoff WORST. If both play Dove, they live in peace, and they each receive payoff GOOD. But if only *one* plays Hawk, and the other plays Dove, the Hawk exploits the Dove and gets payoff BEST, while the Dove gets payoff BAD, which is still preferable to WORST. It is *not* an equilibrium in this game for both players to play Dove. If a player thinks the other player will play Dove, he will (if rational) play Hawk. The only (symmetric Nash) equilibrium turns out to be that both players randomly play Hawk with a certain probability, so as to render the other indifferent between the Hawk and Dove strategies. As a result, wars will occasionally occur.

Now suppose there is some signal, which we will call "the judgment of the sovereign," observable to both players before the game is played, and which has two states: (a) A is in the right, and (b) B is in the right. Now there is a new (symmetric Nash) equilibrium: each player plays Hawk when he is in the right, Dove when the other is in the right, and wars are avoided, even though the sovereign has no power to change the payoffs of the game. Finally, suppose the sovereign *can* change the payoffs, though only negatively. Specifically, suppose the sovereign imposes a PUNISHMENT on players who play Hawk. Now the payoff to playing Hawk when one's opponent plays Dove is BEST MINUS PUNISHMENT. If this payoff is worse than GOOD, the temptation to play Hawk has been eliminated.

Sovereignty, then, is an ideological construct, or fiction, by which people try to guarantee peace, without the need to arrive at an elusive moral consensus about justice. Does it work? In the history of Europe, there have been times of general war and other times where peace was prevalent. Some of the times of general war—the Thirty Years' War (1618-1648), or the French Revolutionary and Napoleonic Wars (1793-1814), for example—were times when no principles of sovereignty and legitimacy were generally accepted, and people were fighting over conflicting principles. Some of the times of general peace—the "Age of Metternich" (1814-1848), for example—were times when certain principles of legitimate government enjoyed dominance, however odd these principles (e.g., hereditary monarchy) may appear in retrospect.

Yet World War I occurred when governmental legitimacy was as well established as it has ever been. And in the early 20th century, it was the absolutism of tsarist Russia, not the liberal constitution of England, which proved most vulnerable to revolution. Anyway, to establish and sustain principles of legitimacy is difficult, and rulers tend to encourage a certain superstitious dread of questioning the reigning principles of legitimacy, not only out of self-interest, but from a plausible fear that the war and revolution which would occur if people ceased to believe in them would be harmful to all.

To give the Westphalian settlement legitimacy, required a philosophical revolution, and Thomas Hobbes wrought it. That said, Hobbes is important less for his direct influence—he had no disciples, unlike Locke—than for articulating an idea whose time had come. He is one of two great political philosophers (the other is Machiavelli) whose greatness consists partly in a sort of moral defectiveness which made them fail to anticipate the horror with which their ideas would be greeted, and therefore to advocate ideas about the amorality of sovereign power which shrewder cynics have understood that it is more advantageous to be reticent about. Yet Hobbes did engage in some tactical obfuscation and deceit.

The insincerity of Hobbes' religion

Hobbes' *Leviathan* is, oddly enough, an *insincere* book. Hobbes was not insincere in his main thesis, about the need for absolutist government; again, he was no mere flatterer. His insincerity (or irony) is in the details of his arguments and examples. What Hobbes writes on the topic of religion, though perhaps less important from today's perspective than in the minds of Hobbes' contemporaries, best illustrates this weird aspect of Hobbes' thought. Hobbes purports to write as a Christian, quotes the Bible as an authoritative source, and refers to God as a real entity, yet there is scarcely a page in *Leviathan* from which his apostasy cannot be deduced. The following definition of religion, by itself, is sufficient to convict Hobbes as an infidel:

> "Fear of power invisible, feigned by the mind, or imagined from tales publicly allowed [is] RELIGION, not allowed, superstition; and when the power imagined is truly such as we imagine, [that is] TRUE RELIGION."

Superstition refers, in ordinary language, to something false. If religion is the same as superstition, but for the historical accident that a sovereign happens to allow it, religion too is false. Lest this conclusion be too obvious, Hobbes adds a line about "true religion." This is for plausible deniability; but Hobbes does not actually affirm that the category of "true religion" is non-empty. And indeed, by Hobbes' definition, if there is "true religion," there must be "true superstition," which sounds like a contradiction in terms and which Hobbes will not admit, since, after all, every religion allowed by one sovereign is disallowed by some other sovereign. The only way to make sense of this definition is to conclude that Hobbes thinks all religion is false. Hobbes also dismisses as nonsensical certain key concepts which have been held by the Catholic, the Orthodox, and most of the Protestant churches since the time of the Council of Nice in the 4th century AD:

> There is yet another fault in the Discourses of some men; which may also be numbred among the sorts of Madnesse; namely that abuse of words... by the name of Absurdity... when men speak such words, as put together, have in them no signification at all; but are fallen upon by some, through misunderstanding of the words they have received, and repeat by rote; by others, from intention to deceive by obscurity... and if any man require, let him take a Schoole-man into his hands, and see if he can translate any one chapter concerning any difficult point; as the Trinity; the Deity; the nature of Christ; Transubstantiation; Free-will &c. into any of the modern tongues, so as to make them intelligible...

When men write whole volumes of such stuffe, are they not Mad, or intend to make others so? (*Leviathan*, Location 840-50)

It gets worse. Hobbes was a materialist, who dismissed as nonsense the idea of an incorporeal spirit. *Leviathan* begins with a psychological inquiry in which man is assumed to be a sort of machine. In view of these prejudices, it is hard to see how Hobbes could believe in life after death. Of course, writing in 1651, Hobbes cannot openly deny the afterlife. But a hint of disbelief appears in a comment on why fame after death is a reasonable motive for human action. Hobbes argues:

And though after death, there be no sense of the praise given us on Earth, as being joyes, that are either swallowed up in the unspeakable joyes of Heaven, or extinguished in the extreme torments of Hell: yet is not such Fame vain, because men have a present delight therein, from the foresight of it, and of the benefit that may rebound thereby to their posterity: which though they now see not, yet they imagine; and any thing that is pleasure in the sense, the same also is pleasure in the imagination. (*Leviathan*, Location 1027)

Hobbes seems here to affirm an orthodox Christian belief in heaven and hell. But the argument makes little sense if this affirmation is taken at face value. If men really face the dilemma of "unspeakable joy" or "extreme torments" depending on their actions in this life, they should dedicate themselves wholly to the pursuit of the one, and the avoidance of the other, and not worry about *any* earthly goods, let alone any as vague and distant as worldly fame after death, except inasmuch as they help him to gain eternal life.

On the other hand, a person who expects his soul to live forever would have little reason to regard the benefits of posthumous fame as limited to this life, since he may have a chance to meet, in heaven, his admirers among posterity. But Hobbes' argument is both necessary and cogent if Hobbes actually disbelieves in the immortality of the soul. In that case, fame after death seems an irrational motive for action, since we will not be around to enjoy it, until Hobbes connects it with the pleasures of anticipation, and then it makes sense.

If Hobbes' Christianity is insincere, does it matter? One response is to dismiss it as an irrelevant foible. Living in an age when Christianity was the dominant and legal religion—so the argument goes—for Hobbes to have written an openly anti-Christian book would have invited the suppression of his book and jeopardized his personal safety. Even if the book were published, the anti-Christian message would needlessly alienate readers. In any case, for purposes of persuasion, adding religious to rational arguments could do no harm and much good. So Hobbes brought the Bible and God into his arguments for plausible deniability and to appeal to religious readers.

But Hobbes' political philosophy can (unlike Locke's) be detached fairly cleanly from his theology, which serves more as a decoration of or a digression from it, rather than supplying its fundamental assumptions. A modern reader can safely ignore Hobbes' theology and focus on his politics.

Not quite. Hobbes' religious insincerity matters for at least three reasons. First, it explains his otherwise baffling insistence on a right to self-preservation so absolute that it overrides every moral obligation. Second, in maintaining this "noble lie" as regards religion, Hobbes acts out the role that he thinks intellectuals ought to play in a commonwealth. Third, though religion is the most obvious example, Hobbes' insincerity seems to extend to other parts of his argument as well.

Principled cowardice: Death is the end, so stay alive at all costs

Christians have always recognized the right to life, and Christian opposition to abortion goes back to Roman times. The right to life, as Christians understand it, constrains others, including rulers, not to kill any person without just cause. Hobbes distorts this principle by turning the first natural law into an individual right to attempt to preserve oneself by every possible means, regardless of the rights of others:

> A LAW OF NATURE (Lex Naturalis), is a Precept, or generall Rule, found out by Reason, by which a man is forbidden to do, that, which is destructive of his life, or taketh away the means of preserving the same; and to omit, that, by which he thinketh it may be best preserved... The Fundamental Law of Nature... is a precept, or generall rule of Reason, "That every man, ought to endeavour Peace, as farre as he has hope of obtaining it, and when he cannot obtain it, that he may seek, and use, all helps, and advantages of Warre." (*Leviathan*, Locations 1360-1372)

Jesus taught: "Do not fear those who kill the body but cannot kill the soul. But rather fear him who is able to destroy both soul and body in hell" (Matthew 10:28). He lived this teaching by accepting an unresisting death at the hands of Pilate and the Sanhedrin, and urged others to "take up [your] cross... and follow

Me, for whoever desires to save his life will lose it, but whoever loses his life for My sake will save it" (Luke 10:23-24).

Many of Jesus's disciples in the centuries afterwards joyfully took this advice, receiving their "crowns" of martyrdom at the hands of angry mobs or the Roman state. Jesus's teaching, that one should be ready to die for the truth and should not worry about self-preservation, is quite logical if one believes that this life is a preparation for an eternal heaven or hell. Hobbes' teaching—preserve yourself by every expedient, no matter how wicked—is equally logical if one believes that death is the end.

The Russian novelist Fyodor Dostoevsky, a Christian, worried that "if there is no God, everything is permitted." Hobbes argues, very explicitly, and as his own view rather than as a warning against it, that if there is no sovereign, everything is permitted:

> Naturally every man has right to everything... Because the condition of man [without government] is a condition of Warre of every one against every one; in which case every one is governed by his own Reason; and there is nothing he can make use of, that may not be a help unto him, in preserving his life against his enemies; It followeth, that in such a condition, every man has a Right to every thing; even to another's body. (*Leviathan*, Location 1366)

This claim, which Hobbes derives from the imperative of self-preservation, is important to Hobbes' philosophy because *it is this right of every man to everything in the state of nature which, in a commonwealth, is retained by the sovereign alone and constitutes his absolute power.* Oddly, Hobbes later develops a different concept of "laws of nature" which are more compatible with Christianity, but he insists that "the laws of nature oblige in conscience always, but in effect then only when there is security... they bind to a desire they should take place; but... to the putting them in act, not always," and again, the right of self-preservation is evoked: "for he that should be modest, tractable, and perform all he promises, in such time, and place, where no man els should do so, should but make himself a prey to others." Jesus, of course, taught that people must be good even when others do not reciprocate, repaying evil with good and turning the other cheek.

The odd thing is that Hobbes showed some courage in writing *Leviathan*, a book both royalist and anti-Catholic, at a time when he was in exile in Catholic France and Parliament had seized power in England; yet he believed in self-preservation at all costs, i.e., in cowardice, *in principle.*

The noble lie

If Hobbes believed that there is no God and death is the end, it was not just for fear of authority, or even of alienating readers, that he masked this belief. Hobbes would have been inconsistent had he renounced Christianity openly. *Hobbes' own philosophy required him to profess Christianity, because all the sovereigns he had lived under or could expect to live under (the House of Stuart, or Oliver Cromwell, or the King of France) were Christian, and Hobbes believed that the Sovereign is "judge of what doctrines shall be fit to be taught" to his subjects.*

Hobbes' insincerity, then, is just what his political philosophy requires of himself and other intellectuals. Had Hobbes lived in the Soviet Union, he would have made a defense, equally insincere, of Marxism. Hobbes' pseudo-Christianity is an important part of his political philosophy because it illustrates how intellectuals in his preferred model of society should behave.

In general, sovereignty depends on just this kind of insincerity or hypocrisy, especially among intellectuals, but to a lesser extent among the people as a whole. In sovereignty, there is always an element of the Platonic "noble lie." Sovereigns must insist that they enjoy rights, in particular the right to exercise force, which are denied to their subjects. They must forbid to others the expedients—revolution, conquest, palace coups, or even free and fair elections—by which they became sovereigns. An ideology, combining general principles with particular historical facts (or fictions), is needed to support these special claims of exemption from the moral law if the sovereign is to be viewed as better than a robber.

A free-thinking intellectual may find that his inquiries lead him to accept the ideology of the regime he lives under, or not. If not, conscience may compel the thinker himself, or others who are influenced by his doctrines, to withhold obedience from, or even to engage in armed resistance against, the regime. Such thinkers are dangerous, and sovereigns may, explicitly, or tacitly, bribe or threaten them into silence or insincerity (and they may resort to silence or insincerity from fear even if the sovereign does nothing).

But thinkers who *sincerely* believe in the regime's ideology may be no less dangerous if they hold the regime to the high ideals that it uses to justify its rule. One who supports the king because he is just will turn against him if he commits an injustice. Thomas Jefferson, George Washington, and the rest of the American revolutionaries rebelled against Britain because they believed *too much* in the Lockean principles of the British constitution as established in the 1688 revolution. Mahatma Gandhi and Martin Luther King likewise opposed the British Raj and American racial policy in the name of British and American principles of consent and equality (respectively). It was the true believers in the dream of communism whom Stalin exterminated most ruthlessly.

The only safe intellectuals for a sovereign are like Hobbes, insincere supporters of the ruling ideology, who espouse what the sovereign commands, but are ready to espouse something else if tomorrow the sovereign decides a different ideology is preferable. The role of pliable court intellectual was not available to Hobbes amidst the turmoil of the English Civil War; but Hobbes amply shows in *Leviathan* that he is willing to play it, as he thinks every intellectual ought. His insincerity, like his cowardice, is principled.

The failure of the argument

The third reason why Hobbes' insincerity must be taken into account is that it does not seem to be limited to religion. The core argument of *Leviathan* is so weak, so easily defeasible at every stage in a long chain of reasoning, that one can hardly help seeing in it the same sort of insincerity, of ironical opportunism, of disbelief in his own arguments, as in the case of Hobbes' purported religion. In defense of the claim that subjects have consented to be subjects of an absolutist regime, Hobbes argues:

> Because the major part hath by consenting voices declared a Soveraigne; he that dissented must now consent with the rest; that is, be contented to avow all the actions he shall do, or else justly be destroyed by the rest. For if he voluntarily entered into the Congregation of them that were assembled, he sufficiently declared thereby his will (and therefore tacitely covenanted) to stand to what the major part should ordayne: and therefore if he refuse to stand thereto, or make Protestation against any of their Decrees, he does contrary to his Covenant, and therefore unjustly. And whether he be of the Congregation, or not; and whether his consent be asked, or not, he must either submit to their decrees, or be left in the condition of warre he was in before; wherein he might without injustice by destroyed by any man whatsoever. (*Leviathan*, 1890)

Hobbes claims to have proven by this argument that "no man can without injustice protest against the institution of the sovereign by the major part." The argument is not merely defeasible, but self-defeating, for Hobbes leaves an opening for men to escape the duties of a subject by not consenting, albeit at the cost foregoing the state's protection; and since lots of people have never participated in a constitutional assembly or taken an oath of allegiance, most men are, it would seem, left in Hobbes' notional condition of war: free to obey particular decrees of the sovereign if they so choose, or to disobey them, while running certain risks.

If their consent is supposed to be *presumed* on the ground that otherwise the state will kill them, the validity of this presumption depends rigidly both (a) on Hobbes' claim that in the state of nature everything is permitted - for if there is a pre-institutional right to life, sovereigns and subjects are morally bound to leave non-consenting individuals in peace - and (b) on a belief that everyone not only may, or even should, but does place self-preservation above every other value. Since (a) is unconvincing and (b) is empirically false, the argument fails. This is not the only place where Hobbes' argument fails—his account of what justice is and why people should be just is, if anything, even less convincing—but it will suffice.

A thief, or a philanderer, might look for arguments against the rights of property, or marriage, with which to justify himself. He will prefer strong arguments but will settle for weak ones if they are all that he can find. And herein lies the importance of Hobbes: that although his case for sovereignty must be one of the weakest arguments a philosopher has ever penned, yet it is the best defense that can be made of the cowardly subservience and statist bigotry with which much of mankind has, for thousands of years and still in the present day, not only submitted to—that might be done in a spirit of meek but unbowed nonresistance, as Socrates submitted to his Athenian jury and Christ to Pilate and the Sanhedrin and Gandhi to the British Raj, hating the sin while loving the sinner—but condoned, endorsed, approved, cheered, praised, honored, respected, believed in and aided even the most brutal, unjust, and lying rulers, and sneered at and persecuted those who spoke truth to power, all of which can, thanks to Hobbes, be summed up in a word: *sovereignty*.

We are all Hobbesians now

Hobbes' argument, very weak on the logical plane, is strong in a different way, namely, *there is lots of evidence that we really believe it*, or at least accept it, whether or not it makes sense. I began this chapter by referring to certain pairs of words, namely *murder/execution, extortion/taxation, abduction/arrest*. That the state is exempt from the moral law is one interpretation, and in some cases (when a state's actions are indefensible in terms of natural law and the social contract, yet the state is still granted semantic absolution by ordinary people who talk about them) this seems to be the only viable interpretation, of the contrasting judgments implied by these words.

Although readers may be misled by Hobbes' pretensions of being a political geometer, starting from definitions like Euclid and proceeding by deduction, *Leviathan* is, in its own way, a richly, albeit tendentiously and selectively, empirical work. Several more examples may be offered to show that we are all at least *ad hoc* Hobbesians.

First, in the months prior to the Iraq war, it was widely argued that the regime-change planned by the Bush administration would violate "Iraq's sovereignty." Not even "Saddam's sovereignty over Iraq," but *Iraq's sovereignty*, as if, after all, Saddam Hussein "bore the person" of the Iraqi people and there was "a real unity of them all" of which he was the representative. Advocates of "Iraq's sovereignty" felt no need to recant, and might not even have been surprised, when Iraqis thronged the streets to cheer the invader and went on to elect a government that hanged Saddam for his crimes. That most Iraqis hated Saddam, and had wanted to be rid of him, did not make him less their representative. All this is quite consistent with Hobbes' ideas.

Second, American college students and others who want to criticize U.S. foreign policy often say that "we" did wrong in overthrowing a Latin American regime or supporting Osama bin Laden in the 1980s, even though they did not participate in these actions, and were usually not born when they took place. Mere enjoyment of boasting might explain why Americans who were born long after World War II will say, proudly, that "we won World War II."

But when Americans use the word "we" in speaking of actions of the U.S. government that they disapprove, and are ashamed of, needlessly accepting responsibility for wrongs done by others, it seems, after all, as if we agree with Hobbes that subjects must "every one... owne, and acknowledge himself to be the author of whatsoever [the sovereign] shall act, or cause to be acted."

Third, Hobbes' theory justifies the idea of territorial sovereignty and the practice of modern states in restricting migration by means of passport regimes. Although only persons, not land, can authorize a sovereign, Hobbes' ideas (a) that consent to the social contract can be justly extorted by fear, and (b) that non-consenting persons who inhabit a sovereign's declared territory can be justly murdered by their fellows, provide a basis for the notion of a state that claims a monopoly of violence within a given territory.

One implication of Hobbes' theory is that illegal immigrants, who are not subjects of the sovereign power, may justly be killed. If that were really true, laws restricting immigration into the United States would be possible to enforce.

Demands for stronger enforcement of migration restrictions often feature the telltale word *sovereignty*.

Fourth, contemporary official attitudes to the right of revolution are exactly the same as those of Hobbes. Hobbes was zealous to legitimize *all* sovereigns, and to close all doors to revolution. Yet he automatically recognizes the legitimacy of a revolutionary regime once it gains physical control. The sovereign is overthrown; long live the sovereign. If this seems like crazy inconsistency, it is also the standard practice of contemporary international diplomacy. Again and again, a government is overthrown by a military coup in Africa, or Asia, or Latin America, and the coup leaders' delegates are immediately allowed to occupy their countries' seats at the United Nations.

These are contemporary examples; but *Leviathan* is full of similar examples from Hobbes' own time and from prior history. By incessant allusions, Hobbes carries the reader through the Bible and ancient Greece and Rome to the Europe of his own day. His conceptual framework is capable, like a sponge, of absorbing a huge amount of substantive experience of the claims and practices of governments.

Hobbes' theory turns out, after all, to be able to explain much in history, and in our attitudes, and our laws. He is able to make a strong case that much of the world regards sovereignty in much the same light that he regards it, or at least speaks and/or acts as if it does. Today, it is often convenient for us to recognize the sovereign rights of regimes whose practices are abhorrent to us, and whose ideologies are absurd, so that we regard them as ruling solely by force and fear; yet we nonetheless treat them as legitimate governments. When we do, we become *ad hoc* Hobbesians.

Popular sovereignty

For Hobbes, it is possible for the sovereign to be one man—a monarchy—an assembly of men—an oligarchy—or, maybe, a democracy, though he writes little of the latter, and at one point seems to hint that he had a low opinion of it:

Tyranny and oligarchy... are not the names of other forms of government, but of [monarchy and aristocracy] misliked. For they that are discontented under monarchy call it tyranny; and they that are displeased with aristocracy call it oligarchy: so also, they which find themselves grieved under a democracy call it anarchy, which signifies want of government; and yet I think no man believes that want of government is any new kind of government...

By not quite contradicting those who call democracy anarchy, Hobbes manages to give the impression that he agrees with them.

Hobbes had reason to be skeptical. For "the people" to "rule," they must be able to make decisions, and so we speak of "the will of the people." But if there is disagreement among the people, what can it mean to speak of their will? The "will of the majority" seems to be a clearer concept; but it turns out also to be flawed.

Suppose there are three voters, A, B, and C, who can choose between three mutually exclusive policies, X, Y, and Z. Their preferences, in rank order, are shown in Table 1:

Table 1: Cycling

	A	B	C
1	X	Z	Y
2	Y	X	Z
3	Z	Y	X

What is the "will of the majority" here? If X, Y, and Z are proposed, and each voter has one vote, there will be a tie. In binary elections, X beats Y, and Y beats Z, *but Z beats X*. This is called *cycling*, and it implies that the majority can never make a decision, or more precisely, that if they arrive at a decision by a series of binary votes the outcome will be determined by the order in which the votes are taken, and the system is not a democracy but a well-concealed tyranny by an "agenda setter" who decides that order. Thomas Hobbes would have gone mad with envy and admiration, could he have foreseen a 20th-century "impossibility theorem" by Nobel laureate Kenneth Arrow, which proves that no group decision-making process can satisfy even the following minimal criteria:

- *Unrestricted domain.* The group is always able to make a choice.
- *Pareto efficiency.* If every voter prefers X to Y, the group chooses X over Y.
- *Independence of irrelevant alternatives.* If every voters preferences between X and Y remain unchanged when alternative Z is offered, the group's preference between X and Y is also unchanged.
- *Non-dictatorship.* No voter is a "dictator" who can determine the group's preference single-handedly.

In short, the idea of *the* people—a collective noun, a reification—as opposing to *people*—separate individuals—choosing, is at bottom incoherent, or at best can only be given an arbitrary meaning in a particular institutional context. In view of these findings, it is weird that literate middle-class capitalist nations like the United States and the leading nations of Western Europe are able to make democracy work. It is not at all surprising that democracy has so often failed elsewhere.

Woodrow Wilson's dangerous idea

A quote which is sometimes displayed on the homepage of the Woodrow Wilson Center is a reminder of the idealism in Wilson and hints at a great might-have-been. "Every people has a right to choose the sovereignty under which they will live," said Wilson in 1916. The trouble here lay in the use of the singular reification—every *people*. How different might history have been if Wilson had used people as a *plural*, and had said "*All* people *have* a right to choose the sovereignty under which they will live!"

That doctrine would have implied open borders, and freedom of migration, with all the people—each individual person—choosing what state to live in, by moving there. That policy might have made the world safe, not so much for democracy, as for something more important: *freedom*.

Alas, in Wilson's day freedom of migration was dying. World War I was the occasion for the imposition at borders everywhere of requirements for passports—those wicked little documents that symbolize an age in which human beings have no rights as such, but only as subjects of some sovereign state—which were never lifted thereafter. Instead, Wilson played the role of sorcerer's apprentice, helping to awaken a new totalitarian tribalism.

Wilson's idea of national self-determination does not make sense. It is impossible to give *every* people a right to choose the sovereignty under which they will live, for two reasons: (a) as shown above, the concept of "a people" "choosing" is not robust, and (b) in Wilson's day and through most of history people of different nationalities live, more often than not, all mixed up together, so that no matrix of compact, nationally homogeneous, territorial states can be created unless lots of ethnic cleansing occurs first.

Yet Wilson and his fellow peacemakers at Versailles faced a genuinely hard problem. By the time President Woodrow Wilson laid the basis for the peace and the post-war world order with his Fourteen Points speech in January 1918, the great multi-national monarchies of Eastern Europe—Russian, Austrian, and Turkish—were crumbling. (The Russian tsars had already been overthrown by the Bolshevik revolution.) A new governing principle was needed to replace the defunct sovereignty of the monarchs.

Americans, naturally, wanted to export their own political model, in which they had always felt a justifiable pride, all the more so now that autocracy had been discredited. But what was that model, and how could it be applied in Europe? Woodrow Wilson saw that model as *democracy*, that is, *rule of the people*, which requires a people, that is, a nation. So the map had somehow to be redrawn to conform to this idea. At that point, the new states would enjoy national sovereignty, and the newly ascendant principle of *national sovereignty* would serve the same function that sovereignty had served since the Peace of Westphalia: to make peace, by drawing lines.

Hardly any of the world's leading states fit the new paradigm. National self-determination pointed to the breakup, not only of the Ottoman, Russian, and Habsburg empires, but of all the overseas colonial empires of Western Europe as well. The breakup of all those empires, which was largely accomplished in the decades following, left people of different nationalities intermingled in the same lands and cities, expected somehow to be sovereign states.

Ethnic cleansing, a logical ramification of Wilson's national self-determination principle, began immediately. Even during the peace conference, Greece tried, with British support, to exercise Greek rights of national self-determination in majority-Greek Anatolian cities like Smyrna. This resulted in the expulsion of over a million Greeks from Asia Minor as Turkey retaliated. Sad episodes of ethnic cleansing and genocide have periodically stained world history in the decades since, as various peoples have responded to the incentives that the principle of national self-determination creates by getting rid of awkward neighbors whom they would otherwise will have to treat as equal fellow-citizens.

The Nazi slogan *Ein Volk, ein Reich, ein Führer* (one-people, one-state, one -leader) was Adolf Hitler's spin on the principle of national self-determination. Early assertions of German power under Hitler—the occupations of the Rhineland, of Austria, and of the Sudetenland—were justifiable, and were justified, as national self-determination, and were accepted by the Allies partly for this reason, greatly strengthening Hitler at home and abroad and facilitating his later conquests. Nazi conquests of Poland, Denmark, France, etc. cannot be defended in the same way, but the worst crime of the Nazis, the Holocaust, can be. After all, if the sovereign people of Germany did not want Jews living among them, why should they have to do so? And if no foreign country was willing to accept many German Jews as immigrants, what choice had they, but to exterminate them? Of course, if we believe what was argued in **Chapter 1**, we will affirm the *habeas corpus* principle, that Jews had a right to life which the Nazis could not justly violate. But that is only to observe that *natural rights are inconsistent with sovereignty*. (Hobbes would say that the Jews had a right to resist the Nazis; but Hitler had a right to kill them; and citizens of Germany and conquered countries had no right to come to the Jews' aid.)

The heyday of national self-determination was also the heyday of racism, of the Ku Klux Klan, of anti-Semitism, of theories of the master race. This is logical enough, since it takes a bit of semantic alchemy even to make a distinction between, on the one hand, "nation" and "nationalism"—these words comes from the Latin *natus*, born, and thus referred originally to people with a common ancestry—and "race" and "racism," on the other.

Strictly speaking, the United States of America has never been a nation-state, which makes it rather odd that Woodrow Wilson should have promoted the idea of national self-determination at all. America has had its share of racism, of course, but it has always been a "melting pot" of people of many different ancestries. The population of colonial America was largely British in stock, but there were always Dutch and Germans, soon joined by Irish and Jews, then Scandinavians and Italians, etc.

And of course, there were the non-white peoples, the Americans Indians and black slaves from Africa, who were not initially treated as equal members of the nation, but whom it eventually became one of America's moral triumphs to integrate and accept as equals. If America is a nation at all, it is a nation united by citizenship—a *state-nation* rather than a nation-state—or perhaps, more nobly, a nation united by a civic creed of freedom.

But the new, post-racial meaning which the word "nation" has acquired in America is not easy to apply in polities for which a revered constitution and pride in democratic success are not available to act as unifying factors, even today, let alone in 1918. And to call for national self-determination, that is, for people of the same *nation* to form a *state*, implies that nationality is more fundamental than citizenship. Without claiming that this is the only reason that people learned to identify themselves largely by their real or imagined race in the decades after 1918, it clearly encouraged the trend. The habit was broken in Europe only after World War II in reaction to the horrors of Nazism. It lingered and did damage in the post-colonial world for some time thereafter.

After World War II, the dissolution of the European colonial empires brought national self-determination to south and southeast Asia, the Middle East and Africa; and many of the same tragedies that had afflicted Europe in the inter-war period—the wars of secession, the expulsions of populations, the authoritarian regimes based on paranoid ideologies and personality cults, the persecution of minorities, the attempts at economic autarky resulting in stagnation and impoverishment—afflicted those regions.

A world safe for pseudo-democracy

National self-determination today is like a volcano that has gone mostly dormant after a series of violent eruptions. The ash and the lava flows—racism, ethnic cleansing, genocide, totalitarian tribalism—have mostly ceased, but have left their marks—the national borders, the regions from which long-established populations have been expelled—on a landscape recently scorched and scarred, but where the greenery—international trade and migration, racial tolerance, cosmopolitan culture—has now begun to recover. The volcano is not wholly dormant, and its occasional eruptions—inter-ethnic violence in the Caucasus or Yugoslavia or Kyrgyzstan or the Great Lakes region of Africa—and fears of another eruption—ethnic tensions, threats of secession—were the first disturbances of the peace to interrupt the liberal idyll of the "end of history" 1990s. But the volcano's main force has been spent, at least for now.

The principle of national self-determination is no longer regarded, for official purposes, as carrying weight in international law and diplomacy. There is little external support for an independent Chechnya, Kurdistan, Catalonia, Corsica, Tamil Eelam, Tibet, Uighurstan, Balochistan, Pashtunistan, Transnistria, or Hawaii. The Armenian-occupied province of Nagorno-Karabakh continues to be regarded, after almost twenty years of *de facto* separation, as the sovereign territory of Azerbaijian. Even Taiwan, a thriving capitalist democracy that was politically separate from the Chinese mainland for almost the entire 20th century, cannot secure international recognition. East Timor's struggle for independence from Indonesia in 1998 only enjoyed international support because its original occupation by Indonesia in 1975 was illegal. Milosevic's genocidal past and the chaos of post-communist Yugoslavia gave Kosovo a special justification for seeking independence, yet even in this case it took ten years before its *de facto* independence received international recognition. Abkhazia and South Ossetia were recognized by Russia as a means of humiliating Georgia's Western allies but otherwise have received negligible international support. The world has tried to *freeze* borders, to treat them as "sacred."

In suppressing the principle of national self-determination, the sovereign peoples of today exhibit the perennial hypocrisy of sovereigns. Nation-states that were born in secession prohibit secession. India, Pakistan, and Sri Lanka seceded from the British Empire. Each then prevented or tried to prevent the secession, respectively, of Kashmir, of Bangladesh, of Tamil Eelam. The United States declared independence from Britain, then blocked by federal force the secession of the Southern states. International relations multiply the hypocrisy.

The independence struggle of the Chechens may resemble that of the Irish or the Greeks, but the Irish and the Greeks do not support it.

National self-determination, though it is the origin of today's nation-states, is inconsistent with national sovereignty, for as long as groups of subjects within a nation-state have a right to secede from it, it does not enjoy sovereignty. With the suppression of this principle, a world order based on national sovereignty has been able to mature. Indeed, Wilson's vision of a world order based on free-market, democratic nation-states living in peace under (not the League of Nations but) the United Nations has been realized, with one difference. Wilson wanted to "make the world safe for democracy." What came to pass instead was a world safe for *pseudo-democracy*.

For almost two thousand years, the memory of Roman power was paid this linguistic compliment: that crowned heads of Europe called themselves *emperors*, after the Latin word *imperator* or (military) commander which became the title of Rome's supreme magistrate, or some variation of the family name of Julius Caesar, such as *Tsar* or *Kaiser*. Today the United States of America receives the same compliment from the whole world, for the preferred title of heads of state is that which was held by George Washington and Woodrow Wilson: *president*.

All but a handful of countries in the world—the monarchies of Saudi Arabia and Thailand are the main exceptions (and Thailand is *de facto* mostly democratic)—claim to be democracies. Odd as it may seem, periodic elections have been regularly held, and falsified, in authoritarian and totalitarian regimes from the Soviet Union to North Korea to Iran to Zimbabwe for decades. Elections are even conducted in countries like Azerbaijan and Syria, where the presidential office is passed from father to son like a crown. To make elections safe for rulers, ballot boxes are stuffed, candidates are disqualified, or jailed on trumped-up charges, political parties are banned or denied access to the media and the right to organize, television and radio, sometimes also newspapers and the internet, are tightly controlled, journalists are arrested or killed—yet the elections are held, nonetheless. That these obviously phony elections apparently confer enough legitimacy to be useful to rulers is a backhanded tribute to how far-reaching the influence of the idea of democracy has become.

For most of the period since 1918, while pseudo-democracy became nearly universal, genuine democracy remained scarce. Wilson's principle of national self-determination might overthrow the great multinational empires, but it contributed nothing to the painstaking work of discerning and defending the rights of each individual and thereby giving rise to *freedom*. And there can be no genuine democracy without freedom. It is too easy, in the absence of well-protected individual rights, to stifle public debate and thwart political competition. Only recently has genuine democracy enjoyed real success and spread to new countries and regions. But it is far from universal, and after a period of democratic expansion during 1975-2000, it is now in retreat in large areas of the world, especially in the former Soviet Union.

An apt phrase has been coined by one of democracy's euthanizers, Vladimir Putin. He calls his authoritarian regime in Russia a "sovereign democracy." Putin has a point. There is a contradiction at the heart of Putin's sovereign democracy, namely that by muzzling the press and preventing the opposition from contesting elections, Putin deprives the Russian people of political choice and therefore of the opportunity effectively to practice democratic self-government. But there is also a contradiction at the heart of liberal democracy, as practiced in America, where an "independent"—which is to say, not democratically accountable—judiciary can overturn laws passed by elected legislatures, without which practice the Bill of Rights would be null and void. How are the people sovereign, when judges can overrule them? Putin's way of combining the two contradictory concepts of *sovereignty* and *democracy* is really no more incoherent than America's. *For democracy to be democratic, it cannot be sovereign.*

Today's liberal democracies and "sovereign democracies" may be roughly characterized as historical instantiations, respectively, of the political philosophies of Locke and Hobbes. In the Hobbesian pseudo-democracies, a sovereign who is above the law receives the formal consent of his people in noncompetitive elections. In the Lockean democracies, there is some recognition, however it is expressed and institutionalized, of human rights which elected governments must respect, and this creates a space for political competition and genuine democratic choice. But the liberal democracies are only *relatively* Lockean. They call themselves sovereign, after all, and the powers they claim extend beyond what Locke envisioned, and probably beyond what can be justified in natural law, especially vis-à-vis the rights of foreign-born persons without representation, and in curtailing the right to migrate.

Territorial jurisdiction in natural law

Hobbes' case for the rights of sovereigns fails as an argument. Its premises are false and its logic unsound. Yet it is perennially relevant because Hobbes manages to rationalize the claims to a special exemption from ordinary moral law which rulers perennially make and subjects too often condone. So pervasive is the idea of sovereignty, so much is it woven into our ordinary ways of speaking and acting about all matters political, that it is difficult, even for the sake of argument, to purge it from our minds and to think about the just powers of governments in a more valid way. Nonetheless I will try to do so here; that is, to think about what kind of territorial jurisdiction, what kind of claims to a local monopoly of force, a government may exercise within the moral law. To this end, I offer and evaluate a series of arguments for territorial sovereignty/jurisdiction.

1. People have a right to defend their property by force. When they delegate that right to a state, the state has the right to defend by force the property of its subjects. In that sense, the property of a state's subjects is the state's territory.

This is valid as far as it goes. But (a) territorial jurisdiction in this sense does not justify excluding non-citizens from the *streets*, and (b) it does not justify the state in excluding non-citizens from the private property of citizens when they have been invited by citizens.

2. People have a right to use pre-emptive violence to defend themselves against an imminent threat. If I see you running at me with a battle ax, your evident intention of killing me absolves me from guilt if I pull out my pistol and shoot you first. Similarly, the state, in order to defend the property of its citizens, may exclude foreigners not only from the private land of its citizens but from other non-private land in the vicinity of its citizens' territory, as strategic necessity dictates.

If this argument is valid, and it surely is at least to some extent, it may even point beyond sovereignty to a doctrine of pre-emptive war. At the same time, though, it does not justify the exclusion of foreigners whose intentions are obviously peaceful. Armed foreigners, criminals, members of hostile armies may be excluded; peaceful workers and traders should not.

3. Since no court can handle all the disputes that arise in the world, there need to be many courts, and a division of labor among them. If a case could be tried in any of several courts, the parties to the dispute might have a further dispute about which court to try it in. So courts should, as much as possible, agree among themselves on clear rules about which of them will try a given case. Among the various means of doing this, drawing physical borders between the jurisdictions of different courts is likely to be an important component.

This is the best argument for one aspect of sovereignty, namely, the precise definition of physical boundaries which are not coincident with the extent of private property of any state's subjects. But even that conclusion is only acceptable if the courts (or states) regard one another as just. Suppose there are two courts, court A and court B. If court A believes that court B is generally just, it can make an agreement with court B that court B will try all cases within territory X, while court A tries those in territory Y. If, on the other hand, court A does not think that court B is generally just, it cannot justly acknowledge court B's jurisdiction (thereby condoning court B's unjust conduct) and ought not to aid it through, for example, extraditing those it has condemned. If courts A and B regard one another as just, they may be wise to define precise jurisdictional boundaries, but it in no way follows that they can forbid people from crossing them. (If Vermont's courts regard New Hampshire's as insufficiently liberal, it cannot therefore exclude New Hampshirites from its territory.)

4. Citizens pay taxes to provide public goods, starting with physical safety. If foreigners are allowed to come in and use the streets, they will free-ride on the tax dollars of citizens.

But if this argument is valid, it clearly implies that foreigners should be *taxed*, not that they should be *excluded*.

None of these arguments can justify the *arbitrary* and *discretionary* exclusion of foreigners who cannot plausibly be regarded as security threats. The state's justification for the use of violence is derived from the just uses of violence by individuals, namely, self-defense, including the defense of one's property, and retribution. Neither self-defense nor retribution is applicable as a justification for coercion of a peaceful migrant.

The conclusion, which is that people have a right to migrate that the state ought to respect, that the illegal immigrant laboring to win a better life for his family is in the right and the INS agent who deports him is in the wrong, ought to come as something of an anticlimax. If the truth be told, it is simply self-evident that a peaceful migrant is harming no one and ought to be left alone, yet we have had to resort to laborious reasoning and historical inquiry in order to uproot and discard the sophistries by which aggression against such persons is rationalized.

The conclusion we have arrived at is not peculiar to the meta-ethical standpoint that has been defended and applied in this book. It would be vain to seek words strong enough to express with adequate force how perverse migration restrictions are from a *utilitarian* point of view. The world's richest countries are, in dollar terms, over a hundred times richer than the poorest. Such income gaps reflect and/or affect life expectancy, nutrition, and literacy; access to electricity, plumbing, clean water; entertainment; education; travel; security from crime; in short, most of what constitutes human flourishing. Migrants who come to the United States quickly close much of this income gap, as well as enjoying, in many cases, greater political and religious freedom.

Nor do American citizens lose by it on the whole, for while some do suffer from competing with immigrants, these losses are offset by others' gains from trade with immigrants. And it is worth noting that, while one might expect the presence of large numbers of poor immigrants in the United States to produce a rise in crime (though it would take a large rise in crime to counter-balance the welfare gains that immigration brings to immigrants and to many natives), in fact crime has fallen in step with the growth in immigration in recent decades. Any plausible utilitarian analysis of migration policy would imply a major easing of immigration restrictions, if not entirely open borders.

From a Rawlsian meta-ethical standpoint, the case against migration restrictions is equally decisive (even if Rawls does not accept this compelling ramification of his theory).[14] No one behind a veil of ignorance would choose to live in a world in which he had, say, a 20% chance of being born into a rich country and shielded by migration controls from a perhaps awkward co-existence with poor immigrants, and an 80% of being born into a poor country where his best chance of gaining a more secure and fulfilling life for himself and his family was blocked by those same migration controls. Any attempt to defend migration controls on communitarian grounds immediately runs into the problem that not only nations but a great variety of communities—families and races, religions and cultures and schools of thought, business firms and professional associations, networks of friends, political parties and movements, hobby clubs, etc.—knit people together, and most of these cross borders, so that migration controls *separate* as well as uniting people, if they do unite people at all.

Who guards the guards, revisited

We have claimed that even sovereign states are bound by the moral law. But a sovereign state is typically the most powerful entity in its territory. If such a state

---

[14] http://gregmankiw.blogspot.com/2006/05/tierney-and-rawls-on-immigration.html. Also see Glover (2009).

violates a people's rights, who can stop it? By whom can a sovereign be held accountable? If Hobbes was wrong, if sovereigns are not exempt from morality, if tyrants have no right to rule, if they are at one with pirates and robbers, if their overthrow is justified, who is to carry it out? The question that we asked before returns, with the stakes now higher than ever: *Who guards the guards?*

6

The Ethics of Liberation

—Americans, of all people, should never be surprised by the power of our ideals. Eventually, the call of freedom comes to every mind and every soul. We do not accept the existence of permanent tyranny because we do not accept the possibility of permanent slavery. Liberty will come to those who love it. (George W. Bush, Second Inaugural, January 20, 2005)

The great *cause célèbre* of the last decade, the Iraq War or "Operation Iraqi Freedom," created a unique pattern of polarization, in which both pro-war and anti-war voices came from both sides of the usual right-left political spectrum. Allies of convenience, though they sometimes had little else in common but their position on the war, promiscuously borrowed one another's arguments and talking points. The analysis in this chapter inevitably was shaped by these polemical battles, and although it is an attempt to apply the principles developed in **Chapters 1 through 5** (pro-freedom, anti-sovereignty) to what is still one of the burning issues of our times, it also reflects a perspective on certain events, trends, and personalities which is separable from those principles.

I suspect that someone else might approach the Iraq War from the same philosophical premises, yet appraise it quite differently. I also suspect that this chapter will become obsolete more quickly than the rest of the book. Still, my effort will at least show how high the stakes are in trying to understand and apply the principles of a free society. While there might be cases where they could be applied more cleanly and non-controversially, I do not think it would be better to go looking for such examples, for applications of theory to practice are usually not clean, but must bring in many judgments that are not informed by the theory. Readers who are sick of the Iraq War, or for whom the issue is too emotionally charged, may skip this chapter. Others are welcome to argue with me about it.

On March 20, 2003, the armed forces of the United States, Great Britain, Australia, and Poland invaded Iraq to overthrow the worst extant tyranny on earth except maybe North Korea. Saddam Hussein began his rule of Iraq in 1979 with a high-profile mass murder, the first in a rule-of-murder which claimed hundreds of thousands of victims in domestic terror—the number will never be known, but has been estimated at 800,000[15] —not to mention the millions who died in the wars Saddam started against Iran and Kuwait.

The United States was culpable in all this from beginning to end. Saddam Hussein joined the Ba'ath party in 1958 and in the following year was involved in a U.S.-backed plot to assassinate then-prime minister Abdul Karim Qassim. Later, in the 1970s and 1980s, the United States supported Saddam as an anti-Communist and a mortal enemy of the Islamic Republic of Iran. In the 1990s, sanctions imposed on Saddam by the United States and its allies took a terrible toll, not on Saddam's regime, but on ordinary Iraqis, which became the subject of the following horrifying exchange in 1996:[16]

CBS journalist Lesley Stahl on U.S. sanctions against Iraq: We have heard that a half million children have died. I mean, that's more children than died in Hiroshima. And, you know, is the price worth it?

Secretary of State Madeleine Albright: I think this is a very hard choice, but the price—we think the price is worth it.

Osama bin Laden listed "the great devastation inflicted on the Iraqi people by the crusader-Zionist alliance, [with] the huge number of those killed... exceeding 1 million" as one of his three reasons for declaring holy war on the United States in 1998.[17] Strangely enough, in this case bin Laden's position was more liberal and humanitarian than that of the United States. U.S. troops stationed in Saudi Arabia to protect that kingdom against aggression by Saddam supplied another of bin Laden's grievances, and again, bin Laden had the liberal high ground, for it was unseemly that U.S. troops were propping up a vicious tyranny like that of the House of Saud.

Probably no event since the Munich conference of 1938 has so damaged the international reputation of democracy as the liberation of Iraq. An estimated 36 million people worldwide participated in protests against the Iraq war between January 3 and April 12, 2003, in vain;[18] and it was overwhelmingly unpopular throughout the world (except in America, where a large majority initially supported it). The war was condemned as "unilateral," "illegal," and "imperialist"

---

[15] http://www.indict.org.uk/newsarticles.php?article=news180603
[16] http://www.fair.org/index.php?page=1084
[17] http://www.fas.org/irp/world/para/docs/980223-fatwa.htm
[18] http://en.wikipedia.org/wiki/Protests_against_the_Iraq_War

"aggression." Global public opinion became sharply less favorable to the United States during the war.

Yet if it was a public relations failure, it was a triple success strategically: (a) it overthrew Saddam, (b) it seems, as of August 2010, to have established a new, democratic regime in Iraq, albeit a still fragile one, and (c) it won the War on Terror by forcing Al Qaeda to shift money and weapons into Iraq, where they lost. It also set a startling precedent which may yet kill Westphalian sovereignty for good. We shall briefly review the history of these important events, then consider the ethics of liberation.

The Islamist challenge

What emerged as the most dangerous challenger to the U.S.-led, liberal world order of the post-Cold War era had roots going back to the resistance of Western-backed *mujahideen* to the Soviet invasion of Afghanistan; to the religious ferment in 1950s Egypt that gave rise to the Muslim Brotherhood; and to the abolition of the Caliphate in Turkey, and thus of a notional pan-Islamic religious state, by Ataturk in 1924.

The Muslim world was the only region which had a potent anti-liberal ideology in the immediate aftermath of the fall of Communism. The moment of worldwide democratic transformation in 1989-91 left the Muslim world largely untouched. Algeria is the exception that proves the rule, for the peaceful dissolution of a typical nationalist-totalitarian regime there in 1989 paved the way, not for an embrace of democracy as in central Europe or Latin America, but for a civil war, as Islamists explicitly opposed to democracy sought to establish an Islamic government.[19]

The existence of similar forces in Egypt, Saudi Arabia and elsewhere, helped deter dictators from granting liberalization and the secular opposition from seeking it. Osama bin Laden had been involved in the Afghan war, and had gained confidence from the defeat and subsequent collapse of the Soviets. Although there have been many historical episodes of adversarial relations between Islam and the West—the initial Arab conquests of the 7th century; the Crusades; the Turkish conquests of the 14th to 17th centuries, and the takeover of Muslim lands by European colonial empires in the 19th and early 20th centuries—the paranoid anti-Western ideology of modern Islamism has more recent origins in

---

[19] http://en.wikipedia.org/wiki/Algerian_Civil_War

writers like the Egyptian Islamist Sayyid Qutb (1906-1966), whose brother was mentor to Ayman al-Zawahiri,the second-in-command al-Qaeda leader.[20]

The pre-eminent grievance of the Islamists is the existence of the state of Israel, which came into being by displacing many Palestinian Arabs; but the disproportionate attention and anger which this has provoked in the Islamic world bears witness to deeper complexes. Islam was born in an explosion of aggressive military expansion—*jihad*—which overran most of the Mediterranean world, Persia, and some of modern Pakistan and central Asia; and Muslims who see their identity as rooted in this history have difficulty accepting the reversal of the process by the establishment of a non-Muslim state in lands that are historically Muslim (though also, earlier, historically Jewish).

Osama bin Laden's terrorist organization, al-Qaeda, launched coordinated terrorist attacks on the World Trade Center in New York, blocks away from Wall Street, and the Pentagon and the White House in Washington, DC on September 11, 2001 ("9/11"). The date was symbolic—911 is the code by which Americans call emergency services—and showed an intent to destroy the centers of American military, financial, and political power.

The attack shocked the U.S. public and transformed U.S. politics. Though bin Laden was angry at the United States for having troops in Saudi Arabia, maintaining sanctions against Iraq, and supporting the Israeli occupation of Palestine, in attacking the "far enemy," America, bin Laden seems to have hoped to strike also the "near enemy," the secular governments in Muslim and Arab countries, especially Egypt and Saudi Arabia, which were (he thought) sustained by American support.

Might the United States have simply "turned the other cheek" after 9/11—made no response, gone on living as it had done before? The suggestion seems contrary to the premise of government, whose primary *raison d'etre* is to protect the rights and safety of their citizens. But how to respond to this *asymmetric* attack presented a difficult problem.

Probably no one, and certainly not al-Qaeda, could defeat the United States on a level-playing battlefield. But though NATO invaded Afghanistan and quickly captured Kabul, al-Qaeda, a secret and global organization, quietly embedded in populations from Afghanistan to the Horn of Africa to Western Europe, was not vulnerable to direct military force in the way that Saddam's regime in Iraq, or the Taliban regime in Afghanistan, was.

---

[20] http://en.wikipedia.org/wiki/Muhammad_Qutb

The sad logic of the war seemed to be that the invasive policing that the U.S. would have to condone, and even to urge governments in the Islamic world to resort to, if al Qaeda was to be hunted down, would provide a golden pretext for the dictators of the Muslim world to become still more repressive. President George W. Bush found a risky high road out of this dilemma.

The liberation

Soon after the fall of Kabul, the Bush administration turned its attention to Saddam's Iraq, even though Saddam had nothing to do with 9/11. The rhetorical and diplomatic buildup lasted over a year. When it finally came, the liberation of Iraq was swift: only 21 days passed from the beginning of the invasion to the fall of Baghdad. As of the end of April 2003, there were even fewer casualties in the second Iraq War than in the first. Many of Iraq's armed forces chose to desert rather than to fight, reflecting both their disloyalty to the dictator and the certainty that America would win. In its early days, the war had the character of a revolution, as the Iraqi people, rather than resist the Americans, seized the opportunity to tear down a hated tyranny.

One of the more sinister aspects of the Iraq war is the attempt by the Western media to persuade Western publics that prewar predictions that coalition troops would be "welcomed as liberators" were false. In fact, coalition troops *were* welcomed as liberators, as any mainstream news article from April 9, 2003 will readily show. Choosing at random, I quote the account of *The New York Times*:

April 9, 2003, the day Baghdad fell. In an old notebook, seeds of the future are there.

By dawn most of Saddam Hussein's military had melted away, leaving a city ripe for the plucking. American troops already controlled the west bank of the Tigris, and their colleagues on the east advanced through the morning toward the city center, hourly shrinking the bubble of Saddamist control...

Iraq's long-suppressed Shiite majority was coming. We saw them looting an abandoned police barracks, carrying out machine gun barrels, tear gas guns and cutlasses.

Saddam City no more. The delight was unmistakable.

"Good, America, good," shouted one young man.

"Have we got rid of the criminal? Tell us," pleaded an old man. "When, where are we going to get rid of him?"

In Sunni suburbs the mood was black. A quarter past noon, a gray-bearded engineer watching looters snarled: "This is the freedom that America brings to us: They destroyed our country. They are thieves. They stole our oil, and they kill our people."...

Around 3:30 p.m. one of the first people to risk crossing the Americans' path was an old Christian woman named Victoria. She ran across the street, kissing her rosary beads and murmuring "al-hamdullilah, salaam, inshallah." (Praise be to God. Peace, God willing.) She did not stop for an instant, heading back to the safety of her house...

At 4 p.m. a group of Iraqis screwed up the courage to run out of their houses and tear down a poster of Mr. Hussein. It was only 50 yards from the Americans, but well out of their sight. An apparently spontaneous gesture, one of many we saw across the city.

"Heroes, heroes the Americans," said one young man, beaming. "They came into the country and occupied it as fast as they could, thank God."...

Beside him another man was ecstatic: "Thank you, thank you Mr. Bush. Gentleman, gentleman. Very gentle man."

But an older man shook his head. "If they just came to liberate us, then a thousand thanks. But if they are coming for something else, well, we are a Muslim country."[21]

Obviously not *all* Iraqis welcomed the fall of Saddam. But these were not uncommon opinions, either. A typical poll taken in March 2004,[22]

---

[21] http://atwar.blogs.nytimes.com/2008/03/18/baghdad-april-9-2003-fear-euphoria-and-hints-of-things-to-come/

[22] http://abcnews.go.com/sections/world/goodmorningamerica/iraq_anniversary_poll_040314.html

for example, found a plurality of 48% to 39% saying the US was right to lead the invasion.

In spite of abundant text and video evidence, in spite of the eloquence many Iraqi bloggers who since 2003 have addressed the world in praise of their liberation by the coalition (and of course there are some on the other side too), the media's ploy seems to have succeeded. Much of the public seems to have been brainwashed into believing that, whatever their own lying eyes may have clearly indicated, the Americans and British were not welcomed as liberators after all.

Nation-building

The vast majority of the financial costs and military casualties that America incurred in Iraq took place after the main war aim, regime change, had been decisively achieved by the capture of Saddam in December 2003. Why? Because a consensus emerged that the liberation was not enough, that the U.S. had a responsibility to install a new regime—of course democratic—to take the place of Saddam's. So U.S. troops stayed, first to keep the peace, then to fight a rising insurgency.

A Coalition Provisional Authority governed Iraq until sovereignty was transferred to an interim Iraqi government in June 2004 by Iyad Allawi. An election took place on 30 January 2005 to elect a government which would draft a constitution under a transitional law. To ensure that people would not vote twice, voters had to get their hands marked with purple ink. This required some courage, since terrorist groups regarded voting as collaboration with the American occupiers, and as a result the election became the "purple finger revolution," a source of national pride for Iraqis.

Iraqi politicians succeeded in negotiating a new constitution which was passed by referendum on 15 October 2005. Ibrahim al-Jaafari became prime minister in place of Iyad Allawi after the January 2005 elections and held the post for a year, before Nouri al-Maliki became prime minister after the first elections under the new constitution. He held the post for four years. At the time of writing, it appears likely that Iyad Allawi will return to power as a result of new elections held, as scheduled under the constitution, in March 2010.

In short, Iraq has a democratic constitution and seems to have developed a tradition of multi-party, competitive elections followed by peaceful, legitimate transfers of power. What makes this achievement all the more remarkable is that Iraq is Muslim, majority-Arab, multi-ethnic and an oil state, all predictors of democratic failure. (Rowley and Smith, 2009).

Yet violence continued throughout the transition - sometimes of a merely terrorist nature - sometimes inter-communal between Sunni and Shia, even as American troops tried to maintain order. The nadir occurred around 2006, after which, thanks to Bush's "surge" early in 2007 involving a new strategy and more troops, with help from the policies of the Iraqi government, and perhaps also thanks to retaliation against Sunni violence by Sadrist militias, violence was reduced and greater security established. In spite of these improvements, Iraq remains one of the most dangerous countries in the world.

The defeat of al Qaeda

One side-effect of the Iraq War was that the United States effectively won the War on Terror that began in 2001. As Michael Totten, writing in 2008, explains,[23]

> The Al Qaeda leadership emphatically has not agreed [with the fashionable charge on the American left] that Iraq is a distraction. It has been their main event for years.

> "The most important and serious issue today for the whole world," Osama bin Laden said on December 28, 2004, "is this Third World War, which the Crusader-Zionist coalition began against the Islamic nation. It is raging in the land of the two rivers. The world's millstone and pillar is in Baghdad, the capital of the caliphate."

> It's only natural that an Arab-led and mostly Arab-staffed terrorist group like Al Qaeda would be more concerned with a strategically critical country in the heart of the Arab Middle East than with a primitive non-Arab backwater in Central Asia…

> Make no mistake: Al Qaeda's manpower and resources have been thoroughly degraded from its disastrous fight with Americans and Iraqis, especially in Anbar Province which was briefly established as Al Qaeda's "capital" of the so-called "Islamic State in Iraq."

---

[23] http://www.commentarymagazine.com/blogs/index.php/totten/31621

Last summer I met with U.S. Army Lieutenant Colonel Mike Silverman in Ramadi, the capital of Iraq's Anbar Province and also what until 2007 was Al Qaeda's key stronghold. "What's the most important thing Americans need to know about Iraq that they don't currently know?" I asked him.

"That we're fighting Al Qaeda," he said without hesitation. "[Abu Musab al] Zarqawi invented Al Qaeda in Iraq. The top leadership outside Iraq squawked and thought it was a bad idea. Then he blew up the Samarra mosque, triggered a civil war, and got the whole world's attention. Then the Al Qaeda leadership outside dumped huge amounts of money and people and arms into Anbar Province. They poured everything they had into this place. The battle against Americans in Anbar became their most important fight in the world. And they lost."

Al Qaeda lost in Iraq partly because American soldiers and Marines outsmarted and outfought them, but also, just as importantly, because the Iraqi people themselves rose up in resistance.

Just as important as Al Qaeda's physical defeat in Iraq was the collapse in support both for al Qaeda in particular and for militant and terrorist methods in general in Arab public opinion.[24] The abstract case against tactics like suicide bombing is not as strong as people in the West tend to insist (a bit self-servingly since they have a huge advantage in conventional military power). It seems to have taken a terrorist war against an Arab people to bring home to Jordanians and Lebanese the horror of terrorism.

No way back

Opposition to the Iraq war was always strong and, since 2003, has increased in breadth, even if time has dulled its intensity. Yet opponents have struggled to find a coherent message and have missed opportunities for electoral vindication. By December 2004, 56% of Americans thought the war was a mistake,[25] compared to 79% in May 2003 who thought the war was justified.[26] Yet the war issue seems to have hurt George W. Bush in the 2004 elections less than it hurt

---

[24] http://pewglobal.org/2007/07/24/a-rising-tide-lifts-mood-in-the-developing-world/
[25] http://www.washingtonpost.com/wp-dyn/articles/A14266-2004Dec20.html
[26] http://www.washingtonpost.com/ac2/wp-dyn/A1155-2003May16

John Kerry, who could not formulate a coherent position on it. Prime Minister John Howard of Australia, another war leader, also won re-election, and Prime Minister Tony Blair of Britain easily won re-election in 2005.

The unpopularity of the Iraq war may have been a factor in Barack Obama's victory in the November 2008 US presidential election, but it was a minor issue, and the Obama administration, once in office, carried out the plans of the Bush administration in Iraq. At bottom, opponents of the war are faced with a *fait accompli*. The invasion is irrevocable. Saddam is dead and cannot be restored to power. More importantly, *America can no longer credibly commit to respect the sovereignty of totalitarian regimes.*

At any time between the end of the Vietnam War and 9/11/2001, the possibility that America would "spread freedom" directly by simply overthrowing a totalitarian regime and establishing a new, democratic one in its place would have seemed fantastic. Yet it happened. And if it happened once, it can happen again, particularly because, even if the war has become retrospectively rather unpopular, it has by no means been unanimously repudiated by either the public or the political class. The old rules are gone, and no one quite knows what the new ones are.

"Iraq's sovereignty"

Turning from the history to the ethics of liberation, the indispensable argument in the case against the war is that it violated "Iraq's sovereignty." Yet war critics rarely make it directly. They make it indirectly when they say the war was "illegal," or an act of "aggression." Only an absolute ethical claim like "sovereignty" can justify a war critic in total *a priori* rejection of the war, as opposed to a more considered approach that weighs the benefits of liberating and bringing democracy to an oppressed people, and arguably of a decisive victory against al-Qaeda, against the net lives[27] lost, the fiscal cost, and the cost to America's reputation in international opinion.

---

[27] One must think in terms of *net* lives lost because the murderous record of Saddam Hussein, and the lethal effects of the sanctions to which Iraq was subjected before its liberation, implies that innocent lives would have continued to be lost in Iraq if the war had not occurred. In the early days of the war the pace of death in Iraq was arguably slower than it had been, on average, under Saddam, so that the war was actually saving net lives. It seems clear that this ceased to be true later, but any appraisal of the war must take into account that Iraqis would have been dying as a result of violence and deprivation with or without the war.

Of course, one might plausibly balance the costs and benefits and conclude that the war was not worth it; but this kind of moderate and considered opposition to the war has been rare. More typically, war critics have tried to *anathematize* the war and its supporters, insisting that it was extremely stupid or "incompetent" or somehow criminal. There is a good reason for this. If the Iraq War made the world a more dangerous place by violating the principle of Westphalian sovereignty, the most basic rule of the global commonwealth in which we live, thus depriving nations all over the world of the sense of security that sovereignty gives them, in order to reverse the damage, it is not enough to persuade the world that the Iraq war was, on balance, not worth it. It is necessary to define the war as a crime and its supporters as fools and villains, and somehow to make America and its allies say *never again*, and believe it, and be believed.

Because sovereignty cannot be defended rationally—Hobbes made the best attempt, and he failed—people must be compelled to regard it with superstitious dread and not to question it. To be moderately against the war, narrowly to oppose it on pragmatic grounds, is in effect to be for it, to accept its legitimacy if not its retrospective advisability. But while *Iraq's sovereignty* is the core anti-war argument, an explicit defense of it is unappealing, since it requires a defense of the proposition that Saddam had a right to rule Iraq.

A war of choice

When Japan bombed Pearl Harbor in December 1941, the U.S., in an obvious sense, had to fight. When Iraq invaded Kuwait in 1990, a clear violation of international law had occurred, and in that sense the U.S. was compelled to act. The U.S.-led invasion of Iraq in 2003 was different. The case for regime change in terms of international law was strong enough. Iraq had violated its treaty obligations by ejecting weapons inspectors and also U.N. Resolution 688, which demanded that Iraq "end the repression of the Iraqi people." But all that had been going on for years, without the U.S. doing anything. And President Bush had done nothing about it before 9/11.

Of course, 9/11 made a difference, but it was not exactly clear why it should have compelled the U.S. to invade Iraq; for Iraq had not been involved in 9/11. In short, the Iraq war was a *war of choice*. It was not imposed on the United States by external events. It happened because the Bush administration, and its allies, wanted it to happen. This puts it vaguely at odds with the idea of a world order based on law and rights. The rule of law implies that those with power behave in a predictable way. The Iraq war points to a world in which every country needs to worry about the caprices of unpredictable U.S. presidents. But while it is a bad thing if democracies have started to worry about the caprices of U.S. presidents, if *totalitarian dictators*, or potential totalitarian dictators, are worried about them, that may be a very good thing indeed.

An assault on international law

Critics are right to regard the Iraq War as an assault on international law, even though, as explained above, the legal case for the war was strong enough. The problem is that (a) *before* the U.N. process began, the Bush administration (backed by the Blair government in Britain) had *already* declared its intention to invade Iraq *regardless of whether it got U.N. authorization or not*, and (b) as soon as it became clear that the second U.N. resolution in support of the war would not be forthcoming, the Bush administration immediately de-emphasized its legal case for the war—Saddam's failure to rid himself of WMDs—and spoke almost entirely in terms of liberating a people from tyranny.

U.N. Resolution 1441, the "first resolution" giving Saddam one last chance to avoid war if he met certain conditions before a certain deadline (he did not), was passed at a time when the U.S. and the U.K. were promising to lead an invasion of Iraq in any case. In effect, the U.N.'s hand was forced by a form of blackmail. And although Resolution 1441 arguably strengthened the legal case for the U.S. to invade, the intention of those who passed it seems to have been to avert, not to authorize, war.

That said, whether an assault on international law is bad depends on whether the integrity of a system of international law that recognizes the sovereignty of totalitarian dictators is a good thing and worth preserving. If Westphalian sovereignty is a bad way of arranging world affairs, the fact that the Iraq war undermined it might be one of the war's virtues.

If liberation, why Iraq?

War critics sometimes ask, as a *reductio ad absurdum* of the claim that liberation was America's war aim in Iraq: If it was just about liberation, why Iraq? Why not North Korea? Or Myanmar? Or Zimbabwe? Syria? Iran? Saudi Arabia? Egypt? Russia?

This *reductio* argument fails, even if the arbitrariness of the choice of Iraq is conceded. If there are ten good actions available to me, and I do one of them, but not the other nine, that does not prove that I had an ulterior motive for the one that I did. But the choice was not arbitrary. First, Iraq was probably *the worst*—the most murderous and totalitarian—of the various dictatorships where the U.S. might have considered regime change, with the exception of North Korea, which would have been much harder to overthrow.

Another reason to choose Iraq was *international law*. Although the international law justification for regime change in Iraq was questionable, and made more so by the Bush administration's conduct leading up to the war, it was stronger than the case against any other of the tyrannies in question. Also, the U.S. was more culpable in Saddam's rise than in those of Kim Jong Il and the rest. And Iraq was good "flypaper" for al-Qaeda, as North Korea was not.

Coalition of the willing

A catchy and appealing phrase that the Bush administration coined to describe the nations that participated in the liberation of Iraq—the "coalition of the willing"—so exasperated Democratic presidential candidate John Kerry that he sneeringly called it a "coalition of the coerced and the bribed," thus insulting America's closest allies and doing himself serious damage in the 2004 presidential campaign. But one can understand Kerry's frustration. The dangers hidden in the concept of a "coalition of the willing" are serious, but so subtle, so hard to explain to voters.

Collective security, as advocated by Woodrow Wilson and embodied in the charter of the NATO alliance, according to which an attack on one must be regarded as an attack on all, makes it *mandatory* for states to act when aggression has occurred. By contrast, the Bush administration's voluntarist approach to war undermines international legality, because there might be just causes for which the coalition of those willing to fight is an empty set. By analogy, one may imagine a city in which the police enforce the law only when they feel like it. In that case, unpopular persons might be deprived of the protection of the law, and citizens who wanted protection would have to try to curry favor with the police.

But then, the world is not a city, and the United States is not a police force, and vigilante justice—if it really is justice, and the overthrow of Saddam was—is better than no justice at all. The real problem may be the opposite: that the Bush administration did not carry the concept far enough. To the extent that the main war aim was to liberate Iraqis, as the Bush administration's rhetoric often suggested, it may not have been a public good *for Americans* which the taxpayers could be required to pay for on the grounds that non-payers would just be free-riding. The expedition, by this account, was a kind of charity operation and should, in principle, have been paid for by private donations.

The Pottery Barn Rule (or Fallacy?)

"You broke it, you own it"—such is the Pottery Barn Rule, or Pottery Barn Fallacy, which summarizes the consensus that emerged in the summer of 2003. According to the Pottery Barn Rule, the U.S.-led coalition, having destroyed Saddam's regime, had a responsibility to stay and reconstruct Iraq. Many Iraqis themselves do not seem to have agreed with this view. From shortly after the end of the war, polls showed Iraqis supporting a quick withdrawal of American troops, and when American troops nonetheless stayed, there was a rapid rise in support for insurgent attacks on coalition troops, even by Iraqis who had favored the coalition's invasion in 2003. Who was right, advocates of the Pottery Barn Rule, or Iraqis saying "Thank you, but go home now" to their liberators?

Assume for the sake of argument that governments derive their just powers from the consent of the governed. In that case, from the fact that Saddam had received no consent from Iraqis and enjoyed no just powers over them, it does not follow that the United States, having removed Saddam, *did* have just powers over them. Even if the U.S.'s exercise of power in Iraq after mid-2003 was somewhat illegitimate, though, it might have prevented worse things. Yet things got bloody enough that it seems plausible that they would have been better off in the event of an immediate U.S. withdrawal. That would also have made the liberation of Iraq a cheaper enterprise for America (and maybe encouraged America to try it, or threaten it, elsewhere).

A quick invasion and withdrawal, without taking too much responsibility for the aftermath, seems to have been what Defense Secretary Donald Rumsfeld had in mind.

The nuanced case for the Iraq War

Future president Barack Obama, then an Illinois state senator, told an anti-war rally in October 2002, "I don't oppose all wars… What I am opposed to is a dumb war. What I am opposed to is a rash war… A war based not on reason but on passion…"

These remarks expressed a view that was fashionable, but not astute. Actually, the war was the brain-child of intellectuals like Condoleeza Rice and Paul Wolfowitz, and was supported by leading pundits from Andrew Sullivan to Tom Friedman to Christopher Hitchens, as well as regional specialists like Fouad

Ajami and Bernard Lewis. A critic who said that the war was too clever by half, and that its critics were stupid in a good way, planting their feet in wholesome prejudices and platitudes and resisting the brave new world of liberation, would have taken a more tenable line.

The case for war, as it emerged in the course of events (for there were good reasons that it could not be fully articulated in advance), was nuanced and subtle, even informed by cutting-edge social science about democratization and the democratic peace. It would take more space than I can spare to do it justice, but at least three separate arguments justified the decision to invade Iraq:

1. *Weapons of mass destruction (WMDs).*

Not only did weapons of mass destruction supply the official case for the war, but the Bush and Blair governments claimed that Saddam's regime *already possessed* weapons of mass destruction. But this claim, which turned out to be false, was necessary neither to the legal nor the strategic case for the war. Legally, Saddam was required not only to rid himself of WMDs, but to prove to the international community, via weapons inspectors, that he had done so. Instead, Saddam had kicked out the weapons inspectors in 1998 and refused to let them back in until well after the deadline set by Resolution 1441, when he allowed token visits as a last-ditch effort to avert war.

Strategically, though it turns out that the sanctions had succeeded in preventing Saddam from acquiring WMDs. However, they could not be sustained forever, particularly given their humanitarian cost, and there could be little doubt that Saddam intended to acquire WMDs when he had the chance.

Why, then, did Bush and Blair (and Secretary of State Colin Powell) claim that Saddam *actually had* WMDs, rather than merely that he had failed to prove he did not have them, and might acquire them in future? Because (a) they thought he did have them, (b) it was the easiest way to scare the public into supporting the war, and (c) finding WMDs would have been a great way to vindicate the war *ex post*.

And the main reason that not only Bush and Blair, but many critics of the war, thought Saddam had WMDs was simply that *he had kicked out the weapons inspectors.* Why would he do that unless he had something to hide? As it turned out, Saddam did not have WMDs, which was fortunate in that he could not use them against allied troops, but politically embarrassing for Bush and Blair.

This raises the question of why Saddam was so reluctant—so fatally reluctant, as it turned out—to admit weapons inspectors when he had nothing to hide. But it does not undermine the real WMD argument for the war, which was that (a) Saddam had violated his treaty obligations, and (b) he was sure to pursue WMDs, once the sanctions were lifted.

2. The freedom agenda

As argued above, to wage "war on terror," America would have to form alliances with many regimes that shared America's aversion to Islamic terrorism but that were otherwise hostile to American values of freedom and democracy. The Bush administration resorted to a number of such compromises, but seems not to have been comfortable with adopting a comprehensively illiberal foreign policy.

For one thing, they saw that such collaboration with dictators had often backfired in the past, enabling America's enemies to take up liberal causes against America—as, indeed, Osama bin Laden had done, though political correctness prevented bin Laden from acquiring the usual Western sympathizers in the immediate aftermath of 9/11; and soon Bush had twisted the geopolitical kaleidoscope so as to make two of bin Laden's three liberal causes obsolete.

The liberation of Iraq, and the resounding advocacy of freedom which followed it, counter-balanced the illiberal tendencies inherent in the war on terror, and made it clear that, even if 9/11 had forced America to be more tolerant of certain illiberal regimes temporarily, it was at least as strongly opposed to totalitarianism as it had ever been.

Meanwhile, US troops in Saudi Arabia (they were withdrawn in 2004 after the threat which Saddam posed to Saudi oil had been removed), and the sanctions on Iraq were removed after the regime change there. Of course, the Iraq War gave al-Qaeda a new liberal-friendly grievance—the U.S. occupation of Iraq—but this was a grievance which was very problematic for al-Qaeda to exploit.

3. The flypaper strategy.

Whatever battlefield successes America might accomplish in Afghanistan, victory by American standards could consist in nothing less than establishing security and democracy there. But Afghanistan was probably the single most unpromising place on earth in which to establish democracy. It was Muslim, ethnically fragmented, landlocked, extremely poor, the scene of decades of civil conflict, and illiteracy was widespread—in all these respects, the worst possible conditions for the emergence of democracy (Rowley and Smith 2009).

America's own conception of governmental legitimacy constrained it from establishing any regime in Afghanistan other than a democracy; but it was hardly conceivable that democracy would succeed there. It was likely, if not inevitable, that Afghanistan would become a quagmire, like Vietnam, as at the time of writing (in summer 2010) it seems to have become.

Iraq was different. There were reasons to be skeptical of U.S. plans to bring democracy to Iraq—there were as of 2003 *no democracies* in the Arab world—but there were also reasons to be hopeful. Iraq was a substantially urban society, more secular than Afghanistan, with higher levels of income and education, with access to the sea and international trade. Moreover, Iraq would be a *post-totalitarian* society, which has some advantages for democratization.

To occupy Iraq was an easier task militarily, because of its terrain and its more concentrated population, than to occupy Afghanistan. U.S. troops quickly became the pre-eminent force in Iraq, able to direct a transition to democracy, as they never did in Afghanistan. The examples of post-World War II Germany and Japan gave reasons for hope that "Operation Iraqi Freedom" could succeed in its own terms.

All this put al-Qaeda in a nasty catch-22. Probably an invasion of Iraq would help al-Qaeda's recruitment. But it would face a terrible dilemma. Either it could fight America in Iraq, or not. If not, it would forfeit its claim to be the vanguard of the Muslim world in the struggle against the infidel. But if it did fight, because of its inferiority to the U.S. military, it could only fight through terrorism that would mainly kill Muslim Arabs, alienating the very group that al-Qaeda regarded as its constituency. Al-Qaeda chose to wage a terrorist war in Iraq, made itself despised and hated in the Muslim world, and became much less of a threat to the United States.

Invading Iraq in 2003 was a very clever plan; and it worked. The moral victory which al-Qaeda and the Taliban may win in Afghanistan has been rendered marginal by al-Qaeda's fatal defeat, physical and ideological, in Iraq. None of that should dispel unease at the tens of thousands of innocents who were killed, if not in most cases by American guns and bombs, then as a foreseeable consequence of the invasion.

Bush lied, people died?

It seems clear that not only President Bush, but most of his Democratic opponents, believed that Saddam had WMDs, and to that extent the popular taunt "Bush lied, people died," is false. It fails to distinguish *making a deliberately false claim*—a lie—from *making a claim one believes to be true but that turns out to be false*—a mistake.

However, it does seem that the Bush administration was less than fully frank about its motives for war. While there seemed to be a chance of getting U.N. authorization for the war, the Bush administration emphasized WMDs and downplayed the war aim of liberating a people from tyranny. From the moment the second U.N. resolution failed, the Bush administration began to emphasize liberation and the freedom agenda. If the "flypaper strategy," described above, was part of the original case for the war as the Bush administration conceived it (perhaps it was just a fortuitous side-effect), it was never clearly and publicly argued.

There were good diplomatic reasons not to be too explicit about the rationale for the war. A war to enforce a U.N. resolution must be far more acceptable to the U.N. General Assembly, which represents *governments*, many of them authoritarian, than a war to liberate an oppressed people. And to openly admit to the "flypaper strategy," which must anticipate there being many Iraqi civilian victims, would not have helped American popularity in Iraq.

The problem is that diplomatic communication and democratic accountability cannot be separated: every presidential speech to the American people is heard round the world. But the result is that many Americans justifiably felt the Bush administration had misled them. It also seems that the Bush administration deliberately underestimated the cost of the Iraq war *ex ante* in order to make it more politically palatable.

Iraq and the police principle

By recent estimates at the time of writing, Iraq war cost the U.S. about $700 billion.[28] Divided by the Iraqi population of about 27 million, the cost per liberated Iraqi has been about $30,000. While $30,000 is not too high a price to pay to free a human being from totalitarianism, the United States would have to carry out a major fiscal policy adjustment if it wanted to liberate all oppressed peoples in the same fashion.

However, liberation might become much cheaper in the future, for two reasons, as a result of the Iraq war. First, the U.S. military will study the episode and learn lessons. Second, once the threat of regime change has been credibly established, it may not be necessary to carry it out. Facing the gallows in December 2006, Saddam probably wished that back in March 2003, he had struck a deal. If he had, he probably would have spent the rest of his days in a palace

---

[28] http://en.wikipedia.org/wiki/Financial_cost_of_the_Iraq_War

on an island in the South Pacific under U.S. protection (or something similar). The next dictator threatened with regime change might take that option.

More importantly, if there is a credible threat that totalitarian dictators will be overthrown and punished, fear may prevent wicked politicians from pursuing a totalitarian course in the first place. A credible threat is the instrument by which police forces maintain order in a city at a relatively low cost. If everyone indulged all their criminal impulses, the police would be vastly outnumbered by the criminals, and could not maintain order. *Law* is, among other things, a device to make police violence efficient.

If the law is known, the police may achieve an equilibrium in which most obey the law, enabling them to focus on comparatively few law-breakers and maintain their credible threat. The first Iraq War was extraordinarily effective in creating a credible threat against *aggression* because it had a firm basis in law. The second Iraq War has probably not created a similarly credible threat against totalitarianism, because it lacks a firm basis in law.

For this reason, *the interpretation of the precedent set by Operation Iraqi Freedom*, and the way that precedent is incorporated into U.S. foreign policy doctrines and/or international law in the coming decades, is crucial for the future of freedom. If definite lines can be drawn about when a regime has forfeited the right to rule and made itself liable to be legally overthrown by any coalition of the willing that sees fit to undertake the task, fear would induce dictators to change their behavior. This may be happening already—no new totalitarian regimes have emerged since 2003—but it is too early to tell.

As an answer to *who guards the guards*, however, the Iraq war just pushes the question one step back. The Iraq war shows that it is possible for a U.S.-led "coalition of the willing" to overthrow a totalitarian dictatorship. It suggests that establishing a democratic regime in the place of a fallen dictatorship may be possible even in unfavorable environments. Had the United Nations provided a clear endorsement of the war - and it might do so under similar circumstances in the future - many of the invasion's legitimacy problems would have been avoided. But if very bad regimes are, or may be in future, answerable to the U.N. or to U.S.-led coalitions, to whom are the U.N. and/or the U.S. accountable? This unanswered question—I think—motivates much of the lingering uneasiness among critics the Iraq War.

7

Free Trade and Globalization

"THE greatest improvement in the productive powers of labour, and the greater part of the skill, dexterity, and judgment with which it is anywhere directed, or applied, seem to have been the effects of the division of labour... [and] the division of labor is limited by the extent of the market."
—Adam Smith, *Wealth of Nations*, 1776, Chatpers 1 and 3

I f the challenge to national sovereignty from the 2003 Iraq War seems like a special case, a quieter but more pervasive challenge to national sovereignty, from economic globalization and the rise of *free trade*, seems almost like a historical law. **Figure 1** shows how, since 1975, the growth of world trade has dramatically outpaced the growth of world GDP.

Figure 1: World trade growth has outpaced world GDP growth since 1975

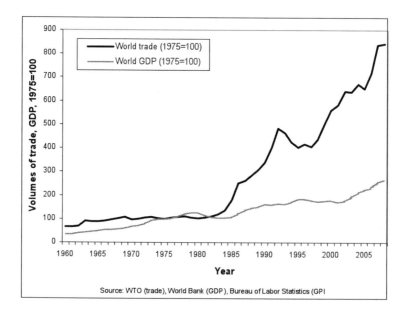

Source: WTO (trade), World Bank (GDP), Bureau of Labor Statistics (GPI

Free trade might be consistent with full national sovereignty if it were adopted (and could be withdrawn) unilaterally, but that rarely happens. Instead, free trade usually emerges through bilateral and multilateral agreements among governments by which they grant market access to one another, that is, by which they *relinquish some of the rights* (*or powers*[29]) *to restrict trade* which, under the doctrine of sovereignty, they would otherwise enjoy.

Why states would want to do this is not too hard to explain. States judge that they stand to benefit less from the powers they relinquish than they stand to benefit from access to a foreign market that they secure in return. The mystery is *how* states can do this. That there is no third-party enforcer for agreements among sovereign states is almost a tautology. A sovereign state is the final arbiter, the ultimate third-party enforcer of agreements. If it is possible to appeal over the state's head to some other arbiter, the state is to some extent not sovereign.

The World Trade Organization (WTO), which enables states to acquire a form of property rights in market access to foreign countries, is beneficent, yet problematic. Like many other international agencies—the U.N., NATO, the World Bank, the I.M.F.—it can serve as a valuable check on the abuse of power by governments; but at the same time, the modes of accountability for the emerging "global commonwealth" of such institutions are unclear.

Globalization

Were the 1990s an age of "globalization," as the popularity of this buzzword during that decade suggests? Certainly they were, if the term "globalization" is used with its usual vagueness, to lament or celebrate the diffusion of everything from language (e.g., English) to cuisine (e.g., McDonalds) to culture (Hollywood, rock-n-roll) to money (the U.S. dollar) to technology. By that account, most of recorded history was an age of globalization. There was globalization even in prehistoric times, at least within the Afro-Eurasian landmass: wheat spread from the Middle East to Scandinavia and China; and Indo-European languages were spoken from Lithuania to Ireland to India even before there was writing. Ancient galleys carried silks and spices to Rome from China, India, and Southeast Asia.[30]

---

[29] I will use the word "powers" throughout this chapter to speak of what might elsewhere be called the "rights" of sovereign states, to avoid a metaphysical confusion with natural rights enjoyed by individuals, which, unlike the "rights" claimed by and typically imputed to sovereign states, have an ontological reality directly rooted in human nature.

[30] Before 1492, the Americas were isolated from Afro-Eurasia by the Atlantic and Pacific oceans, so globalization in ancient and medieval times was not quite global; and Australia was only discovered by Europeans (Captain James Cook) in 1770, but this is inessential.

For a more useful periodization of globalization we can distinguish (a) *cultural diffusion* by migration or imitation, (b) long-distance *natural resource trade, (c) a global division of labor,* and (d) *global governance.*

Cultural diffusion is as old as human history by definition, since history begins with writing, and writing was invented in certain places and diffused elsewhere, and older, for the spread of languages, of agricultural techniques and arts and crafts, of stories and beliefs began long before that.

Long-distance trade in natural resource such as spices, precious metals, and silk occurred in ancient times, when Romans bought pepper from India and silk from China, and was extended to the Americas after 1492, when Europeans began to import gold, silver, sugar, tobacco, and cotton. Natural resources began to be traded over long distances early, because they cannot be produced *at all* in certain places and are highly valued at the margin where they are absent.

World trade based not on natural endowments but on a global division of labor in production emerged only when a revolution in technology and industrial efficiency in the most advanced societies, and innovations in navigation that reduced the cost of shipping, made it cost-effective to make a thing in Place A and carry it thousands of miles to Place B, even though there was no physical obstacle to making it in Place B. Factory-made cloth from Manchester could undersell handspun cloth in Madras. It is largely this kind of trade rather than trade in natural resources that explains the steep rise in world trade shown in **Figure 1**. This kind of globalization is sometimes blamed for the rich-poor gap worldwide, but informed people know that what is today seen as world poverty—low life expectancies, malnutrition, disease, high child mortality, illiteracy, and so on—is just the normal condition of life that has prevailed for most of human history. On the contrary,[31] plugging into globalization with an export-oriented economy, adoption of foreign technology, and a welcoming environment for foreign investment, is the best way for poor countries to grow.

Global governance structures like the League of Nations, U.N., GATT/WTO, I.M.F, World Bank, etc. first emerged in the early 20th century; but for decades their effectiveness was impeded by great power rivalries. The end of the Cold War in 1990 gave these agencies more scope to pursue ambitious agendas throughout the world, which became one reason for the late 1990s anti-globalization angst. Meanwhile, the global division of labor was shifting and intensifying, natural resource trade continued apace, and cultural diffusion

---

[31] See, for example, Dollar and Kraay (2001).

accelerated in the wake of the fall of communism. In that sense, the 1990s were an age of globalization to a more than usual degree.

Comparative advantage

It is no surprise to economists that free trade works. Economics was born in free trade advocacy. Adam Smith's *Wealth of Nations* was, among other things, a masterful critique of the prevailing mercantilist economic doctrine of Smith's day, and a generation later, David Ricardo formulated the comparative advantage argument which is the major argument economists use in favor of free trade down to the present day. But while this argument is useful for refuting certain crude popular fallacies—for example, "buy American" to "keep jobs at home," to which it is enough to say that one trades goods for goods, and therefore, in the end, jobs for jobs—it has two serious flaws.

First, comparative advantage theory ignores the possibility that free trade can lead to *increased specialization and division of labor*, with resulting increases in productivity. This causes comparative advantage to understate the benefits of free trade. Second, the argument lacks proper foundations in utility theory. In particular, the refrain that free trade "makes both countries better off" has no clear meaning. But before expanding on these flaws we must review the traditional argument.

The comparative advantage principle applies not only to countries but to individuals. Suppose an executive (wage: $200/hour), whose main job is management and negotiations, can also type 80 words a minute, while his secretary (wage: $20/hour) can type 60 words a minute. It is still best for the executive to focus on management and negotiations, because while he has an *absolute advantage* in both skills, he has a *comparative advantage* in the job, management and negotiations, that his secretary cannot do, or cannot do nearly as well.

The same argument may be applied to countries. Suppose that:

America produces **five times** as many bushels of corn per man-hour as Japan; and

America produces **twice** as many cars per man-hour as Japan;

Ignoring the existence of other goods, other factors of production, differences in quality, and so on, America should—this is the comparative advantage argument—sell Japan corn in exchange for cars, even though it has an *abso-

lute advantage in both goods. America would hurt itself, as well as Japan, if it slapped high tariff barriers on Japan's computers in order to keep its high-wage car sector "competitive."

Steve Landsburg, in *The Armchair Economist*, makes this argument in a way that is particularly amusing and cogent. There are two technologies for producing cars. Call them the Michigan technology and the Iowa technology. The Michigan technology starts with metal, plastic, rubber and so on, from which workers make tires and engines and carburetors and so on, and assemble them into cars. The Iowa technology starts in the cornfields of Iowa. Corn is the raw material from which the cars are made. The corn is harvested, put on trains, sent to Los Angeles, then placed on ships, which sail off into the Pacific Ocean. A few months later, the ships reappear with Toyotas on them. (That an entity called "Japan" may play a role in this process is irrelevant.) Why—this satirical version of the comparative advantage argument concludes by asking—should the federal government prefer Michigan-made cars to Iowa-made cars?

Why comparative advantage understates the gains from trade: specialization as nature versus nurture

The comparative advantage argument takes countries' relative productivities as given. But why does the U.S. produce corn, or cars, more efficiently than Japan? Why are different countries—or different people—more or less productive in making different things? Two distinct types of causes may be labeled "nature" and "nurture." In agriculture, mining, and tourism, natural endowments are crucial. Maui has a natural superiority to Minnesota in producing pineapples and honeymoons. Alaska has a natural comparative advantage in oil production compared to Alabama. By contrast, Japan's prowess in making cars and cameras has little to do with nature.

As it is with countries, so with it is with individuals. Some specialization is a function of "nature"—a lot of us are just not smart enough to be nuclear physicists, or strong enough to be football players—but "nurture" is probably more important. I could have been a farmer or an auto mechanic or a soldier or a graphic designer, if I had made different choices years ago, and could learn a lot of narrow specializations—selling cell-phones, fixing printers, roofing, driving a limousine—in a few months or weeks.

It is far from obvious that the same logic applies to countries, yet the "new trade theory" championed by Paul Krugman (Krugman, 1997), Elhanan Helpman (Helpman, 1987) and others has shown convincingly that it does. At the level of particular products and brand names, countries specialize, and Finnish consumers (for example) benefit from the fact that all their cell-phone-making prowess is concentrated in one company, Nokia, while at the same time Finnish cell phone buyers have a global array of phones to choose from.

Adam Smith did not formulate the idea of comparative advantage. That was left to David Ricardo. Yet in a way Smith was ahead of Ricardo, because his theory emphasized that specialization is a *cause* as well as an *effect* of differences in productivity. If productivity gains due to international division of labor are important, free trade is much *more* beneficial than anyone would guess from the theory of comparative advantage alone.

The Achilles' heel of comparative advantage: utility theory

Why, we asked, should the government prefer Iowa-made cars to Michigan-made cars? Superficially, the rhetorical question makes protectionism seem arbitrary and absurd, for why should the U.S. government favor Michigan over Iowa? Actually, there are any number of reasons why the federal government might prefer to put $1 in the hands of a Michigan family than to put a bit more than $1, e.g., $1.25,[32] in the hands of an Iowa family. There are bad reasons for this—maybe Michigan is a swing state in the Electoral College; or the automakers hire good lobbyists—and not-so-bad reasons—maybe Michigan families are poorer than Iowa families and need the money more—but we cannot say, in general, that the government's preference is necessarily irrational.

And this is the problem with the comparative advantage argument: free trade has winners and losers; and even if the gains to the former exceed the losses of the latter in monetary terms (which can be proven to be the case if some conditions hold, e.g., an absence of externalities), utility theory provides no basis for the kinds of interpersonal comparisons that would allow us to aggregate utility across persons so as to say that "the nation as a whole" is better off from free trade.

It is often said that the winners gain more (in monetary terms) than the losers lose, so that winners can "compensate" losers; but this is only true if it is naively assumed than money can be transferred among citizens without creating inefficiencies. In practice, taxing the winners and subsidizing the losers from free trade must involve not only administrative costs but also, more importantly, perverse incentives, which may be worse than the deadweight losses from tariffs.

---

[32] It can be safely assumed that the Iowa family gets more than the $1 the Michigan family loses, because only if the Iowa process is more efficient will free trade cause it to occur.

If, for whatever reason, the government wants Group A to be better off than it would be under free trade, even at the expense of Group B, a tariff may be the most efficient way to achieve this end. A wide variety of market imperfections— positive and negative externalities; learning-by-doing effects that differ by sector; natural monopolies—provide further valid reasons why ignoring the comparative advantage argument and restricting trade might be preferred by a rational government that values the welfare of its citizens.

Natural rights and free trade

Quite different than comparative advantage in its premises, but similar in its conclusions, is the case for free trade from natural rights. By this account, the natural property rights which people acquire through labor and trade include the right to *alienate* property. Governments, instituted to protect natural rights, can justly intervene only when rights are being violated. When individuals trade among themselves by mutual consent, no rights are being violated, and the government has no just pretext for intervention. It makes no difference whether the trading partners are members or non-members of the social contract. The pure natural rights case for free trade is perhaps most applicable to agriculture, a sector where property rights arise directly from the mingling of labor with the gifts of nature, but which, unfortunately, is one of the sectors most distorted by protectionism.

We said in **Chapter 4**, however, that it is unrealistic to regard all property rights as purely natural. Although the idea that property rights originate in mixing one's labor with materials thus appropriated from the commons is valid as far as it goes, there is enough vagueness in its application that avoidance of conflict and achievement of economic efficiency require the definition of property rights by a judiciary in a fashion that is inevitably partly discretionary.

This reality makes it tricky to apply natural rights to free trade. A person who imports goods *imports (a claim to) property rights* in those goods. If a state permits imports, they will soon be exchanged and become impossible to disentangle from property rights that originated domestically. For State B to impose a tariff may be interpreted as imposing a charge for the translation of State A-originated property rights into State B-valid property rights. This pretext for revenue collection seems at least as plausible as those which are used to justify ordinary tax collection, if not more so.

It is clear in which direction the argument from natural rights points. A world of states with constitutions of natural liberty would impose, at most, few and/or light restrictions on trade. The pursuit of economic autarky violates citizens' natural rights to trade with foreigners. Yet it is not clear how strong this case for free trade is, or how far it goes, when the origins of the property rights to the goods being traded are complex and heavily affected by positive law. The position of the American colonists, who held that the British had a right to regulate their trade but not to tax them, is perverse from the perspective of utilitarian economics, but makes some sense in terms of natural rights.

Economic sanctions

One surprising implication of applying natural rights to trade policy is that *economic sanctions against unjust regimes are not only a legitimate policy tool, but may be morally obligatory*, because property rights originating in such regimes are not just, and to allow them to be imported is to recognize them. To trade with a *kleptocrat* is to buy stolen goods. Since, under the common law, possession must be presumptive evidence of ownership, a state that permits imports from such regime at the border can hardly avoid recognizing them later. The state may have an obligation to identify unjust foreign regimes and ban trade with them, in order to avoid becoming an accomplice in crime.

Just proportionality in enforcing smuggling laws

We proposed in **Chapter 3** that retribution must be regulated by a norm of proportionality. If this admittedly vague rule is accepted, it gives rise to the question of what punishments a state that restricts trade may justly impose on smugglers who evade its trade restrictions. If smugglers are doing business with brutal foreign tyrants, corporal punishments such as imprisonment may be warranted, since whatever crimes the tyrants are committing against their peoples, those who supply their needs and get some of the loot have a share in. If, on the other hand, tariffs are imposed on goods imported from other countries that are more or less free and just, it is hard to see what harm smugglers have done that could be a basis for retribution. At most, non-recognition and/or confiscation of property might be warranted, and that would probably be an inadequate deterrent if smuggling is difficult to detect and has large economic payoffs. This line of argument reinforces the natural rights case for free trade.

The logic of mercantilism and the tariff revenue treadmill

Comparative advantage implies that *unilateral* free trade is the best policy; but we should not be surprised that this argument has proven unpersuasive in practice, since even in theory it falls short. Historically, governments rarely adopt free trade unilaterally (Britain's ending of the Corn Laws was an exception that proves the rule). Instead, they do so through treaties, whereby Country A agrees to allow certain imports or reduce certain tariffs *in return for* Country B doing the same.

Now, if we believe in the comparative advantage theory, this is odd. If my tariffs hurt *me*, why should I refuse to lower them unless you lower your tariffs as well? If, however, we accept that there plenty of reasons why a rational state might to want to restrict trade, we still face the puzzling fact that in trade negotiations, states almost invariably treat every reduction in foreign tariffs as a point gained, and every reduction in their own tariffs as a *concession*. It seems as if they believe that *exports are good, imports are bad*.

We may call this belief the *mercantilist fallacy*, and it is subjected to a reductio ad absurdum, since it implies that a state should, ideally, try to export everything and get nothing in return. Even if the optimal tariff is not always zero, is not the typical mercantilism of trade negotiators clear evidence of irrationality?

No, it is not.

Imagine the government as a unitary entity with preferences in *net tariff space*. By "net tariff" I mean the sum of all taxes on a foreign product before it reaches a consumer minus the sum of all taxes on an equivalent domestic product before it reaches the consumer. For example, if Spain's domestic excise tax is $5 per widget, France's is $2, and the tariff at the Spanish-French border is $5 per widget, the *net tariff* on Spanish widgets sold in France is $5+$5-$2 = $8 ($10 of taxes on the Spanish widget minus $2 of taxes on the French widget equals $8 net tariff). Each net tariff is a scalar value in some kind of units and can be conceived of as a dimension in an n-dimensional[33] space.

Governments have some objective function defined over this net tariff space, that is, for any two vectors of net tariffs A and B, the government knows whether it prefers A, prefers B, or is indifferent. Governments also prefer more revenue to less.[34] In trying to achieve more preferred points in net tariff space, governments can use two policy instruments: excise taxes and tariffs, both of which

---

[33] The letter n refers to an arbitrary number.

[34] Regarding a government as a unitary actor is less problematic than it seems, since it really only means that the government is able to make decisions in response to different situations. The government's objective function can be observed, in principle, through "revealed preference": depending on what the government does in different situations, we can guess what it *wants*.

may be negative. (A negative excise tax is a subsidy to domestic production; a negative tariff is a subsidy for exports.) Subsidies always reduce revenue. Taxes and tariffs may increase or decrease it, depending on the relevant elasticities.

The framework is general enough to take into account governments' desires with respect to all sorts of distribution and externality effects. Governments' optimal net tariffs may be positive, negative, or zero. If the widget industry is a heavy polluter, Spain's government may prefer that the net tariff on French widgets be negative and the net tariff on Spanish widgets in France be high, so as to minimize widget production in Spain.

Now, Spain can always raise the net tariff on French widgets sold in Spain. It can do in one of two ways: (a) by raising the widget tariff, or (b) by lowering the widget excise tax. One or both of these policies is likely to have a positive effect on Spain's revenue and, in the worst case, Spain will lose no more than the whole tax revenue it had been earning on French widget imports. Spain can also lower the net tariff on French widgets sold in Spain, by raising the excise tax on domestic production. And Spain can raise the net tariff on Spanish widgets sold in France, by raising its excise tax on widget production, which, again, is probably revenue-positive and at worst mildly revenue-negative.

The one thing that Spain cannot do unilaterally and while maintaining revenue is to lower the net tariff on Spanish widgets sold in France, or in other words, *to secure greater access for its widgets to the French market.* Spain can reduce this net tariff by lowering the excise tax on domestic production, but that will typically reduce revenue. Worse, if France does not want to see this net tariff reduced, it can raise it back by raising its tariff, while increasing revenue at the same time. If Spain keeps trying to secure market access unilaterally by reducing excise taxes (perhaps to negative levels, i.e., subsidizing the industry), France can counter-act this policy by raising its tariffs, and Spain will find itself on a *tariff revenue treadmill*, wasting resources without achieving its aims. In fact, the only effect of Spain's policy is to transfer revenue from itself to France.

The above argument fully explains why governments involved in trade negotiations behave *as if* they believed the mercantilist fallacy that *exports are good, imports are bad.* Such behavior is not at all inconsistent with governments having subtle and well-informed trade policy objectives which include the deliberate outsourcing—*imports are good, exports are bad*—of certain domestic industries, depending on industry-specific distribution, externality, and learning-by-doing effects.

The reason such objectives are not pursued in trade negotiations is that for the pursuit of such objectives, trade negotiations are not needed. Oil is an example of a good which the United States has made a policy decision to import more of, while producing less at home. Because oil production is dirty and damaging to the environment, the U.S. government has been reluctant in recent decades to allow the creation of new refineries or the exploitation of known oil fields, such as that in the Alaska National Wildlife Reserve.

There is no need for the U.S., in addition to these policies, to make trade pacts with Saudi Arabia or Russia to secure oil imports. The U.S. simply restricts domestic supply unilaterally, after which a shift towards imports is automatically mediated through price system. States behave like mercantilists in trade negotiations, not because they believe the mercantilist fallacy in general, but because it is only when they happen to desire more access to foreign markets that they have to resort to trade negotiations.

Concentrated benefits and diffuse costs

There is a well-known argument developed in the *public choice* school of economics that purports to explain why governments do not embrace free trade (Rowley, Thorbecke and Wagner 1995). According to this argument, the benefits from any particular tariff are *concentrated*—they go to producers in a given industry, who can sell for higher prices—while the costs are *diffuse*—they are paid by the entire citizenry in the form of higher prices for a good which, however, comprises an insignificant fraction of a typical consumer's income. Because a small price change can heavily affect producers' fortunes, they have a strong incentive to lobby the government for protection. By contrast, consumers will pay little attention to a small increase in price on a minor item.

While the "concentrated benefits-diffuse costs" argument is plausible, once we leave behind the naïve comparative advantage argument, it is an answer in search of a question. There is no reason to be surprised that states want to restrict trade. There is no reason to be surprised, either, that they usually sound like mercantilists when they are engaged in trade negotiations, because the tariff revenue treadmill blocks them from getting access to foreign markets unilaterally.

(Quasi) property rights in market access

The logic of mercantilism points to a different argument for free trade. While a given trade restriction may benefit a particular state, it will almost certainly harm foreigners in the process. There could in principle be cases where industry X generates negative externalities in Country A, but positive externalities in Country B, so that a tariff on imports of X from A to B would benefit both countries, but it is implausible that such cases are at all common. Typically, A's tariffs harm B, and B's harm A; typically, too, A, B, or both, suffer harms from foreign tariffs that exceed the benefits they derive from their own tariffs.

It is possible and likely that pure free trade, the origin (all zeroes) in net tariff space, is preferred by most or all governments to the outcome that will emerge if each state takes advantage of its sovereign powers to set domestic tariffs on imported goods so as to optimize its own objective function.

The trade policy commitments that states give and receive through trade negotiations may be regarded as (quasi) *property rights in market access*. States possess sovereign powers sufficient to control access to their own markets; in trade negotiations, they surrender some of these. The fact that State A has surrendered sovereign power X to regulate trade results in market access for State B. But are sovereign powers alienable like this? Not really. The abrogation of a trade treaty, for example, would hardly be regarded as a sufficient basis for a declaration of war. Who can make states keep their promises? Who guards the guards?

The problem may be illuminated by an analogy. Suppose there is a city with laws similar to those of a typical American city but for one difference: it recognizes no legally enforceable property rights in automobiles, i.e., no one owns cars. A resident of this city, Jim, has a snazzy sportscar. That is, he physically possesses the only set of keys to it, but not a legal title. Another resident, Jake, has a powerful truck. One day Jake meets a hot girl whom he wants to impress, and Jim decides he wants to open a landscaping business. Jim wants Jake's truck and Jake wants Jim's sportscar. But there is a problem. If Jim gives Jake his sportscar, he can always keep a spare set of keys and take his car back whenever he wants it. Jake can do the same with his truck. If Jim and Jake trust each other enough, they may be able to do the deal; but if not, the mutually beneficial trade may be impossible to execute.

Countries that engage in trade negotiations are in a similar position to Jim and Jake. To exchange secure market access is mutually beneficial, but states do not have a good way, according to prevailing doctrines of sovereignty, to commit to relinquishing their powers to restrict market access.

The GATT/WTO

The General Agreement on Tariffs and Trade (GATT), which emerged after World War II, and the World Trade Organization (WTO), which succeeded it in 1995, try to help states solve the commitment problem and create a form of property rights in mutual market access. A similar organization, the International Trade Organization, was proposed decades earlier in 1944, but was rejected by the U.S. Congress on the grounds that its powers would impinge on national sovereignty. The fact that the GATT emerged and evolved into the WTO in spite of this initial rejection of the scheme is evidence that the GATT and WTO are not historical accidents, but expressions of some kind of historical law.

The above argument that states seek mutual market access, and need third-party enforcement to help them secure it, points to the nature of that law. The WTO strengthened the GATT by (among other changes) extending its scope from goods to intellectual property and services, and introducing a binding dispute settlement system.

The GATT/WTO is based on the principles of *reciprocity* and *non-discrimination*. *Reciprocity* means that states lower tariffs multilaterally, by agreement, in effect trading market access rights, and especially that they *must not raise tariffs unilaterally*. *Non-discrimination* means each country's policies are applied uniformly to all other countries: America cannot impose a 10% tariff on Spanish cloth and a 20% tariff on French cloth.

The reciprocity rule creates a form of *property rights in market access*, as discussed above: each country is protected from being arbitrarily deprived of access to other countries' markets. But why does the non-discrimination principle apply?

One reason for non-discrimination is that discriminatory tariffs create openings for weird and inefficient forms of arbitrage. If the United States imposes a 10% on Spanish cloth and a 20% tariff on French cloth, Spain will be tempted to impose a 5% tariff on French cloth, import it, then pass it off as Spanish cloth and re-export it, keeping as revenue the 5% tariff, minus the extra transactions costs of shipping through Spain instead of directly. It would be difficult for the United States to expose the fraud, while on the other hand, it would be easy for the United States to *claim* fraud as a pretext for not honoring out of its agreements with Spain even if Spain did not engage in this practice.

Another reason for nondiscrimination is that it blocks states from engaging in *blackmail* and imposing exorbitant tariffs far above even their own preferred levels, in order to have more room to negotiate for the reduction of other countries' tariffs. There are exceptions to the nondiscrimination rule, of which the most important are free trade areas. When countries form a free trade area, they can stop imposing tariffs on one another's goods without at the same time removing tariffs on all other countries' goods. The U.S. has 17 free trade agreements in force.[35]

But the non-discrimination principle gives market access something of the character of a "public good," and as such it will tend to be underprovided. For example, if two big countries, say, the United States and China, agree to a mutual reduction of tariffs, WTO rules require (unless they form a free trade area) that the same tariff reduction be extended to all other countries as well, even if the other countries do not lower *their* tariffs. But the obligation to extend their concessions on tariffs to the whole world raises the "cost" (in lost trade protection) of the trade agreement as perceived by the U.S. and China. If the trade agreement happens, non-discrimination makes it more beneficial, since all countries benefit, rather than only the U.S. and China. But nondiscrimination makes it more likely that a given bilateral trade agreement will not occur at all.

Free trade versus sovereignty

In addition to non-discrimination and reciprocity, another of the WTO's principles is *national treatment*: once goods are inside the country, domestic regulations cannot be applied in such a way that foreign-made goods are treated differently than domestic ones. So the influence of WTO rules does not stop at the border. To ensure national treatment, a variety of other changes in domestic policy, in tax administration for example, may be required as well. When domestic policies like these can be dictated by outside actors, it is clear that sovereignty is being curtailed.

Agreements on intellectual property rights and services require adjustments of domestic regulation. The dispute settlement mechanism makes the infringements of sovereignty more serious and systematic.[36] It has been invoked, as of the time of writing, 411 times since the establishment of the WTO, in many cases because a member country has a complaint against a *domestic* regulation by another country.

The WTO cannot use force to make countries comply with its rules. Instead, if the WTO rules in favor of a complainant, and the defendant refuses to comply with the ruling, the complainant is authorized to impose special punitive tariffs against the defendant. This mechanism may not work. For example, in 1998 the U.S. and Canada filed a complaint against the European Union for

---

[35] http://www.ustr.gov/trade-agreements

[36] http://www.wto.org/english/tratop_e/dispu_e/dispu_status_e.htm

imposing a ban on meat containing artificial beef hormones. The WTO ruled in favor of the U.S. and Canada, requiring the E.U. to lift its ban; but it continues to refuse to comply. The WTO authorized the U.S. and Canada to retaliate, and ever since the US and Canada have imposed punitive tariffs on various E.U. industries in an effort to break the E.U.'s political will to maintain the ban. But the E.U. is holding its ground.

The WTO and natural rights

What, if anything, do natural rights and the WTO have to do with each other? The natural rights case for free trade implies that there are limits, perhaps very tight limits, on the extent to which states can justly limit trade. The WTO, by contrast, begins by imputing to states full sovereign powers to limit trade, and then tries to create a mechanism for which they can trade these away in return for market access. The effect of the WTO, however, has been to curtail sovereign power, "binding" states to keep their tariffs down, and thus working in favor of natural liberty.

Logically, deal-making among states might operate for or against liberty. States might make deals to raise minimum wages, that is, to curtail the natural right to work, rather than to reduce tariffs. Possibly, though, a weak organization like the WTO is better equipped to facilitate commitments to *relinquish* powers than to *extend* them. If Country A's exporters encounter illicit tariffs in Country B, they know it, and can alert their governments and trigger a complaint to the WTO. If Country B fails to enforce a minimum wage which it negotiated with Country A, this will be harder for Country A to discover. It has been difficult for the WTO to enforce international agreements on intellectual property, and an extension of WTO sway to labor and environmental standards might require it to assume new policing and investigative functions. Sovereign states might well refuse to relinquish such powers to the WTO.

A global commonwealth?

The WTO's power to hold governments accountable for their trade policies is a new element in a global system of what the framers of the United States Constitution called "checks and balances," whereby some branches of power are checked by others. If the public choice school is right that "concentrated benefits and diffuse costs" distort states' policies to the detriment of the citizenry as a whole, people may benefit from their own governments being constrained by WTO rules, even if the trade policies of other countries were held constant. *A fortiori*, they benefit from other governments being constrained by WTO rules.

The Framers of the United States Constitution deliberately established a separation of powers among three branches of government, the legislative branch, the executive branch, and the judicial branch, and regarded the inevitable overlap and tension between these branches of government, and between the upper and lower houses of the legislature, as a *virtue* of the new constitution. They thought that each branch of government would check abuses of power by the others.

The WTO, an autonomous agency which constrains the way governments can use their power, extends the "checks and balances" principle to a global level, as do other institutions like the U.N., the World Bank, and the I.M.F., transnational judicial institutions like the International Criminal Court, and regional organizations like NATO, APEC, the E.U., and so forth. States today find their decision-making hemmed in by all sorts of international agencies and treaties.

A development along these lines was foreseen, and advocated, by Woodrow Wilson, who, in addition to national self-determination, had another big idea. He wanted to found a League of Nations, a sort of *global commonwealth* or what is now called "the international community," able to hold governments accountable on a global scale. That such an entity exists today may be seen if we consider one of Hobbes' arguments in *Leviathan*, which, true enough in Hobbes' own times, has since become intriguingly obsolete. Hobbes argued that sovereigns are, with respect to one another, in a perpetual state of war:

> In all times kings and persons of sovereign authority, because of their independency, are in continual jealousies, and in the state and posture of gladiators, having their weapons pointing, and their eyes fixed on one another; that is, their forts, garrisons, and guns upon the frontiers of their kingdoms, and continual spies upon their neighbours, which is a posture of war. (*Leviathan*, Part I, Chapter XIII)

It is not plausible today that all sovereign states are in a "posture of war" with respect to one another. In particular, the democracies are clearly not in a posture of war. The very idea that a war might between the contemporary United States and United Kingdom, for example, is absurd. Even to describe relations with and among non-democracies as a "posture of war" seems like an exaggeration, thanks in part to global institutions like the United Nations and the WTO which bind the world together in an ever-growing web of bilateral and multilateral treaty obligations.

World peace and *free trade* sounds like good things. *World government* sounds scary. Yet they are connected. It would be an exaggeration say that world peace and free trade require a world government. But to establish and maintain peace and free trade tends to involve the emergence of structures and agencies that serve first to facilitate the negotiations among states, later to arbitrate among them, and finally to make rules for them.

The U.N., NATO, the G7, the G20, the OECD, the European Council, the WTO, the World Bank and the I.M.F., and the International Criminal Court are agencies of this kind. Once created, these structures are subject to both centripetal and centrifugal forces which are difficult to keep in balance. They tend either to fall apart, or else to accumulate more and more power.

Wilson's League of Nations fell apart, not least because the United States refused to join it. By contrast, both the United States and the European Union began as bargains among states that were once autonomous, but which jointly created institutions—the U.S. federal government; and the European Coal and Steel Community / European Community / European Union—that gradually usurped more and more power and made the "sovereignty" of the subordinate political units increasingly obsolete.

The same process is probably happening today on a global scale, though of course it is much less far advanced. The Iraq War, though it was a sort of mutiny against the rules of the global commonwealth, may ultimately strengthen it by putting another weapon—regime-change—in the arsenal of global governance, and by highlighting the U.N.'s role as the touchstone of international legitimacy.

This emerging world government is benign enough that some of the world's least fortunate people—people living under totalitarian rule, or in failed states and war zones—have reason to welcome it. The 2005 Human Security Report[37] found that there was a sharp drop in the number of wars in the decade after the end of the Cold War, as well as in the average number of casualties in each one, and gave much of the credit for this to U.N. peacekeeping operations.

But for those who can afford to take the long view, and to indulge in the wise paranoia of liberty, the emerging patterns of global governance point back to the question we have persistently asked—*Who guards the guards?*—and with a new urgency, since, when the guard in question is an emerging world government, it is no longer possible to appeal upward.

---

[37] http://www.hsrgroup.org/human-security-reports/2005/text.aspx

James Madison's answer to "Who guards the guards?" was, in effect, "They guard each other." The framers turned the infinite regress into a circle.

Checks and balances are no panacea

Lest a high regard for the wisdom of James Madison and the U.S. Constitution tempt us to think of checks and balances as a panacea, Hobbes' view on the separation of powers is worth revisiting. He thought that:

> These... Rights, which make the Essence of Soveraignty; and which are the markes, whereby a man may discern in what Man, or Assembly of men, the Soveraign Power is placed... are incommunicable, and inseparable... If we consider any one of the said Rights, we shall presently see, that the holding of all the rest [without that one], will produce no effect, in the conservation of Peace and Justice, the end for which all Common-wealths are Instituted.

> And this division is it, whereof it is said, "A kingdome divided in it selfe cannot stand." For unless this division [of powers] precede, division into opposite Armies can never happen. If there had not first been an opinion received of the greatest part of England, that these Powers were divided between the King, and the Lords, and the House of Commons, the people had never been divided, and fallen into this Civill Warre... (*Leviathan*, 1950-60)

The United States having proven to be a highly successful polity, the Framers' "checks and balances" strategy appears, in hindsight, very wise. Yet Hobbes points out the obvious danger, namely that the government will be divided against itself, making it ineffectual or even allowing it to be torn apart by civil war. In fact, the United States was torn apart by civil war in 1861-65, and Hobbes might easily have shown how that event confirmed his view of the separation of powers as a disastrous mistake; for a conflict between the Supreme Court, with its *Dred Scott* decision, the presidency and Congress, which came to be dominated by a Northern majority, and the states, some of which refused to accept the threat of abolition after the 1860 election, was precisely what led to the Civil War. But fortunately, so far at least, there turned out to be only one Civil War.

There are several historic constitutions which featured a division of powers, checks and balances, and which eventually failed partly for that reason. The elective monarchy of early modern Poland, and the generous rights enjoyed by the Polish nobility, made that kingdom an easy prey for the more centralized monarchies of Hapsburg Austria and especially of Prussia and Russia. For much of the 17th century, the unsettled nature of the British constitution, and the conflict between Crown and Parliament, often made Britain ineffectual and a pawn of foreign powers; and at one point, as Hobbes was keenly aware, led to civil war.

The ancient Roman republic had a particularly ingenious system of checks and balances. The Romans were led by consuls, *two* of which were elected every year, and each of which had a power to veto the acts of the other. Although it was under this system of government that Rome achieved its most spectacular victories and extended its rule over most of the Mediterranean. But in the 1st century B.C., the republic was paralyzed by its built-in checks and balances, and more and more power passed to strong military commanders like Marius, Sulla, Pompey, and Julius Caesar, after whom the institutions of the Republic were eviscerated by a new system called the Empire.

While the checks and balances in the United States constitution have sustained some form of free institutions for over two centuries, they have failed to keep the U.S. government within the bounds the drafters of the Constitution had in mind. In 1789, the drafters of the U.S. constitution thought a Bill of Rights was unnecessary, because they had enumerated only quite limited powers in the constitution, and thought the government simply lacked the authority to overstep these bounds.[38] It had not been given the *power* to violate the rights which a Bill of Rights would protect (it was thought) superfluously.

Since then, certain clauses, like the "commerce" clause and the "necessary and proper" clause, have been stretched to the limits of plausibility and beyond in order to justify a continual usurpation of new powers by the federal government. A critical moment came in 1936-7 when President Franklin D. Roosevelt, frustrated by the Supreme Court overturning unconstitutional legislation, threatened to pack the Supreme Court so as to make it more pliable; and ultimately he forced the Court to yield to his whims.

In spite of this, the federal courts, combined with the Bill of Rights, which has proved to be more necessary than the framers guessed since the failure of the "enumerated powers" strategy for limiting government, remain a useful check on demagogues. For example, in Arizona in 2010, a state law which would have overturned generations of *habeas corpus* tradition by forcing people to carry

---

[38] See Smith (1998).

identification papers domestically, was overturned, though unfortunately only in part, on appeal to the federal courts.

World Migration Organization?

The WTO presents one model of how a transition to generalized open borders might work. The idea would be that, just as states want their exporters to get access to foreign goods markets, they may want their citizens to get access to foreign labor markets as well. Each state has sovereign powers that enable it to control its own *labor* market (illegal immigration excepted). Already, reciprocal agreements sometimes occur, hereby citizens of State A get to travel to State B visa-free. A World Migration Organization would recognize each state's sovereign powers to control its own labor market, but would push for migration to be regulated in a non-discretionary way, through migration taxes—the equivalent of tariffs, rather than quotas—and then "bind" migration tax rates by mutual agreements.

A decline in free trade?

If free trade is partly a result of multilateral negotiations among states, idealistic motives, too, have had their place. Historically, the two great eras of trade liberalization were the middle decades of the 19th century and the second half of the 20th century. In each case, trade liberalization emerged through negotiation and reciprocity, but it was spearheaded by a major power—Great Britain in the 19th century, the United States in the 20th—which favored free trade ideologically, and for which free trade served to advance broad geopolitical goals.

The great 19th-century free-traders Richard Cobden and John Bright saw free trade as a means to world peace, while the U.S. in the Cold War era wanted to spread prosperity in order to halt the spread of communism. The rise of revisionist powers in Europe and in the United States in the late 19th century broke the momentum of 19th-century free trade. The failure of the Doha round of trade talks during the past decade represents a similar, ominous loss of momentum for free trade today.

How serious a problem is this decline of free trade? After decades of trade liberalization, most countries' average tariff rates are now only 10-20%. According to one influential model known as the "Harberger triangle," welfare losses from tariffs at this level are small. But the Harberger triangle model is probably wrong, for it focuses only on comparative advantage, taking productivities as given.

Moreover, when a complex global division of labor "splits up the value chain," goods may cross borders several times at consecutive stages of production, and the tariffs add up. Also, differences in industry standards among countries impede trade. (Americans who have traveled in Europe and brought electronic devices with them, only to find they could not use the local electrical sockets without an adapter, have encountered one minor instance of this phenomenon.)

A well-known 1995 paper by Engel and Rogers[39] asks "How Wide is the Border?"—that is, if we observe the behavior of prices in places that are physically close but are on the opposite sides of the borders of the U.S. and Canada, what amount of physical distance would be needed to cause the same degree of price dispersion? They find that the border is virtually at least 2,500 miles wide. This reflects various causes, but is at least suggestive of the amount of trade liberalization and trade facilitation (e.g., by coordinating standards and regulations) that remains for a strengthened WTO to bring about. But the powers of a strengthened WTO might well be abused.

Globalization and freedom

Most of what is referred to under the vague heading of "globalization" has been good for freedom, so far. Opportunities to trade, travel, and communicate across international borders, which have become available to more and more people, in themselves are a contribution to freedom. Meanwhile, a loose global commonwealth of international agencies has emerged as a side-effect of the pursuit of worthy aims like peace and free trade through international negotiations and treaties, and so far has mostly acted as a beneficent check on the abuse of power by governments.

But the global commonwealth is only an accidental friend of freedom, and as economic integration feeds more power to global institutions because states depend more on international factors to achieve their aims, it may become a threat. At that point, it would no longer be possible to appeal *upwards*. The old *who guards the guards* regress has nowhere else to go. Globalization is welcome in the short run, but worrisome in the longer run as the world runs out of higher levels of authority.

---

[39] "How Wide is the Border?"... [get citation]

8

Civil Disobedience

Fortunately, there is one more force that can check the abuse of power by national governments and international bureaucracies alike, and this one, though it appears only intermittently in history, is always and necessarily on the side of freedom. That force is *civil disobedience.*

A brief history of civil disobedience

Civil disobedience is the public and conscientious refusal to obey laws which one regards as wrong and wishes to see changed. Some examples from the grim yet glorious history of civil disobedience will illustrate before we make this definition more precise. I begin with two examples of individuals who set a pattern of civil disobedience admired and emulated by others, then go on to describe large social movements based on civil disobedience.[40]

Socrates.

The Greek philosopher Socrates was tried by a jury in democratic Athens in 399 B.C. and condemned to death for "failing to acknowledge the city's gods" and "corrupting the young." The event was uncharacteristic of free-thinking and tolerant Athens, and Socrates, in *The Apology*, makes clear the absurdity of the charges by pointing out that the books of Anaxagoras, a philosopher far more atheistic than himself, were being sold at the public theater in Athens.

But Socrates's goal at his trial seems to have been, not to establish his innocence, but to display before the jury—Athenian juries consisted of hundreds of jurors, probably the largest audience Socrates had ever had—the art of subversive inquiry to which he had dedicated his life. The ways Socrates' characteristically penetrating questions make fools of his accusers would only have alienated a jury probably comprised mostly of just the kind of complacent bourgeoisie whom Socrates subjected to devastating cross-examination.

---

[40] For brevity's sake I omit the prophet Daniel, and the three holy youths Shadrach, Meshach and Abednego, from the Old Testament, but they are also excellent examples of civil disobedience.

Worse, he justifies his life-work by means of a story about how the oracle at Delphi had told him he was the wisest man in Greece, and how he, knowing himself to be ignorant, set out to prove the oracle wrong by cross-examining people who were reputed to be knowledgeable. Then he describes how he questioned various people who were thought wise and found that they knew nothing, and concludes that the oracle was right after all, since he, Socrates, though he knows nothing, has at least the advantage of *knowing* that he knows nothing.

When the jury condemns him to death and Socrates has an opportunity to propose an alternate sentence which the jury can then accept or decline, he exasperates the jury further by first suggesting a public stipend and then, at the urging of Plato and other of his disciples, a small fine to be paid for by friends. The jury votes for the death sentence by a larger margin than that by which they found him guilty. Finally, given a chance to escape death by flight with the help of wealthy friends who would bribe the guards, Socrates (in the *Crito*) refuses. Anticipating modern social contract theory, he personifies the Laws and says that he has tacitly consented to them by remaining in Athens and cannot justly disobey them.

Yet in *The Apology* he argues that he *must* go on questioning people, whatever the jury may order him, because it is a divine calling and a service to the state. Socrates' civil disobedience consists in a principled refusal either to yield to the jury's desire that he be silent, or to resist his punishment in any way. Socrates has since become a kind of secular patron saint of free inquiry.

Jesus of Nazareth.

The Jewish Sanhedrin, or supreme court, held that Jesus of Nazareth committed the capital offense of blasphemy, from the perspective of the old Jewish law, by making claims about His own divinity. That Jesus did make such claims is most strongly indicated in the Gospel of John, where at one point Jesus makes a claim about Abraham, the Jews ask mockingly how He could have seen Abraham when He is not fifty years old, and Jesus answers "Before Abraham was, I AM"—an allusion to what Jews took to be the name of God on the basis of Exodus 3:14. Outraged, the Jewish crowd tries unsuccessfully to stone Him.

Later, brought to trial before the Sanhedrin, Jesus, like Socrates, makes things easy for His accusers by repeating His claims. Asked if He is Christ, the Son of God, He says: "It is as you said. Nevertheless, I say to you, hereafter you will see the Son of Man sitting at the right hand of the Power, and coming on the clouds of heaven" (Matthew 26:64).

Jesus also repeats, before Pontius Pilate, the claim most likely to get Him in trouble with the Romans. Asked by Pilate whether He is the king of the Jews, Jesus says "It is as you say" (Matthew 27:11). Jesus makes no physical resistance to his arrest and execution, and orders a disciple who tries to fight to put his sword away (Matthew 26:52).

While Socrates' and Jesus's trials are similar in some ways, in one respect there is a striking role reversal. In Socrates' trial, certainty is on the side of power, doubt stands bravely in the dock. In Jesus's trial (if it deserves the name) it is *Pilate* who is the skeptic, asking "What is truth?" while Jesus knows the truth and is determined to tell it to the world (John 18:38).

The Christian martyrs.

In the almost three centuries between Christ's ministry and the conversion of Constantine, many Christians, probably numbering in the thousands, were "martyred" at the hands of officials of the Roman empire for refusing to participate in the imperial cult. The Christian martyrs provide a more exact example of civil disobedience than Socrates or Jesus, because it is clear that they conscientiously broke a specific law by refusing to give divine honors to the Roman emperors.

Because persecution varied in intensity, and Christians usually had the option of flight, only a small fraction of Christians were actually faced with the stark alternatives of sacrilege or martyrdom. During the more intense periods of persecution, some Christians participated in the imperial cult to save themselves, while remaining secret believers, and then tried to return when persecution subsided. Others, like St. Ignatius, rejoiced in the chance to be martyrs.

Unlike Socrates, who died by a painless poison, the Christian martyrs were often tortured in order to compel submission, and then suffered a variety of gory deaths, including crucifixion (the apostle Peter), being eaten by wild beasts (St. Ignatius), and roasting alive (St. Lawrence). The martyrs' impact was out of all proportion to their numbers and seems to have been the opposite of what the Roman emperors had hoped. The Christian writer Tertullian (160-220 AD) claimed that "the blood of the martyrs is the seed of the church"—that is, that far from deterring people from joining the Christians, the deaths of the Christian martyrs fascinated others and facilitated its spread.

The word martyr means "witness," and certainly a person's willingness to suffer martyrdom bore powerful witness to the sincerity of the martyr's belief and the value he or she placed on Christ's promises of salvation. Christian martyrs have appeared in other places where political authorities have tried to suppress or prevent the spread of the Christian faith by force, down to the present day.

Henry David Thoreau.

We owe the word "civil disobedience" to Henry David Thoreau's 1849 essay of that name, in which, in his inimitable style, he urged men to obey conscience rather than law, and illustrated the idea by recounting his own experience of refusing to pay his taxes as a protest against the Mexican War and Southern slavery. However, civil disobedience played a limited role in the abolition of slavery. The network of abolitionists who helped runaway slaves, known as the Underground Railroad, was not quite a case of civil disobedience inasmuch as it operated secretly.

Mahatma Gandhi.

Mohandas K. Gandhi (1869-1948) led non-violent resistance to British policies in South Africa and later to British rule in India. When a 1906 law required the registration of all Indians—a forerunner of the *apartheid* regime that matured later—in South Africa, Gandhi convinced the Indian community to defy the new law by nonviolently submitting to the punishments for doing so. After a seven-year struggle the government yielded.

Gandhi returned to India and led the Congress Party through several phases of non-violent struggle, including the Non-Cooperation Movement (1920-22), the Salt Satyagraha (1930-31), and the Quit India movement (1942), and his non-violent tactics also inspired local efforts such as the Bardoli Satyagraha in 1928. Gandhi's commitment to non-violence was dramatically demonstrated in 1922, when the Non-Cooperation movement was going from strength to strength until protestors in Uttar Pradesh killed 23 police officers, and Gandhi immediately called it off. Gandhi was willing to negotiate with the British and settle for more limited goals without abandoning the long-term goal of independence.

Though the relatively liberal nature of British rule in India was an important factor in the success of Gandhi's movement, many tens of thousands in South Africa and India spent time in jail for participating in Gandhi's civil disobedience movements. Hundreds of nonviolent protestors were killed in the Amritsar massacre of 1919, though this action was not typical of the British Raj, and the officer responsible was relieved of his command.

India became independent in 1947, and Gandhi was assassinated shortly afterwards by a Hindu extremist. In hindsight, Gandhi may *not* have brought India independence much faster than would have occurred without him, but he probably *did*, by establishing strong traditions of political nonviolence, lay the foundations of India's enduring democracy.

Martin Luther King and the civil rights movement.

Before the 1950s, blacks in the United States were excluded from schools, jobs, most white residential areas, the front seats in the public transit system, restaurants and clubs and other public places, and in the South were disenfranchised and intermittently terrorized by extra-legal violence from lynch mobs and the Ku Klux Klan. Reverend Martin Luther King advocated racial justice through nonviolent tactics such as boycotts, beginning with the Montgomery Bus Boycott of 1955, and protests, such as those in Birmingham that led to King's arrest and was the occasion for the famous "Letter from Birmingham Jail," and the March on Washington in 1963, scene of King's famous "I Have a Dream" speech.

Other initiatives included the Freedom Rides, groups of whites and blacks who traveled together on (segregated) public transportation around the South to challenge segregation laws. The Civil Rights Act of 1964 enacted as law much of what the movement sought to achieve, and in the course of the next generation racism became taboo even in private conversation in the United States. King himself was assassinated in 1968.

The military draft.

Military conscription is a violation of a person's physical right to possess his own body; but more importantly, it violates freedom of conscience. The decision of whether the use violence is justified in a given situation is always complex, and there will never be consensus. In the 1960s, many young American men, subject to the draft, regarded the Vietnam war as wrong, and some responded with civil disobedience, including burning draft cards and blocking traffic in Washington, D.C., during a protest on May Day, 1971. The draft has not been used since the end of the Vietnam War.

Pope John Paul II and the fall of communism.

European Communism was brought down by a Polish trade union and civil disobedience movement called Solidarity. Communism was imposed on Europe east of the "Iron Curtain" by the Soviets after World War II, and had never been popular. Twice before, in Hungary in 1956 and in Czechoslovakia in 1968, popular reform movements initiated by members of Communist governments, had moved in the direction of independence and liberalization, only to be crushed by Soviet tanks.

Solidarity, by contrast, originated outside the Communist Party in networks of Catholics energized by a visit from a new Polish pope, Karol Wojtyla / John Paul II. Solidarity adhered to Catholic social teaching and practiced non-violence. In 1980-81, a series of strikes by Solidarity displayed its power to paralyze the country as it pushed for a variety of goals including rule of law and freedom of conscience. The Soviet-backed Polish communist government imposed martial law, arrested Solidarity's leaders, and forced it underground, but it survived and continued to enjoy international support, particularly from John Paul II.

A relatively young and comparatively liberal Soviet leader, Mikhail Gorbachev, was elected in 1985, who was willing to let eastern European countries govern their internal affairs, depriving the Polish communist government of an important rationale for repression. At last, hoping to legitimize its rule by a democratic mandate, the Communist government legalized Solidarity in 1989 and held elections. Solidarity's sweeping victory ended the regime in Poland, and triggered similar revolutions in Hungary, East Germany—scene of the symbolic destruction of the Berlin Wall by glad crowds—Czechoslavakia and Bulgaria. All the revolutions were non-violent, and the label "velvet revolution" which has been applied to Czechoslovakia is a good description of all.

The above history (of course incomplete) includes five mass civil disobedience movements—the Christian martyrs, the Indian independence movement, the American civil rights movement, the burning of draft cards, and the velvet revolutions of 1989—all of which achieved their aims. Christianity became tolerated throughout the Roman Empire, and the imperial cult was abolished. India gained its independence. Segregation was abolished and American blacks gained equal rights. America stopped using military conscription. Communism fell.

But none of the mass movements really paralyzed or overwhelmed the sovereign power. However appealing nonviolence is, a cynic could argue, in each case, that their success was *accidental*, and in particular, was the result of sovereign power falling into the right hands. Not the Christian martyrs, but the Roman Emperor, Constantine, brought about legal tolerance for Christianity in the Roman Empire. Not Gandhi or *satyagraha*, but a Labour Party victory in the British elections of 1946, brought about Indian independence.

Not Martin Luther King or the Freedom Riders, but President Lyndon B. Johnson passed the legislation that gave American blacks equal rights. The draft continued for years in the face of protests and burnt draft cards, and its disappearance after Vietnam can be accounted for in terms of changes in military technology and tactics.

Communism collapsed in eastern and central Europe when (not John Paul II but) Mikhail Gorbachev said the Soviets would no longer intervene to prop it up. In each case, the regime's coercive power was intact. It could have resisted change if it had been sufficiently determined, and the civil disobedience movement just got lucky that it did not. But there are several rebuttals to the cynic's argument.

First, while the *timing* of victory may have been accidental, because these civil disobedience movements were resilient and durable, they could continue resisting indefinitely until sovereign power fell into favorable hands. Had Winston Churchill won the 1946 election in Britain, Indian independence might have been delayed for a decade. Gandhi might have died of old age, his vision unattained. But the Indian independence movement would not have disbanded, and new *satyagraha* efforts would probably have continued to be tried.

Similarly, if Constantine had been defeated by one of his pagan rivals, by Maximian or Licinius, the legalization of Christianity in the Roman Empire might have been delayed; but the Church had endured two centuries of intermittent persecution and could have endured one or two more centuries if necessary. Robust civil disobedience movements know how to wait.

Second, if we consider the character of the leaders who eventually gave these civil disobedience movements their success, it seems clear that most of them were not the kind of men who would have tried to enact, let alone succeeded in enacting, visionary societal transformations merely for the sake of justice, if the movements had not been pointing the way and pressuring them to do so. Lyndon B. Johnson was a Southerner and a consummate politician, who had become Senate Majority Leader on the strength of the recommendation of archsegregationist Richard Russell. Constantine was an ambitious soldier whose conversion story, amidst one of Rome's chronic succession struggles, underlines his opportunism: supposedly he saw a vision of the cross with the words, "In this sign, conquer." Mikhail Gorbachev could be ruthless: he waged bloody war in Afghanistan for four years, and Soviet troops killed 300 civilians in Azerbaijan on his orders while suppressing a push for independence there in 1990. Each of these leaders saw political advantage to himself in yielding because of the conditions the civil disobedience movement had created.

Third, prior to complete victory, each of these movements had forced the regimes, either to adapt, to compromise, to yield ground, or else to expend political capital by cracking down. Roman Emperors had learned the hard way how difficult Christianity was to kill. The British had resorted to all manner of constitutional tinkering from 1919 onward in their efforts to accommodate some of the legitimate aspirations of Indians and defuse opposition to their rule. The Polish Communist government's imposition of martial law had damaged the economy and deepened its unpopularity.

Fourth, what the victory of each of these movements led to was something more than a change of policy or even of government. It was a true transformation, a social revolution, something new under the sun. The color-blind society advocated by Martin Luther King, and by now largely realized in the United States, is a phenomenon that few if any societies have realized in the past.

Some past societies have been racially homogeneous; in others there has been a friendly symbiosis among races; but a society in which the law insists that a person's race be no barrier to professional advancement in either the public or private sectors, while etiquette demands that personal interaction be just as egalitarian, in short that black and white and Asian and Indian and Native American all be treated the same and "judged not by the color of their skin but by the content of their character," is a revolution. To anyone of Thomas Jefferson's generation it would have been all but inconceivable.

In the same way, one does not adequately comprehend what an event the advent of a Christian Roman Empire, or of an independent, democratic India, or of Europe whole and free, was, if one does not appreciate that until not long before it was achieved, it would have been difficult even to imagine.

Fifth, each of these movements laid the foundation for a new consensus. In this respect, the outcome of civil disobedience differs from the outcomes of most wars, as well as of ordinary democratic politics. Franklin D. Roosevelt's New Deal produced a political realignment, but not a new consensus. Conservative and free-market critiques persisted and eventually the political pendulum swung the other way. Ronald Reagan, too, achieved a political realignment and restored capitalist prosperity for a generation, and his liberal opponents gave ground, but never gave up or converted.

The North's victory in the Civil War was resented by Southerners for a hundred years, and inter-war Germans resented the Allied victory in World War I. By contrast, essentially *no one* in America publicly regrets the end of segregation; *no one* in central Europe wants Soviet communism restored; *no one* in India regrets the fall of the British Raj. No one would have regretted the Christianization of the Roman Empire for a thousand years from, say, 600 A.D. to 1600 A.D.; and even post-Christians today would dismiss throwing Christians to the lions as an absurd and horrible practice. The victories of civil disobedience are lasting.

Civil disobedience defined

What distinguishes civil disobedience from other kinds of disobedience to the law, like stealing, or murder? The three distinguishing features of civil disobedience are:

1. *Kantian universalizability.*

This decorous but cumbersome phrase means that a civil disobedient wants the law he is breaking to be changed. The philosopher Immanuel Kant taught that a person ought to behave according to maxims which he willed to be universal. A thief - who steals the possessions of others but hopes that others will not steal his, or a murderer - who kills others but hopes not to be killed by them - is not a civil disobedient.

2. *Non-violence.*

Civil disobedience is non-violent, that is, it does not violate the natural rights of others. Whether crimes against property, such as the Boston Tea Party, can be excluded from the category of civil disobedience on this ground, depends on the extent to which any particular instance of legal property rights has a basis in natural rights.

3. *Truth.*

An essential aspect of civil disobedience, albeit somewhat hard to define, is that civil disobedience must be more or less honest and open. Gandhi's term for civil disobedience, *satyagraha*, from *satya* = truth and *agraha* = holding on to or insistence, emphasizes this aspect of civil disobedience exclusively. Often, civil disobedience is not merely honest but deliberately public and conspicuous, as it tries to change the law by moving public opinion. But even if the primary motive for civil disobedience is, as it was for Henry David Thoreau, to *avoid complicity in* rather than to change the law, a civil disobedient must not *pretend* to obey the law, lest he thereby acknowledge its legitimacy.

Openly to disobey the law is to risk, or even to invite, state coercion and violence. A civil disobedient may regard this as an inconvenience, as Thoreau did, as a duty, as Socrates did, or even as an honor and glory, as some of the early Christian martyrs did; but in any case he accepts it without resistance, *while not regarding it as punishment*, because punishment implies guilt.

To the civil disobedient, it is the state, not himself, which is guilty. Because it is easy for the state to make life, or at least the external conditions of life, wretched for a non-resisting individual, civil disobedience typically requires *motives that transcend (narrowly defined) self-interest*. Thoreau insisted that the demands of conscience must be obeyed at all costs. For Gandhi, Socrates, the early Christian martyrs, or Martin Luther King, civil disobedience was demanded by God.

In principle, civil disobedience requires greater courage than any military heroism. A soldier runs a risk of a torturous death, but only by accident. The enemy wants to kill him, but probably not to make him suffer, and even a sadistic enemy will not usually have the luxury of killing slowly and painfully as a deliberate military policy. By contrast, a civil disobedient puts himself entirely in the power of an adversary which may torture him either from hatred or in order to break his will. In practice, however, civil disobedience against moderate and liberal regimes may involve little risk of such extreme penalties. The British never tortured Gandhi.

Civil disobedience is distinct from other forms of non-violent political activism, such as *protests, boycotts, strikes* and *hunger strikes*. Often non-violent political movements use all these tactics. Civil disobedience is distinctive, however, in that involves *breaking the law*, so an ethical defense of civil disobedience therefore requires some kind of distinction between human and natural law.

Protests and strikes may involve breaking laws. If they do so, they are a form of civil disobedience; if not, not. Boycotts break no laws and are fairly unproblematic ethically, unless the causes they are used for are bad. (Hunger strikes are, in the logical limit, a form of suicide, and therefore unethical.) Civil disobedience typically involves a higher degree of sacrifice for its practitioner than other forms of political nonviolence - even, in principle, than hunger strikes, since a hunger striker is typically not tortured while a civil disobedient might be.

Why civil disobedience can only be used in pursuit of libertarian causes

Civil disobedience can only be used to advance freedom. The reason for this is that in order to practice civil disobedience at all, one must be subject to some form of coercion. The state wants to draft me; I burn my draft card. The state declares a salt monopoly; I march to the sea and start distilling salt. The state orders me to sit in the back of the bus; I sit in front. Strikes, protests, and boycotts can be used to advocate, as well as to oppose, coercion. A union may strike to demand a minimum wage—that is, to prohibit, by coercion, certain kinds of private labor agreements—or to demand protective tariffs. Any policy, good or bad, pro-freedom or anti-freedom, could be demanded by a protest or made the condition for ending a boycott. But civil disobedience is only available to certain causes.

The political cause which excites the most intense and conscientious advocacy in America today is *abortion*. Of the millions of Americans for whom ending abortion is the great moral cause of our times, it seems a safe bet that at least thousands would be willing to make sacrifices even to the point of death and torture to stop abortion through civil disobedience. *But they cannot.* There is no law for them civilly to disobey. What the pro-life camp wants is an *increase* in government coercion, a use of government coercion to prohibit behaviors currently allowed. Civil disobedience cannot be used for such an end.

As another example, there was very strong opposition to the Iraq War in 2003, and some opponents of the war would probably have been willing to make great sacrifices as civil disobedients in order to prevent it. Those of them who were American, British, Polish, or Australian citizens could, like Thoreau, have refused conscientiously to pay taxes to a warmongering state. Aside from that, however, Iraq War opponents were not subject to any coercive laws related to the war, and so could not civilly disobey them. *Iraqis* could have resisted the Coalition Provisional Authority through civil disobedience if they had been so inclined; but even they could not have used civil disobedience directly in support of the coercive power of Saddam's regime.

Civil disobedience can always be used to try to dissolve a state, since every state deploys coercion, to collect revenue if nothing else. Ironically, though Gandhi was no economic liberal himself—he was a strong protectionist, for example, obsessed with reviving India's inefficient cloth spinning industry which free trade with industrial Britain had rendered obsolete—his *satyagraha* efforts were inevitably libertarian in character, being directed against taxes, state monopoly, mandatory registration and the like, because his chosen tactic was necessarily directed against state coercion. Segregation and the draft were coercive institutions and could therefore be opposed by civil disobedience, with similarly libertarian results. Whatever the Christian church may have done later when it became wedded to temporal power, in the age of the martyrs its aims were perfectly libertarian.

New frontiers for civil disobedience

Is civil disobedience being practiced today? Is there a need for it, are there opportunities for it, in contemporary America? To find out, we can think of the main forms of disobedience to the law that are common today, and match them against the three criteria we established for civil disobedience. As a warm-up, consider the case of *speeding*. Is speeding civil disobedience?

1. *Kantian universalizability.* It is clearly *possible* for a person to will that everyone drive, say, 80 or 90 miles per hour on major highways. It seems doubtful that most speeding drivers really do want that.

2. *Non-violence.* A grey area. While speeding is not "violent" in the ordinary sense of the word, it may be regarded as violating of the rights of other motorists if it needlessly puts their lives at risk.

3. *Truth.* A civilly disobedient speeder must not slow down when he sees a police car. If pulled over, he must neither deny or apologize, but say what he was doing and explain why. The behavior implied by our third criterion would be so odd that we can probably rule out speeding as an instance of civil disobedience.

What about the use of illegal drugs? This may meet the standards of Kantian universalizability—most users of illegal drugs probably want to see them legalized—and of non-violence—A does not violate B's rights by smoking marijuana—but it hardly ever meets the standard of truth, since those who use illegal drugs almost always do so behind closed doors and most are probably ready to lie about it to avoid punishment if necessary. Drunk driving is certainly *not* civil disobedience, because it puts the lives of others at risk and therefore should not be regarded as non-violent.

But by far the most interesting and important case of possible civil disobedience today is *illegal immigration*.

One unique feature of illegal immigration vis-à-vis other kinds of disobedience to the law is that illegal immigrants break laws *to which they in no way consented through the social contract*. We have seen already that "government by consent of the governed" is more myth than reality, but to the extent that the argument "you should obey the laws because we all agreed to them through the democratic process" has any force, it cannot possibly apply to illegal immigration, as illegal immigrants had no say in making the laws that they are breaking. Immigration restrictions are the logical limiting case of undemocratic law, since the set of people who have a say in making such laws—natives and naturalized citizens—is the exact inverse of the set of people who are on the receiving end of them—foreigners.

Illegal immigration may be qualified as civil disobedience in some but not all instances, depending on how it is done, as may be seen by revisiting the three criteria we defined above.

1. *Kantian universalizability.* An illegal immigrant satisfies this criterion if he wills some form of generalized freedom of migration. Of course, he might not: an illegal immigrant might complain about the state's failure to keep out *other* illegal immigrants (for example, because competition from them drives down his wages) or he might want his native country to enforce its migration laws. In that case, his behavior is not civil disobedience. But to judge from some of their protest slogans, it seems that many illegal immigrants do support generalized open borders.

2. *Non-violence.* Although it is obvious that illegal immigration is a non-violent behavior, it is worth pausing to refute a thought (it does not rise to the level of argument) which might be suggested by the analogy of property. We have said that where there are property rights, a sort of inversion of *habeas corpus* may properly be regarded for legal purposes as having taken place, so that a person who defends his own land against a trespasser is regarded as acting in self-defense, as if his land were an extension of his body. Trespassing and stealing might therefore be characterized as forms of "violence" even though no human body is harmed thereby.

By the same token, someone might feel the nation has a natural right to its own land, and an illegal immigrant is acting "violently" inasmuch as he accesses the nation's land without permission. The confusion here lies in the ambiguity of the possessive, since "one's own" has a different meaning in the two cases. No collective property right of the nation in its territory exists. For one thing, it has no way justly to originate, since the labor of which property is a material embodiment belongs to individuals, not states or nations. For another, this collective property right would be inconsistent with individual property rights.

Illegal immigration violates neither persons nor property and is therefore unambiguously non-violent.[41]

3. *Truth*. This one is problematic. Visa over-stayers would seem not to meet this criterion, for they give their word to leave the country and then fail to do so. This might be a minor, excusable lie, or even not a lie at all (if a visa over-stayer sincerely planned to leave and then changed his mind) but it draws a line between the visa over-stayer and the rigorous commitment to truth of a Gandhi. An immigrant who crosses through the deserts of Arizona is in a more truthful position—he has told no lies to get to America—but those who want to work typically use forged documents. A forged document may not be a lie if the use of forged documents has become a convention. For example, suppose I show you a Social Security card that says my name is John Jacobson and my Social Security number is XXX-XX-XXXX. If in showing you this card, I intend to be understood as *claiming to be* John Jacobson with SS# XXX-XX-XXXX, then I am lying. But if I neither desire nor expect that you will believe I am John Jacobson, but simply know that you have to see a Social Security card of some kind in order to hire me, there may be no dishonesty in the action.

Nonetheless, to be an illegal immigrant is to run a risk of being put in situations where one has to choose between telling an outright lie and facing jail and/or deportation. To be in an entirely truthful position, an illegal immigrant would have to intend to tell the truth if such a situation should arise. Certainly he would have to refrain from volunteering lies about his immigration status in less dire situations. It does not seem likely that most illegal immigrants are in an entirely truthful position.

I do not say this to condemn them. No American who ever speeds, or under-reports his income for tax purposes, or tells white lies to his friends, or exaggerates on a resume or in a job interview or on a date, or bends the truth to keep a boss or a customer happy, is in a position to judge an immigrant who is prepared to lie to the police if that is necessary to avoid having his family torn apart by deportation. But most immigration falls short of the "truth-insistence," the *satyagraha*, that made Gandhi's movement so powerful.

---

[41] Of course, I am speaking of the general case here. In particular cases, an illegal immigrant may violate private property rights by crossing the border onto private land, without permission of the owner.

If illegal immigration in the United States does not yet constitute a mass civil disobedience movement, it is not far from it. The large protests that immigrants have begun to conduct raise the visibility of illegal immigrants as human beings, though individual participants do not typically court arrest since illegal immigrants are mingled with sympathetic legal immigrants and native citizens like myself. A *satyagraha* approach might involve illegal immigrants openly advertising their status in order to court arrest and deportation.

Native-born Americans can engage in civil disobedience, too, by providing jobs and accommodations to illegal immigrants, without an intention to deceive the state if questions are asked. For example, I might choose to sublet rooms without asking to see the tenants' documents.

Conclusion

To review the argument so far, people have natural rights, and violence is only permissible in special cases, such as self-defense or retribution. The delegation of rights to self-defense and retribution through a social contract is, ideally, the origin and function of just government; and real governments are just to the extent that they conform to this standard (all fall short). Property, which has some basis in natural rights but is also shaped by positive law, justifies exclusion by individuals, of individuals, from private land.

Since the role of a just government is to protect its subjects' rights, it has no occasion to intervene when non-citizens enter private land belonging to its citizens with the owners' consent, since no violation of rights occurs in this case. Nor can the government justly exclude either citizens or foreigners from the streets, because the streets are not the government's property, but places where the private non-exclusive transit rights of habitual users overlap and prevent (just) private appropriation, and which consequently remain in the commons for purposes of transit.

The general liberty to use the streets therefore has a basis in natural rights, applies equally to citizens and non-citizens of a state, and cannot be justly restricted by a government except when the streets are used in ways that constitute an objective danger to its citizens' safety (e.g., drunk-driving, gang-warfare, or the transportation of hostile armies). Illegal immigrants are (at least in some cases) conducting a form of civil disobedience against an unjust law. It is the law, not the immigrant, which is in the wrong, and the law should be changed, rather than the immigrant removed. But what should the law be changed *to*?

9

Freedom of Migration

"A specter is haunting Europe – the specter of communism," wrote Karl Marx in the *Communist Manifesto*. For some people, the idea of open borders may be as scary as communism. Europeans were right to be afraid of communism, as events proved. But open borders are not communism. It is true that if the United States instantly and completely opened its borders—if, for example, it took the advice of a 1984 *Wall Street Journal* editorial and passed a five-word constitutional amendment, "There shall be open borders"—the resulting influx would probably strain public order to the breaking point and beyond. The results of a recent Gallup poll,[42] shown in **Table 2**, show just how large the demand for migration is:

Table 2: Hundreds of millions worldwide desire to migrate permanently to another country
Employment, Migration, and Age Around the World
Percentage who would like to move permanently to another country

	Employed	Underemployed	Not in workforce
Sub-Saharan Africa			
Aged 15 to 29	43%	44%	45%
Aged 30 to 65	31%	32%	22%
Europe			
Aged 15 to 29	27%	28%	26%
Aged 30 to 65	17%	23%	11%
The Americas			
Aged 15 to 29	27%	25%	26%
Aged 30 to 65	13%	20%	10%
Asia			
Aged 15 to 29	12%	14%	12%
Aged 30 to 65	8%	10%	5%
Middle East and North Africa			
Aged 15 to 20	25%	31%	14%
Aged 30 to 65	14%	23%	6%

Based on surveys in 105 countries in 2009 and 2010.
Results are projected to total population of each country aged 15 and older
GALLUP

---

[42] Gallup, September 8, 2010. "Employed or Not, Many Young People Desire to Migrate." http://www.gallup.com/poll/142901/Employed-Not-Young-People-Desire-Migrate.aspx

If over 40% of the youth of sub-Saharan Africa and over 30% of their elders, over 25% of young people in the Americas and 10-15% of their elders, over 25% of young people in Europe and 15% or more of their elders, about 10% of Asians and 20% of Middle Easterners and North Africans want to migrate, global demand for migration is several hundreds of millions. Not all of these would come to the United States, but America has always been the biggest magnet for migrants, and another recent Gallup poll found that 165 million foreigners would like to settle specifically in America.[43] This is at a time when America is unusually unpopular in the world and when U.S. unemployment is the highest it has been in three decades.

Probably, even if the borders were opened, not all of these would come. On the other hand, "chain migration"—one immigrant comes, then friends and family, who now have a contact in America, follow—might amplify the number. As English continues to spread as a global *lingua franca* and as the economy recovers, demand for migration to America will only increase. The reason the actual number of immigrants is so much smaller than the number desiring to immigrate is that America excludes them by force, or the threat thereof. They are denied visas, or they do not apply because, given the way US immigration officials discriminate on the basis of criteria like education, economic status, occupation, and national origin, rejection would be the near-certain result. The result is that most of mankind is excluded from America permanently, from birth.

Yet it is not too difficult to design an immigration policy that would protect public order, and even the living standards of the native-born, while abandoning discretionary migration control and recognizing, perhaps in a somewhat attenuated form, the right to migrate. Such a policy, called "don't restrict immigration, tax it" (DRITI), is outlined later in this chapter.

But first I will show that the idea that there is a *right to migrate*, that is, that a migrant has the same right to enter and move about in the streets of a host country as do its native-born citizens, is both more and less radical than it sounds—more radical in its consequences, but less so because the idea of a right to migrate is already implicit in much of American patriotic mythology and political discourse.

First, the Statue of Liberty, a gift to the United States from France dedicated in 1886, which in the late 19th century was the first sight that immigrants arriving in New York by sea saw in the New World, still stands in New York harbor

---

[43] http://www.gallup.com/poll/139391/roughly-million-mexicans-express-desire-move.aspx

and bears a plaque with a poem, "The New Colossus," that has come to represent the meaning of the statue. The poem runs:

Not like the brazen giant of Greek fame,
With conquering limbs astride from land to land;
Here at our sea-washed, sunset gates shall stand
A mighty woman with a torch, whose flame
Is the imprisoned lightning, and her name
Mother of Exiles. From her beacon-hand
Glows world-wide welcome; her mild eyes command
The air-bridged harbor that twin cities frame.
"Keep, ancient lands, your storied pomp!" cries she
With silent lips. "Give me your tired, your poor,
Your huddled masses yearning to breathe free,
The wretched refuse of your teeming shore.
Send these, the homeless, tempest-tossed to me,
I lift my lamp beside the golden door!"

Based on its immigration policies today, America is unworthy to take pride in the Statue of Liberty and in what, thanks to this poem and the immigrant experience at Ellis Island, it has come to represent. Not only does America shut out most foreigners who want to come, but it deliberately discriminates in favor of the affluent and educated, and against just those whom, in the poem, the Statue of Liberty welcomed: the poor, the homeless, the wretched, the desperate.

Yet Americans have not commissioned a couple of tugboats to drag the Statue of Liberty into the sea. We have not even chiseled away "The New Colossus" from the Statue of Liberty's walls. Americans still revere the Statue of Liberty as a national symbol, and even cite the Statue of Liberty poem with a patriotic pride, weirdly unmixed with shame, at how far we have departed from the ideal it so beautifully expresses.

The Statue of Liberty today holds a position in America's national psyche similar to that which the Declaration of Independence held in the times when slavery and segregation mocked the brave manifesto that "all men are created equal and endowed with their Creator with ... inalienable rights." We love it, we take pride in it, we would hardly know who we are supposed to be as a nation without it. Yet we do not live by it, paying a certain price in cognitive dissonance and self-deceit for our hypocrisy; and we may someday find it in ourselves to return to it; yet there is bitter resistance to any such plan.

Again, the idea of a right to migrate was expressed in Ronald Reagan's Farewell Address in 1989:

> I've spoken of the shining city all my political life, but I don't know if I ever quite communicated what I saw when I said it. But in my mind it was a tall proud city built on rocks stronger than oceans, wind-swept, God-blessed, and teeming with people of all kinds living in harmony and peace, a city with free ports that hummed with commerce and creativity, and if there had to be city walls, the walls had doors and the doors were open to anyone with the will and the heart to get here.[44]

According to Reagan, the factor determining whether someone gets into America should be the "will and heart" of the migrant—*not* the arbitrary decision of a bureaucrat. In other words, there is, or ought to be, a right to migrate.

Again, the idea of the right to migrate is back-handedly expressed when politicians promise, or voters demand, that when illegal immigrants are given amnesty, they will have to "go to the back of the line." The phrase appeals to a sense of fairness and a desire to avoid rewarding people who cheat the system. Yet it betrays a revealing misconception, namely, that there is a "line" to get into the United States, and that if you wait your turn, you will get in—in other words, a right to migrate.

One waits in line for something one has a right to. Concert tickets, for example: if there were no line, I could buy one, and might be able to sue the organizers of the concert if I were arbitrarily refused. Because there are many buyers and few cashiers to sell them, it takes time to process the transactions, and I have to wait; but eventually I will get to the front of the line and buy my ticket. The "back of the line" rhetoric implies that Reagan's "city on a hill" with "doors... open to anyone with the will and heart to get here"—legally—is a reality.

The fact that America excludes most foreign-born persons from birth makes America's claim to be a beacon of freedom and equality, a land where merit rather than birth determines a person's station in life, hypocrisy; or if you prefer—to put it more charitably at the cost of entertaining a hope that the future may disappoint—aspirational. And it makes certain arguments that are used to justify measures against illegal immigrants quite spurious. For example, journalist Mary Kate Cary argued in *US News and World Report* that:

---

[44] Ronald Reagan's Farewell Adress, http://old.nationalreview.com/document/reagan200406052132.asp

Our [ancestors] all came to this country legally, [some of them after] considerable delay and difficulty. My grandparents already spoke English, [others] did not and they had to learn the language before they could become citizens—something that has become controversial these days. "They had to go to some trouble to become citizens, and that's all we're asking now," said one guy. "Just put forth some effort, and come in legally, like our families did. That's all we're asking." Maybe a mainstream consensus is emerging from the debate over this unreasonable law in Arizona: that securing our border has to come first—and then fair, reasonable but well-enforced immigration rules should follow. It's like he said: "That's all we're asking."[45]

In order legitimately to claim that "all we're asking" is that immigrants "put forth some effort, and come in legally," we would have to ensure that legal channels are available, not just to some, but to all aspiring immigrants, and in particular to any immigrants whom, when they come in illegally, we would be inclined to blame. The truth is that the U.S. makes hardly any visas available for unskilled workers, despite the high demand for them in the service, agriculture, and other sectors; and that the vast majority of illegal immigrants never had the option of coming in legally.

"All we're asking," in reality, is that immigrants permanently relinquish the rich opportunities that the American economy offers them (at least, relative to what they had at home) in order to obey laws to which they never consented and in which they had no say, which were not made with their interests in mind, and of the effects of which the people who *did* have a say in making them, namely, the American people, seem to be so ignorant that they think "all we're asking" is for these immigrants to come into the country through non-existent legal channels.

Articles like Mary Kate Cary's are regularly published in reputable and widely-read newspapers, magazines, and journals. Such falsehoods as the claim that "all we're asking [is that] they come in legally" would not ordinarily get past the fact-checkers of a prominent publication. But the explanation of this weird ignorance and inaccuracy is not far to seek. Why should Americans know anything about our immigration laws, when they will never be subject to them?

---

[45] http://www.usnews.com/blogs/mary-kate-cary/2010/05/04/Arizona-Immigration-Law-May-Lead-to-Consensus.html

"Rational ignorance" of voters is a general problem for democracy—why invest time and effort into choosing the right candidate, when no one's vote ever changes the outcome of an election?—but one factor that mitigates rational ignorance is that people have an incentive to discover what the laws are when they personally are, or stand to be, affected by them. Since the people who have a say in making laws regulating migration is the exact mathematical inverse of the set of people who are subject to them, this partial antidote to voter ignorance is not operative in the case of migration restrictions.

The obliviousness of the "sovereign" American people as typified by Mary Kate Cary to the real nature and effects of their immigration laws is reminiscent of another sovereign person, Queen Marie Antoinette of France just before the revolution. According to legend, when told that the peasants had no bread, she said, "Then let them eat cake"—cake (*brioche*) being a luxury bread enriched with eggs and butter. Whether or not Marie Antoinette really said this (the phrase may be apocryphal from the malevolent pen of Jean Jacques Rousseau), the anecdote usefully illustrates the Queen's ignorance of the condition of the people she (and her husband Louis XVI) ruled.

In defense of Marie Antoinette, though, her ignorance somewhat excuses her unconcern, for if she thought the peasants could all afford to eat cake when their bread ran out, she might well indulge in courtly luxuries without guilt. It was not so much Marie Antoinette who was to blame, as the system which gave people like her powers that they ought not to have had. Similarly, Americans who think that legal channels were available to illegal immigrants, and they simply disdained to use them, can be partly excused for getting angry at them for not "going to some trouble" and waiting in "line." The blame lies less on them than on a system that gives American voters, through their representatives and government bureaucracies, powers that they ought not to have of deciding who is and is not allowed to come into the country.

We have argued above that *civil disobedience* is the just and appropriate response to the migration control regimes of the U.S. and other countries. But what should the civil disobedient want the United States to do? What form should the concessions by enlightened Americans take, to make such civil disobedience unnecessary? What should U.S. immigration policy be?

The "comprehensive immigration reform" acts that came before Congress in 2006 and 2007 would have opened up new opportunities for, and given new dignity to, millions of people. They would have done much to restore the rule of law in America by giving undocumented residents legal status. But only temporarily. They would probably have triggered a surge in illegal immigration as foreigners sought to take advantage of the amnesty before the window of opportunity closed. And they would surely have attracted, over time, more illegal immigrants, hoping to take advantage of the (anticipated) next amnesty. Amnesty,[46] though a good thing, is not a sustainable answer to the immigration question, because it does not recognize the right to migrate.

Of course, politicians in 2006 and 2007 made vague promises to "secure the border" while creating a path to citizenship for those already here. That is, they promised to render thousands of miles of frontiers on land and sea physically impermeable to highly motivated individual migrants, and presumably at least somewhat humanely, without resorting to, say, the murder or torture of migrants. Such a feat has never been achieved and is probably impossible.

Experts like Douglas S. Massey[47] insist that all the increases in immigration enforcement since the 1980s have failed not only to stop, but even to *slow* illegal immigration, and even that they have *increased* permanent illegal migration by making the alternative of seasonal migration more difficult. I find it hard to believe that enforcement has been *that* ineffective; yet there is an easy way to make sense of the claim. Border enforcement increases the *cost*, in money and hardship, of migrating, but that cost is still small compared to the value of migrating.

If U.S. GDP per capita is $46,400,[48] while Mexico's is $13,500, and if we assume the economic growth rate in both countries is about the same and the discount rate is 1% more than economic growth, the benefit of living in the U.S. rather than Mexico for a typical migrant might be on the order of $1.3 million. The rewards, then, may just be too large for the border enforcement measures applied so far to make much of a difference in the incentives for migration.

Would a border fence solve the problem? From a human rights/civil liberties point of view, this is the closest thing there is to an acceptable way of enforcing migration restrictions, since it involves no violence against persons. A border fence near San Diego seems to have had some success in reducing illegal immigration there. But it has probably only *diverted* illegal immigration to the Texas and Arizona borders, rather than stopping it.

---

[46] Some advocates of comprehensive immigration reform will, perhaps, not thank me for calling it "amnesty." They argue that because it imposes fines and other penalties, comprehensive immigration reform is not amnesty, and that to call it "amnesty" is to play into the hands of its critics. I think it is amnesty and this word needs to be rehabilitated.

[47] http://www.freetrade.org/pubs/pas/tpa-029.pdf

[48] From the CIA World Factbook

Economically, the United States is rather homogeneous: GDP per capita differs from state to state by a factor of two or less. For a prospective illegal immigrant, one way into the country may be about as good as another; but there is a strong incentive to get in somehow. If there is a fence at one point on the border, a rational migrant will go to another part of it. If there were a fence along the whole border, it would be time to go over or under or around. A person can get over a fence with ladders, or tunnel under it, go around it by boat through the Gulf of Mexico or up the Pacific Coast, or fly over it in a small plane, or perhaps even as a human cannonball with a parachute.

The last whimsical suggestion might not work, but who can guess what methods human ingenuity would devise when the stakes are as high as a million dollars in lifetime earnings for each immigrant who gets through?

Shipping containers might be one means of transport for the next wave of illegal immigrants if a border fence turned out to be effective. There are already cases of people getting into the U.S. by shipping container.[49] Several million cargo containers arrive in the United States each year. A standard shipping container is 40 feet by 8 feet by 8 feet, and may spend 3-4 weeks at sea *en route* from China to the United States. It is typically not opened for inspection in either the port of departure or the port of arrival, but is lifted by a crane onto a truck and delivered to a final customer. To inspect every incoming shipping container would raise prices on all kinds of imports and be crippling for the US economy. The cost of shipping one container from China to the US is around $5,000.

Not many people resort to immigration by shipping container now, of course. But for a person who is willing to live in a shipping container for a little over a month, this might be the next best way to get into the United States, if the Mexican border is effectively closed. The biggest problems are feces and the lack of fresh air, but technology might find solutions to those problems if there was enough demand for them. Anyway, would you spend four weeks in a stinking shipping container to raise your lifetime earnings by one or two million dollars? I would. But it would take a certain human infrastructure—front companies, internet forums—to help people come into the United States by shipping container on a large scale. A border fence and an amnesty for the illegal immigrants still here might be just the thing to trigger the emergence of this industry.

What is needed is a policy that decriminalizes immigration, along the lines of the "don't restrict immigration, tax it" (DRITI) policy outlined below. DRITI is a serious policy proposal in the sense that I believe, both that enlightened

---

[49] http://seattletimes.nwsource.com/html/localnews/2002914004_smuggling.html

self-interest should motivate, and that justice demands, the adoption by the United States and other countries of a policy along these lines. But since the policy is not politically feasible at present, in another sense the proposal is a mere thought-experiment.

I offer it partly in order to evoke in the reader's mind a certain kind of moral, or pseudo-moral, objection, which I will then refute. For false moral ideas can do as much harm as deliberate evil. Nothing inflicts as much suffering in today's world as the false notion that when our fellow man is in need *nearby*, we must not only help him but coerce others to do so, yet we can justly avoid this obligation only by keeping our needy fellow men at a distance by force.

Don't restrict immigration, tax it

DRITI would establish a new visa, available to any foreign-born person whom it is implausible to accuse of any connection with or propensity for terrorism. Depending on how this criterion was applied, large populations in many parts of the Muslim world might be excluded; but virtually everyone in Western Europe, East Asia, Latin America and Australasia, and most Indians and Russians, would be eligible. The new visa—call it the DRITI visa—would entitle a person to live and work in the United States indefinitely, provided that several conditions were met:

1. *Deposit.* Prior to receiving a DRITI visa, each intending immigrant would have to register with a US consulate and make a deposit equal to the estimated cost of deporting him from the United States. This deposit would "pre-reimburse" the government for deporting him or her if he or she became destitute and requested repatriation. A DRITI immigrant who returned home using his own resources could reclaim his deposit.

2. *Surtax.* A special surtax would automatically be garnished from the wages of all DRITI immigrants.

3. *Mandatory savings.* For any prospective immigrant who applies for and receives the DRITI visa, a special savings account would be created, managed by the US government but owned by the immigrant. This savings account would have the following feature: *money could only be withdrawn from it when the immigrant is physically present in his home country.*

As long as the immigrant would work in the United States, mandatory savings (over and above the surtax) would be garnished from his wages at a certain rate and deposited in the account. Money can only go into the account by this mechanism, that is, by being deducted from wages earned in the United States. It cannot be deposited in the account from other financial resources the DRITI immigrant may possess. (Regulations would need to address the issue of how much self-employed DRITI immigrants would have to/would be allowed to deposit into the account.)

4. *The path to citizenship.* A certain threshold would be established beyond which mandatory savings would cease to be collected from the DRITI immigrant. For example, if the threshold were $50,000, the government would garnish the immigrant's wages until such time as there was $50,000 in his account, then cease to do so. Thereafter the immigrant would still be subject to the surtax, but not to mandatory savings. Also, he would presumptively have the right to become an American citizen, *but only at the cost of forfeiting the savings account to the government.* Other conditions—knowledge of English, character witnesses, an oath of allegiance—might also be added as conditions for citizenship. Of course, having become a citizen, the immigrant would have all the rights of other citizens and would not be subject to the surtax.

5. *Compensation of natives.* Because some natives would lose out by competition with DRITI immigrants, revenues from the surtax and from savings forfeited by new citizens would be distributed among American natives and naturalized citizens to ensure that none (or very few) of them are made worse off by DRITI. Payments (money to keep it simple) might be distributed among all Americans, or—because competition from immigrants would most affect the relatively uneducated and unskilled, who have the lowest incomes—on a means-tested basis.

6. *Children.* The children of DRITI immigrants would enjoy birthright citizenship under the 14th Amendment. That would tempt many parents to come to America under the DRITI policy so as to give their children access to birthright citizenship. Would this be a problem? Up to a point, no. America *needs* more children to finance the retirement benefits of the older generations. If the education of children of DRITI immigrants were regarded as too much of a burden, state expenditures incurred for the education of U.S.-born children of DRITI immigrants could be deducted from the mandatory savings accounts of DRITI

immigrants. If this were not sufficient, extra surtaxes might be imposed on *all* DRITI immigrants to offset the costs incurred by the government in educating U.S.-born children of the more fertile ones.

The purpose of the deposit—to provide a sort of social safety net for immigrants without costing the American taxpayer money—and the surtax and compensation of natives—to prevent any Americans from losing out by DRITI—are evident enough, but it may be useful to further elucidate the motives for the mandatory savings program, and its role in the path to citizenship.

One reason for the mandatory savings element in the policy is to make migration a more effective instrument for promoting international development. This aspect of the policy will give DRITI immigrants an incentive either (a) to return home regularly to withdraw money, and thus maintain ties to their homelands, or (b) eventually to return home permanently. Also, it will ensure that returning migrants will bring home not only new skills, ideas and connections, but also money with which to help the economies of their home countries develop. Many may start businesses. Others will be ideal agents and partners for global corporations or international NGOs. Still others may start civil society organizations, establish political parties, or run for office.

Meanwhile, DRITI immigrants who do choose to stay and become citizens will self-select so that they value America for more than just the superior earning power they enjoy there. It will be (disproportionately) those who value American culture, or American liberty, or American landscapes, or American friends, who will prefer to stay rather than to return home where they might be relatively wealthy, by the standards of their home countries. A nation is more than just an economic machine, and those who become Americans should probably regard that change as being worth some sacrifice.

DRITI in no way involves "buying citizenship." It is not proposed that anyone should be able merely to deposit private money in their account. Rather, DRITI immigrants would *earn* citizenship through labor, that is, through becoming part of that great division of labor, that web of interdependence which is the U.S. economy, those bonds of mutual service which are the basis for the American community.

Although DRITI would involve the federal government surrendering its claim to be able to regulate, in discretionary fashion, all entry and exit into the United States, the government would retain considerable powers to regulate immigration through its three new policy instruments: (a) the DRITI surtax, (b) the DRITI mandatory savings rate(s), and (c) the citizenship threshold.

For example, a high surtax, a low mandatory savings rate, and a moderate citizenship threshold would tend to attract many immigrants intending to become citizens while generating substantial revenue. A low surtax, a high mandatory savings rate, and a high citizenship threshold would attract large populations of sojourners and function as a powerful mechanism for development aid, while creating few new citizens. The government would regulate immigration in arm's-length fashion, rather as the Fed regulates the money supply, rather than through bureaucratic micromanagement and an invasive police state.

Would DRITI solve the problem of illegal immigration and restore the rule of law? It might seem not, for, after all, immigrants might still want to sneak across the border to avoid paying the deposit. Realistically, though, illegally crossing the border is generally harrowing, dangerous, and costly, and few would choose to do it if they had another way into the country. And crucially, *under DRITI, the logical punishment for illegal entry would be different.* An illegal immigrant's crime would be, not that he was present in America, for he would have a right to be in America, but that he had failed to pay the deposit.

The logical punishment would be, not deportation—coercion against his person—but a fine—coercion against his property—equal to the deposit (but that would remain his property) plus a little extra as a disincentive. If the police caught an illegal immigrant, they would exact a fine and then give him a DRITI visa. In effect, there would be an automatic and regular version of the amnesties that passed in 1986 and that were considered by the Senate in 2006 and 2007. It is because illegal immigrants would be punished by coercion against property (a lower-order right, which the state has some leeway to define) rather than by coercion against their persons (a violation of the higher-order rights of *habeas corpus*) that DRITI is **MORE JUST** as well as more efficient than discretionary migration control.

Of course, it is possible in principle that migrants would come without the DRITI visa and be unable to pay the fine when caught, but it is not plausible that this would remain a serious problem. To enter the country illegally is to forgo the benefits of modern transport, making a costly and dangerous trek through the Arizona desert. Very few would choose this course if there were a quick, reliable, and fairly cheap way to get a visa and then hop on a plane or, from Mexico, bus. Once here, it would be difficult for non-DRITI immigrants to find work, since employers could easily recruit DRITI immigrants for jobs native Americans do not want, avoiding the risks of doing business illegally. If traditional illegal immigrants were caught, in the case of Mexicans the DRITI deposit would only be a few hundred dollars, and it is unlikely that the assets even of poor immigrants would be worth less than this amount. It is a safe bet that DRITI visas would put the *coyote* out of business.

The effects of "don't restrict immigration, tax it" would be many and various, and cannot be predicted in detail, but the following three predictions, at least, can be made with some confidence:

1. DRITI would alleviate a great deal of poverty and suffering in the world.

There are still countries in the world where much or most of the population is subject to early death from malnutrition and preventable disease is rampant. There are other countries where a small upper class enjoys a Western standard of living and a larger middle class, though poor by Western standards, is fairly safe from actual hunger, but a substantial part of the population lives by subsistence agriculture or in a precarious state of urban underemployment.

Probably an absolute majority of the world's population lives under conditions that would strike a typical Westerner, either at first glance or upon more intimate familiarity, as shockingly deprived and vulnerable. "Don't restrict immigration, tax it" would enable many of these people to come to America and earn enough money better to satisfy basic needs and simple aspirations. Others would lack the means or the initiative to come themselves, but would benefit indirectly as their more able or fortunate compatriots sent back remittances or returned with money and ideas that would help grow local economies. Probably DRITI would do more good for the world's poor than all the foreign aid in history has ever done or could ever do.

2. DRITI would greatly increase the amount of economic inequality and visible poverty and suffering within the United States.

The DRITI visa would open America's doors to tens of millions, not of the world's poorest for the most part—they would not be able to afford the deposit or the plane ticket—but of people very poor by American standards, many of whom might willingly become poorer in the short run by coming.

It would be easy, at first, to hire unskilled or moderately-skilled workers at minimum wage—and there would be pressure to lower it—for even the most unpleasant jobs, and as firms and households adjusted to take advantage of the new abundance of labor, a new underclass would emerge, first crowded into any makeshift, dingy, dilapidated dwelling available, then creating a demand for builders to erect acres of new, spartan tenements to house the huddled masses.

A new gulf of inequality would open up between the entrepreneurs who would command this new labor supply, on the one hand, and their workers, on the other, but also between the unskilled American-born, who could work and keep his wages and even receive transfers from the government to compensate him for the diminution of his wages due to new competition, and the unskilled DRITI migrant, who, earning the same small wage, would see much of it taxed away as a surtax or into a mandatory savings account, in addition to ordinary taxes.

The presence of large masses of legal, resident non-citizens would challenge Americans' democratic norms. There would be complaints of "taxation without representation," although the truth is that whatever merit there was in that old slogan was due precisely to the lack of consent of American colonists to be taxed, and DRITI immigrants will have *explicitly consented* to pay certain taxes in return for receiving the DRITI visa. Americans would have to get used to having their consciences troubled by scenes of deprivation which, though milder than those which are very common elsewhere in the world, today's migration restrictions prevent us from seeing in person.

3. *America would become a far more racially diverse country.*

Critics of immigration always insist that racism comprises no part of their motives. Perhaps most of them deserve the benefit of the doubt. Yet there is no doubt that racism was a major motive for the adoption of a strict regime of immigration control in the 1920s. And today's immigration control regime, though it has undergone some modifications, is mostly continuous with and still has the same effects as the immigration control regime as that of the 1920s— keeping America largely white.

How are we to interpret this situation? Is the requirement of a passport to enter the United States racist because the motive for establishing this rule was racist, and the law continues to achieve the aims of its racist authors, or is it not racist because those who support and enforce the rule now (and can hardly imagine doing otherwise) no longer feel animosity towards other races? In any case, to establish the DRITI visa would accelerate a change in the racial composition of the American population, with the immigration of tens of millions from non-Muslim Africa and Asia, and probably a sharp rise in marriages between Americans and foreigners with darker complexions.

Other consequences of the DRITI policy might include: acceleration of the global spread of English, while on the other hand, foreign languages would be much more widely spoken within the United States; more foreign tourists and students, for whom, since they do not intend to work, the DRITI taxes would be irrelevant and the DRITI visa would simply be the most convenient way to enter the country; greater cooperation of foreign governments in the fight against terror, lest U.S. inability to certify their citizens as non-terrorists lead to their exclusion from the DRITI program; the emergence of lobbies for the liberation of foreign countries from tyrannical regimes (like the Cuban-Americans in Florida); the appearance of new goods and services in the economy; and greater diversity in cuisine and the arts.

Immigration and Islam

Unless it were deliberately modified to avert this result, DRITI would lead to large-scale immigration of Muslims in search of freedom and economic opportunity, and this is one of the more legitimate reasons to worry about it. Worldwide, Islam exhibits a large democracy deficit vis-à-vis the rest of the world (Rowley and Smith, 2009), partly because of the historical lack of a tradition of freedom, and especially of religious freedom, in Islamic societies. On the other hand, there are now quite a few Muslim-majority democratic countries, suc as Indonesia.

In the past, Islamic jurisprudence held that apostasy from Islam is punishable by death. This is clearly an intolerable practice which every just state has a duty to prevent at all costs. And many Muslims still believe in the death penalty for apostasy today, as the cases of Salman Rushdie, whose murder the Iranian government commissioned as punishment for his alleged apostasy, and of Abdul Rahman, an Afghan convert to Christianity whom an Afghan court nearly sentenced to death before yielding to foreign pressure, show. Mass Islamic immigration could lead to Muslim majorities in host countries, able to replace freedom with Islamic *sharia*.

The most drastic response to this threat would be simply to exclude Muslims from eligibility for DRITI visas, or perhaps from the path to citizenship associated with it. It is tenable that the mere fact of adherence to Islam is evidence of a commitment to values inconsistent with respecting the rights of others that justifies excluding a person as a security threat. This would be unfair, however, to those Muslims, probably constituting a large majority, who have no inclination to accept and/or to act on this (arguable) tenet of their faith. It would also be hard to reconcile with America's (and other Western states') sometimes risky but absolutely indispensable traditions of religious freedom. (Yet it must be said that even nominal Muslims may be exposed to dangerous ideological influences through their religion to which others are not prone.)

A more moderate approach might be to screen carefully for known terror suspects and extremists, to keep a close watch on Muslim immigrant communities, and to inquire into the ideology of Muslim DRITI migrants applying for citizenship to make sure they convincingly disavow the death penalty for apostasy and other traditional Islamic beliefs inconsistent with the principles of a free society, perhaps with the help of oaths or signed statements to that effect.

Mass immigration of Muslims offers two large potential advantages for a country like the United States: (a) emigrants from Islamic countries might absorb the values of freedom and transmit them, through return migration, or relatives, back to the Islamic world, and (b) emigrants from Islamic countries could provide a valuable resource for the intelligence services of the West in their fight against Islamic terrorism. The transformation of the Roman Catholic Church from one of religious freedom's greatest enemies to one of its leading proponents, partly as a result of America's example and the historical experience of Roman Catholics in America, suggests the possible upside to using migration as a way to give Islam a tutorial in freedom.

Immigration versus the social safety net

Aside from special worries about Muslim immigration, I can anticipate two main lines of argument against the proposed DRITI policy. First, one might argue the economics and deny that the consequences would be as beneficial as was claimed in the description of the policy and its impact presented above. I will not devote much attention to this possible objection because I do not think the people with the relevant expertise, economists, are likely to make this argument. The DRITI policy is, in fact, a mere adaptation to *migration* of the uncontroversial argument that the best way for governments to regulate international *trade* is through tariffs and not through discretionary mechanisms such as quotas. Even if some economists do object to the DRITI policy, I think their objections will be political or ethical rather than narrowly economic.

The main moral (or pseudo-moral) objection to open borders has been stated by Paul Krugman: "open immigration can't coexist with a strong social safety net; if you're going to assure health care and a decent income to everyone, you can't make that offer global." [50] That is true, but is it an indictment of open immigration, or of social safety nets? We may unpack Krugman's argument as follows:

Argument A

1. Americans have a moral duty to assure health care and a decent income to everyone who is located in the US.

2. If open immigration is allowed, so many people will come in that it will be impossible to assure health care and a decent income to everyone.

3. Therefore it is necessary to restrict immigration.

As an alternative, we can reverse the order of the steps and negative the first and last:

Argument B

1. Americans have a moral duty not to curtail the right to migrate, but to accommodate those who want to immigrate to the United States for purposes of peaceful labor.

2. If open immigration is allowed, so many people will come in that it will be impossible to assure health care and a decent income to everyone who is located in the U.S.

3. Therefore we must abandon the goal of providing a strong social safety net to everyone who is located in the U.S.

If Argument A—Krugman's argument—and Argument B—which is advocated here—are both compelling in their internal logic, which conclusion (if either) is right depends on which premise (if either) is right. If the US has a moral duty to provide a social safety net for everyone located within its borders, Argument A is true, and immigration must be restricted. If Americans have a moral duty to accommodate immigrants, Argument B is true, and a social safety net for all residents, though not necessarily for all citizens, must be abandoned.

And here I face a difficulty. I think that the premise of Argument A is, in fact, widely accepted; yet I am completely unable to understand why anyone

---

[50] http://krugman.blogs.nytimes.com/2010/04/26/the-curious-politics-of-immigration/

would accept it. That is not to say that I find the moral case for a social safety net per se incomprehensible.

Two strong arguments for a social safety net are (call it "Premise C") that the marginal utility of a dollar's worth of income or in-kind assistance for the very poor is much greater than the marginal utility of a dollar for the middle and upper classes, so compulsory transfers to the very poor are justified because they raise overall social welfare; and (call it "Premise D") that the satisfaction of certain basic needs like health care, food, and shelter is a good of a higher order than the property rights, so the state acts rightly in violating property rights to ensure that basic needs are always satisfied.

I do not agree with either of these arguments, but I understand them. Neither of them, however, is of the slightest use in making the case for a welfare state *whose scope is limited to those who are physically present in the United States* when the needs of people who live abroad are far more intense and urgent, and when restricting immigration does tremendous harm to the foreign-born by cutting them off from the opportunity to improve their lot through migration.

Let us suppose that we reject the premises of both Argument A and Argument B; that we accept an argument for the welfare state from Premise C or Premise D; but that no agency is capable of administering a global welfare state. That would lead us to something like Argument E:

Argument E

1. Because the marginal utility of a dollar is greater for the poor than for the rich; OR Because people have a right for their basic needs to be satisfied; the government should adopt policies that raise the welfare of the poorest people.

2. Because the government's resources are limited, the following two policies are incompatible: (a) open borders, and (b) a domestic social safety net which provide health care and a "decent" income (defined as well above the world average) to everyone located on the territory the government controls.

3. A domestic social safety net without open borders will, at best, transfer money to the poorest native and naturalized citizens. Since even the poorest native and naturalized citizens are relatively well-off in global terms, this does not raise the welfare of the poorest people.

4. Open borders will allow a set of people generally much poorer than any American to enter the country and, even if no public assistance is pro-

vided, they can enjoy large gains in income through participation in private labor markets.

5. Therefore, an open borders policy should be adopted in preference to a comprehensive domestic social safety net.

In short, the strongest arguments that could be used in support of a social safety net, if we ignore the existence of the rest of the world, become arguments for open borders, or for some form of the DRITI policy, as soon as we take the rest of the world into account. So what an argument like Paul Krugman's really has to assume is that America's moral obligation to "assure health care and a decent income" for a person is completely non-existent when that person is located outside America's borders, then magically appears when a person crosses the Rio Grande.

The only guess I can offer as to why anyone would hold this belief is that people want to avoid, not actual guilt, but *feelings* of guilt that result when one has to see poverty close up. Migration controls serve as a *blindfold*, enabling Americans to ignore most of the poverty, deprivation and vulnerability that exist in the world by keeping it physically at a distance. In the past, people lived without this blindfold. The wealthy lived amidst poverty, sometimes engaging in generous charity to the poor, sometimes learning, perhaps callously, to ignore them.

Citizens of a modern welfare state, by contrast, feel that the state should coerce people to give to the poor so as to remove from the streets the kind of visible poverty that would make them feel obliged to give, allowing them to feel conscientious and affluent at once. The price of this moral complacency is paid by would-be immigrants who are not allowed to come to America to better their condition by honest labor, lest their poverty trouble the consciences of affluent Americans.

The trilemma: apartheid, growing illegality, or open borders

The apartheid regime in South Africa mimicked the global state system, and the resemblances between the two are real and instructive. South Africa recognized the "autonomy" or "sovereignty" of a number of "tribal homelands" within the internationally recognized borders of South Africa. The country's black people could stay in their "tribal homelands," but in the rest of the country they had to carry "pass books" as a means of regulating their movements, rather as international travelers have to carry passports.

Migration control limited opportunities for the black population and exacerbated economic inequality. Interestingly, one South African leader, Jan Christian Smuts, played a key role in designing both South Africa's apartheid regime and the United Nations structure that formalized on a worldwide scale the Westphalian sovereignty which the United States exercises when it restricts migration. It would be tendentious and an exaggeration to call the global state system, with its migration controls, *world apartheid*, but the characterization would have more than a kernel of truth in it.

There are also, of course, some important differences between apartheid and migration control in a country like the U.S. First, the scale of human rights abuses in apartheid South Africa was worse. In the U.S., an estimated 1 million families were separated by deportations between 1997 and 2007;[51] but this is still less atrocious than the South African apartheid regime, which tortured people to death.[52]

Second, apartheid was explicitly *racist*, while U.S. immigration policy is not; but this is less of a difference than it seems. Racism is a terrible injustice, but the *reason* it is unjust is that it judges a person and determines their station in life on the basis of a factor outside their control: race. But since place of birth is equally outside a person's control, it is not clear why racial discrimination is worse than discrimination on the basis of place of birth.

The fact that race is *externally visible* makes racism especially oppressive. When a person is discriminated against on the basis of traits not externally visible, they may sometimes be treated as an equal by virtue of their anonymity. But the push for national IDs and requirements to show papers, pointing towards an internal passport regime, tend to make a person's identity more easily ascertainable and thus, if it succeeds, will narrow the gap between U.S. discrimination on the basis of national origin and the explicit racism of South African apartheid.

Third, birthright citizenship as required by the 14th Amendment of the U.S. constitution marks a clear difference between the U.S. immigration regime and that of apartheid South Africa, where blacks could never become citizens with equal rights.

But if the U.S. government continues to yield to pressure to "secure the borders," these differences will be eroded. Assuming that America does not physically prevent illegal immigration (probably impossible to do, as argued above),

---

[51] http://www.hrw.org/en/news/2009/04/15/us-deportation-splits-families
[52] http://findarticles.com/p/articles/mi_m1309/is_v21/ai_3073322/

there will be a continuing influx of immigrants, accelerating as the economy recovers, and the question is how to deal with them.

Already there are millions of people in the United States who were brought by their parents as children. They are citizens of other countries but may not remember or speak the languages of those countries; the U.S. is the only home they have ever known; yet they lack the ordinary legal rights of Americans, even the right to work. Millions more are U.S. citizens thanks to the 14th Amendment, but their parents are illegal immigrants. This creates a difficult problem since the parents are subject to deportation but the children cannot be.

A decisive step towards the establishment of an apartheid regime in America would be the repeal of the 14th Amendment to the U.S. constitution, which grants birthright citizenship to everyone born in the U.S.. That would create a permanent underclass of American-born persons without legal rights. Such measures might curtail immigration by making it unappealing for foreigners, but at the price of deeply degrading the free and democratic character of the American republic.

So one course America can take is apartheid. A second is growing illegality. By this option, America would relax enforcement and/or pass some kind of amnesty. Amnesty would create expectations of future amnesties and accelerate immigration. A large share of the population at any given time would lack legal status, complicating social policy and law enforcement. "Crime"—not real crime but illegal immigration—would often "pay"—many illegal immigrants would end up better off than if they had obeyed the law—making suckers of the law-abiding and undermining the *ethos* of the rule of law.

The only answer to the immigration question which is consistent with freedom and the rule of law is some kind of open borders policy, such as DRITI.

10

Christianity and Freedom

"Ye shall know the truth, and the truth shall set you free."
—Jesus Christ in John 8:32.

"He breaks the spirit of rulers, He is feared by the kings of the earth."
—Psalms 76:12

Religious arguments have this disadvantage: that part of one's audience will not be convinced, because they do not accept the religious premises. For that reason, I have postponed all religious arguments until this chapter. But there are several reasons that the theme of Christianity and freedom must be addressed.

First, there is a strong correlation between Christianity and freedom. Correlation is not causation, and there is "multicollinearity" here; that is, lots of good things tend to go together, making it hard to tell which causes which. The (historically) Christian nations of Western Europe and North America are rich *and* free. Are they free because they are Christian, or free because they are rich, or for some other reason? If we want to control for wealth, Christian Latin America is (mostly) free and democratic, while the Muslim Middle East, with similar average incomes, is not. But is that because Christianity is good for freedom or because Islam is *bad* for it? Professor Charles Rowley and I have showed statistically that there is a deficit of freedom and democracy in Islamic countries (Rowley and Smith, 2009), but the sample sizes are too small to compare Christianity with other religions besides Islam. Still, the correlation between Christianity and freedom and cannot easily be explained away by other factors.

Second, although Christian countries' advantage in democracy is of recent origin—democracy with universal manhood suffrage did not exist anywhere before the 19th century—and might prove transient if democracy spreads, the Christian advantage in *freedom* is much older. Slavery was a universal human institution before the birth of Christianity, and in most places was only recently banned—in 1906 in China, in 1962 in Saudi Arabia.[53] The ancient Greeks and

---

[53] http://en.wikipedia.org/wiki/Abolition_of_slavery_timeline

Romans and Jews had slaves; there was slavery in China, Japan, Korea, Thailand, and Burma, among the Germanic and Celtic peoples of northern Europe and in sub-Saharan Africa. Islam used and traded slaves on an enormous scale.

By contrast, slavery "had essentially disappeared from Europe by the tenth century… because the church extended its sacraments to all slaves and then managed to impose a ban on the enslavement of Christians (and of Jews)" (Stark, 2005, p. 28), and was never reintroduced there on a large scale, though it was later practiced by Europeans when they settled overseas. Also, while despotic government remained the rule in Islamic civilization, in China, and most other parts of the world, the medieval Christian west had developed feudalism, a notionally consensual political order that limited the power of kings. There is nothing recent or transient about the correlation between Christianity and freedom.

Third, in modern times, the movements most hostile to freedom have also been hostile to Christianity as well. The Jacobinism of the French revolution, which rejected Christianity, was radically repressive and terrorist. Communism, a fierce enemy of Christianity, totally crushed free expression and murdered millions in the Soviet Union, China, and Southeast Asia. Nazism and Islamism are also anti-Christian. Christianity is the enemy of freedom's enemies.

Fourth, Christianity provides a firmer basis for believing in natural rights and freedom of conscience than secular reason can offer. We *do* know that theft and violence are wrong from the evidence of conscience, an innate faculty whose evidence a rationalist can accept without submitting to any broader cosmogony; and we can see by reason that people cannot morally commit to do what is wrong or leave undone what is right; and therefore that the validity of a social contract depends on its respecting freedom of conscience.

I think the signers of the Declaration of Independence were right when they wrote that "we hold these truths to be self-evident: that all men are created equal and endowed by their Creator with certain inalienable rights." We can *just see* these things. The trouble is that these meek intuitions are so easily dispelled by the sophisms of Hobbes or of the utilitarians, choked by aristocratic scorn and Nietzschean scoffing, or smothered by brutal customs.

Christianity, by asserting the infinite worth of each individual person, gives natural rights a new basis, and enables Christians to assert them with a special self-confidence. As for freedom of conscience, Christianity properly understood requires it, for to baptize a resisting unbeliever is sacrilege, and only a willing soul can accept salvation.[54]

But—fifth—that is not to say that the New Testament contains anything like a blueprint for Lockean free society in the sense developed in this book. On the contrary! Locke's argument for a free society based on property and social contract drew more on the Old Testament than the New Testament for its arguments, suggesting that Judaism might be an even better religious foundation for political freedom than Christianity, a suggestion which, however, is not borne out by history.[55]

How exactly the Church and the Gospels could have given rise to modern free institutions is a mystery to be elucidated. The society implied by the Gospel ethics is indeed a free society, but in quite a different, a stronger and stranger, sense than Locke's. Indeed, as I shall show, there is a strong *prima facie* contradiction between Christian civilization, even in its better moments, and what might be described as the *holy anarchy* to which key passages in the Gospels, such as the Sermon on the Mount, point. The very phenomenon of Christian civilization is profoundly *ironic*.

Sixth, this Gospel ethics turns out to be refreshingly clean and consistent compared to the dubious expedients that I and others have typically had to resort to in order to make social contract theory work, even if from a worldly perspective it is a crazy consistency, and even if Christians are far from consistent in living by it. There is no "ends justify the means" in the Gospels, no compromises, no fictions. The perfection of the Gospel ethics, compared with the imperfection of liberal ideology, suggests the intriguing possibility that the latter may be a kind of dilution of the former; which is not to deny that it may be the best that (most of) sinful mankind can achieve for the time being. "The perfect is the enemy of the good," the saying goes; but the perfect may also help us to understand the good. It seems that mankind can only achieve lasting progress towards justice by aiming above it and falling short.

---

[54]There have, alas, been many Christians who have argued that, even if souls cannot be saved by force, the forcible suppression of heresy might create conditions more favorable to souls saving themselves. Aside from being morally erroneous, history has shown again and again how *inexpedient* this plan is. Augustine of Hippo suppressed the Donatists by force and immediately North Africa was invaded by the Arian Vandals and subject to the rule of heretics for 90 years; it is Muslim today. The Spanish Inquisition was no sooner instituted than the Protestant Reformation erupted.

[55]This is not to deny that Judaism is compatible with political freedom, but only to point out that political freedom emerged in Christian, not Jewish, nations.

Seventh, the main result of the ministry of Jesus in historical terms was to give rise to a new institution, *the Christian church*, at first small, but soon encompassing nations and outlasting empires; and it is this institution that finally provided a sufficient answer to our recurring question, *Who guards the guards?* I am referring to historical facts here. The Roman emperors, after centuries of despotism, sometimes desperately wicked, and sometimes benign, but always unchecked, finally encountered, in the Christian church, an institution which they could not destroy, and could not enslave, and to whom they at last let themselves be held morally accountable.

And *even to this day* the Christian church (as an institution and as a community) remains the ultimate guardian of the guards in free societies, the refuge in times of tyranny, the reformer—though often a sadly tardy one—overturning bad old customs to advance the frontiers of freedom, and sometimes—this is also an important service to liberty—the ally of an imperfect order against threats of revolutionary chaos and carnage. That is why freedom has, for more than a thousand years, gone from strength to strength, especially in those places, and at those times, where/when Christianity is strongest.

Eighth, Christianity is the main reason to have hope for freedom's future, for in spite of incessant diagnoses and forecasts of its decline, it is as strong as ever and getting stronger.

Ninth, to present the specifically *Christian* case for the free society may help to persuade Christian readers. This means two different things. First, I might persuade a Christian reader who finds the thesis of this book appealing, but who is afraid that it contradicts his religion, that the free society advocated here is *not against* Christianity. Second, a Christian reader who is inclined to resist the thesis of the book may be persuaded that his religion actually *compels* him to accept it, wholly or in part.

I write as a Christian, believing in the Father, the Son, and the Holy Spirit, in the virgin birth and divinity of Christ, the communion of saints, the resurrection of the dead, the changing of water into wine at Cana in Galilee, and the rest of the teachings of orthodox Christianity. The pious convention of capitalizing pronouns that refer to God or Jesus Christ will be observed throughout this chapter as a reminder of this.

I assume that my own Christian commitment will influence how readers receive what I write, making Christians more likely and non-Christians less likely to accept it as an unbiased argument, and rightly so. However, what I write should be of interest to non-Christian readers, for inasmuch as it sheds light on Christianity-in-history, its importance does not depend specifically on accepting the miracles, teachings, or divinity of Jesus of Nazareth.

A higher law

Christianity offered the world an ethics which was new and not new: it accepted what came before, but carried it further. This is most clearly seen in the Sermon on the Mount, where Jesus declares that the Law and the Prophets—the great religious and ethical traditions of the Jews, well known to His hearers—will not pass away, but will be "fulfilled" (Matthew 5:18), and much of the sermon that follows consists of examples of how His disciples might "exceed the righteousness of the Pharisees" (Matthew 5:20), the Jewish sect of His own time which regarded itself as a moral elite. The old and new teachings are contrasted in Table 3:

Table 3: The fulfillment of the law

You have heard that it was said…	But I say to you…
"You shall not murder." (Matthew 5:21)	… whoever is angry with his brother without a cause shall be in danger of the judgement… And whoever says "You fool!" shall be in danger of hellfire. (Matthew 5:22)
"You shall not commit adultery." (Matthew 5:27)	… whoever looks at a woman to lust for her has already committed adultery with her in his heart. (Matthew 5:28)
"You shall not swear falsely, but perform your oaths to the Lord." (Matthew 5:33)	… do not swear at all… but let your "Yes" be "Yes" and your "No" be "No." For whatever is more than these is from the evil one. (Matthew 5:34-37)
"An eye for an eye and a tooth for a tooth." (Matthew 5:38)	… do not resist an evil person. But whoever slaps you on your right cheek, turn the other to him also. (Matthew 5:39)
"You shall love your neighbor and hate your enemy." (Matthew 5:43)	… love your enemies, bless those who curse you, do good to those who hate you, and pray for those who spitefully use you and persecute you. (Matthew 5:44)

In each of these cases, Jesus cites a teaching from the Old Testament, then contrasts it with a new teaching that extends it. When Jesus counsels against (not only murder but) anger (Matthew 5:12-22) and (not only adultery but) lust (Matthew 5:27-28), He points towards an ethics, at once more sublime and more difficult, not only of right action, but of right thought and feeling as well.

We can see why this is desirable—who would want to live in a world in which people acted morally only out of fearful obedience to a religious law while they hated each other and longed for the sins from which they refrained?—but since we can control by our will only our actions, not our thoughts and emotions, Christians have had to insist ever since that no one can by his own efforts be perfect. I can resist the urge to kill or fornicate, but *God's grace* is necessary to change my heart, and remove from it lust and anger. Here Jesus's teachings force us to revise our ideas of individual moral responsibility.

Some of Jesus's new teachings are subversive of the institutions of social order to which we are accustomed. In Jesus's teaching "do not swear at all," the old law is "fulfilled" by being superseded by a new command, not inconsistent with it, that extends it. We might even argue that the new command was implicit in the old one all along. The old law forbids *false* oaths; the new forbids *all* oaths; but then, since we can never be sure what we will be able to perform, not to swear at all may be in any case the only way to be sure of not swearing falsely.

But oaths, promises, vows and contracts underpin the economic and political order of civilized societies. For Hobbes, justice ultimately consists in *nothing but* the faithful performance of oaths, and any social contract theory of government depends on people making and keeping promises. Capitalism, too, depends on contracts to support long-term projects and involving collaboration and uncertainty.

Jesus's teaching on violence and coercion is even more subversive:

> You have heard that it was said, "An eye for an eye and a tooth for a tooth." But I tell you not to resist an evil person. But whoever slaps you on your right cheek, turn the other cheek to him also. If anyone wants to sue you and take away your tunic, let him have your cloak also. And whoever compels you to go one mile, go with him two. Give to him who asks you, and from him who wants to borrow from you do not turn away. (Matthew 5:38-42)

To see how this new teaching of non-resistance fulfills the old law of proportional retribution, one must recall that the principle of retribution is meant to *limit*, not to demand, revenge. One might want to kill a man who had gouged out one's eye, but the law says *no*, the most one can do is "an eye for an eye."

The law does not forbid revenge that is *less* than proportional to the injury, nor does it prohibit sheer forgiveness. But so fallible are we, and so prone to judge in our own favor, to exaggerate injuries done to us and forget those we have done to others, that the only way to be sure of avoiding excessive revenge is to give up all revenge, and we can only be sure of avoiding unjust violence if we abjure violence altogether. But to abjure violence is to abjure the state, which by definition is an agency of violence and coercion.

Aware of these problems, some Roman Catholics have sometimes argued that the Sermon on the Mount is not directed to Christians in general but only to certain disciples who were called to a special ministry. The physical setting of the Sermon—"seeing the multitudes, He went up on a mountain, and when He was seated His disciples came to Him" (Matthew 5:1)—weakly suggests that this message was for His disciples only.

On the other hand, what has been called the Sermon on the Plain, in the Gospel of Luke (Luke 6:20-49), and which contains many of the same teachings including "turn the other cheek" and "love your enemies" and "judge not that ye be not judged," seems to be aimed at Jesus's disciples but to take place in the midst of the multitude: "And the whole multitude sought to touch Him, for power went out from Him and healed them all. Then He lifted up His eyes towards His disciples, and said: 'Blessed are you poor, for yours is the kingdom of God...'" (Luke 6:19-20).

Moreover, the logic of the Sermon does not support this Roman Catholic interpretation. Jesus warns that "unless your righteousness exceeds the righteousness of the scribes and Pharisees, you will by no means enter the kingdom of heaven" (Matthew 5:20), then goes on to describe how they can do so, by following a new teaching which fulfills the old law. It seems, then, that if we may all hope to enter the kingdom of heaven, we all ought to live by the Sermon on the Mount.

That Jesus follows His call to nonviolence and non-self-defense with calls for His disciples to give up the use of the legal system to seek redress of wrongs (Matthew 5:40), and to forsake the claims of property on demand (Matthew 5:42), is an instance of the rich consistency of Jesus's teaching. To use the courts is to try to get someone else (the courts, and the police) to use coercion on one's behalf. To assert property rights is to rely implicitly on the state's commitment to enforce property rights through coercion.

If we are to truly relinquish violence even in self-defense, rather than merely outsource it to others, we must give up law courts and property rights as well. And Jesus's next teaching, "love your enemies," extends "turn the other cheek" from the realm of action to that of desires and emotion. One must not only not avenge, or resist, injuries; one must love those who commit them.

Jesus's exhortation to secret charity—"when you do a charitable deed, do not let your left hand know what your right hand is doing" (Matthew 6:3)—is another instance of Jesus's concern with *motive* as well as action, though in this case (unlike in the cases of anger and lust) the teaching can in principle be obeyed by an act of will.

Jesus is also concerned with *humility*. In the praises that public charity will evoke, He sees danger. Jesus's exhortation to secret prayer has the same motivation—to safeguard the believer's pure motives and avoid temptations to pride—but as a side-effect, the practice helps Christianity to endure times of persecution and survive under hostile regimes, for Christians who are already in the habit of praying privately are less easy to detect and persecute.

In the Lord's Prayer, the words "Thy will be done on earth as it is in heaven" (Matthew 6:10) point to the existence, not only in the future but somehow in the present, of *heaven*, a world where God's will is done perfectly. It is in this other world that Jesus urges people to seek their rewards, and not on earth:

> Do not lay up for yourselves treasures on earth, where moth and rust destroy and where thieves break in and steal; but lay up for yourselves treasures in heaven, where neither moth nor rust destroys and where thieves do not break in and steal. (Matthew 5:19-20)

Economists define money as (among other things) a "store of value." Jesus insists that it is not an effective one, and that the divine economy—the phrase is justified by the mention of "treasures" in heaven, as well as by many of Jesus's parables—offers one infinitely better. Reputation, too, is a store of value, and Jesus tells His disciples not to invest in it by engaging in prayers and almsgiving in public for the sake of human praise. This comes through still more strongly in the Gospel of Luke, where Jesus warns "Woe to you when all men speak well of you" (Luke 6:26). Jesus's warning against saving, piling up wealth, and becoming rich, is reinforced by one of the most startling teaching in the Gospels:

> No one can serve two masters; for either he will hate the one and love the other, or else he will be loyal to the one and despise the other. You cannot serve God and money. Therefore I say to you, do not worry about your life, what you will eat or what you will drink; nor about your body, what you will put on. Is not life more than food and the body more than clothing? Look at the birds of the air, for they neither sow nor reap nor gather into barns; yet your heavenly Father feeds them. Are you not of more value than they? Which of you by worrying can add one cubit to his stature? So why do you worry about clothing? Consider the lilies of the field, how they grow: they neither toil nor spin; and yet

that even Solomon in all his glory was not arrayed like one of these. Now if God so clothes the grass of the field, which today is, and tomorrow is thrown into the oven, will He not much more clothe you, O you of little faith? Therefore do not worry, saying, 'What shall we eat?' or 'What shall we drink?' or 'What shall we wear?' For after all these things the Gentiles seek. For your heavenly Father knows that you need all these things. But seek first the kingdom of God and His righteousness, and all these things will be added unto you. Therefore do not worry about tomorrow, for tomorrow will worry about its own things. Sufficient for the day is its own trouble. (Matthew 6:24-34)

Forethought distinguishes man from beast and civilized man from primitive man. A hunter-gatherer may think only for the following day; the farmer must think ahead to the harvest; the industrial capitalist surveys and plans for the years and decades in which he will enjoy the returns on his factory or railroad. Parents constantly urge children to think about their future, to secure their career or their health by studying or by eating well and exercising, to ignore the instant gratification of candy or video games or being cool, or later, of sex and alcohol and drugs.

To urge people to "think not for the morrow" seems perversely to oppose all this, to reduce civilized man to the state of the savage, or even to that of the beast, as Jesus Himself suggests with His references to the birds and the lilies of the field.

Against this, Jesus has already urged His disciples to "lay up treasures in heaven." For those who believed in immortality, as did Jesus, and the Pharisees too, and as Jesus was teaching His disciples to do, to place value on any merely earthly rewards when they are weighed against heavenly ones is to lack forethought and a sense of proportion. And Jesus does not reduce men to the level of the birds or lilies of the field, for He asks rhetorically, "Are you not of more value than they?"

Earlier in the Sermon, Jesus has compared men to "the salt of the earth," that is, to the element in food which, even in small doses, brings out the flavor of everything, and which in his day was scarce enough to fetch a high price. But the value of men over and above that of beasts consists not in their capacity for self-seeking forethought, but in their ability consciously to love and serve God. Still, it is very hard for us of little faith to suppress the sense that Jesus's teaching to "think not for the morrow" is somewhat reckless.

The Sermon on the Mount is consistent without being repetitive. Its verses allude to one another in intricate and startling ways, and enrich one another's meaning. The advice not to think for the morrow echoes, explains, and elaborates the advice not to lay up treasures on earth; but it is also consistent with, and reinforces, the teaching against oaths, for oaths are directed to the future and require us to think for the morrow. Similarly, the advice to "love your enemies," and the mention in the Lord's prayer of forgiveness—"forgive us our debts, as we forgive our debtors" (Matthew 6:12)—followed by Jesus's comment that "if you forgive men their trespasses, your heavenly Father will also forgive you, but if you do not forgive men their trespasses, neither will your Father forgive your trespasses" (Matthew 6:14-15) are expanded upon by the command to "judge not that ye be not judged" (Matthew 7:1), followed by the beautiful and amusing (almost like a cartoon) metaphor of one who tries to remove a speck from his brother's eye when he has a wooden beam in his own.

But there is another echo here, too: "judge not" echoes "if someone sue thee at the law…" It is too literal to read Matthew 7:1 as a condemnation of courts and judges, yet to reason that disciples of Christ who ought not to judge others privately ought not to judge professionally, either, or that disciples of Christ who ought not to defend themselves in lawsuits ought not to make a career of participating in lawsuits is an application of the Sermon on the Mount difficult to escape. There is no reason to single out lawyers, though. Most worldly professions are at odds with "think not for the morrow" or "give to the one who asks you."

Jesus alternates between and weaves together the themes of trust in God and of an ethics so gentle and generous as to transcend all prudence, which only a person with great trust in God would dare to live by. Thus, it is as the conclusion of a series of verses encouraging people to trust in God that Jesus states one of the most famous Gospel teachings, the Golden Rule.

> Ask, and it will be given to you; seek, and you will find; knock, and it will be opened to you. For everyone who asks receives, and he who seeks finds, and to him who knocks it will be opened. Or what man is there among you who, if his sons asks for bread, will give him a stone? Or if he asks for a fish, will he give him a serpent? If you, then, being evil, know how to give good gifts to your children, how much more will your Father who is in heaven give good things to those who ask Him! Therefore, whatever you want men to do to you, do also to them, for this is the Law and the Prophets. (Matthew 7:7-11)

It seems like a non-sequitur that the word "therefore" connects the Golden Rule to "Ask, and it will be given you," as if it were a consequence. What it may suggest is that humans' following the Golden Rule is an imitation of divine providence. In this it echoes Jesus's comment on "love your enemies': "[do so] that you may be sons of your Father in heaven; for He makes His sun rise on the evil and on the good, and sends rain on the just and on the unjust" (Matthew 5:45). The Golden Rule is offered as a summary of the Law and the Prophets, and seemingly, of His own teaching as well.

Elsewhere Jesus teaches "Love thy neighbor as thyself" (Mark 12:31), which is a quote from Leviticus 19:18, and which extends to the sphere of feeling what the Golden Rule commands in the sphere of action. The Golden Rule has more explicit generality than the other teachings in the Sermon on the Mount, as it turns every desire vis-à-vis others—"*whatever* you want men to do to you"—into a command—"do also unto them"—whereas other verses, e.g., "turn the other cheek," deal with particular situations.

Yet the Golden Rule has—however its status as a *cliché* makes us forget it—the same wildly idealistic and impractical character as the rest of the Sermon. It implies yielding in every quarrel (for one always wishes the other person would), giving away one's property (if one is at all inclined to covetousness), forgiving injuries (one wants one's own forgiven), secret almsgiving (most recipients of charity would rather not be known as the dependent of a particular benefactor), and certainly nonviolence, for none of us wants to suffer violence.

A Gospel society

It is appropriate to ask of any system of ethics: what would the world be like if all lived by it? Clearly the universal practice of the ethics of the Gospels would *not* result in a Lockean free society in which the functions of defense of the rights of person and property, and retribution of wrongs, are delegated to a government. What makes the teachings of the Sermon on the Mount so difficult, as Jesus Himself admits—"narrow is the gate and difficult is the way which leads to life, there are few who find it" (Matthew 7:14)—is Jesus's insistence that His disciples must utterly relinquish the ordinary prerogatives of self-defense and the pursuit of economic security.

But to do so would be no hardship in a Gospel society, because people would be peaceful and would practice a form of decentralized, voluntary social insurance. A person has little reason to fear hunger, thirst, or nakedness, if he can ask for whatever he needs from any of his fellow men, and rely on them to "give to the one who asks you." Likewise, a person need not fear aggression when, by forbidding even revenge and self-defense, the Gospels have taken away all pretexts for violence. When Jesus teaches, elsewhere, "I did not come to bring peace but a sword" (Matthew 10:34), He is referring to the violence that Christians will *suffer*, not inflict.

There would be no government in a Gospel society, no agency claiming a monopoly of legitimate violence, but there would be plenty of leadership, subordination, *governance*, order, and obedience. Leadership can be asserted peacefully and accepted voluntarily, and most interesting human endeavors require it. Buildings need architects, choirs and plays and movies need directors, projects need managers.

Would there be *property rights* in a Gospel society? Jesus's command to "give to the one who asks you" seems to imply property rights, for to give is to transfer property rights, though on the other hand, giving can sometimes be a physical act unrelated to legal claims ("pass the salt"). It is noteworthy that the early Christians tried to live without property, holding everything in common (Acts 4:34-37).

While this suggests that Jesus's most immediate disciples thought a form of voluntary socialism was the best way to realize His teachings, they did not insist on the point, for the New Testament never imposes a socialist economic order on Christians in general. The experiment seems neither to have succeeded nor to have been much regretted, though a form of Christian socialism was later revived in the monasteries, where it was much more successful. To own property, while giving generously, seems to have been accepted as consistent with the Gospels as well.

Would a society that lived by the Gospels be a *wealthy society*? There are reasons to think it would be rather austere. First, socialism is typically inefficient. A person committed to "give to the one who asks you" might feel little motivation to labor, save, and innovate to acquire property which he would only have to give away to all comers. Worse, the exhortation to "think not for the morrow" would seem to forbid capital investment, which is directed to the future, and which is essential to the creation of wealth. That Jesus urges His disciples not to "lay up treasures on earth" further suggests a society virtuously and gladly poor.

Against this, however, is Jesus's comment that though the lilies of the field neither toil nor spin, "even Solomon in all his glory was not arrayed like one of these." Would the adherents of the Gospels, too, be gloriously arrayed in rich raiment—as Christian clergy, in their gorgeous vestments, have often been? And if so, will they enjoy the same luxury in eating and drinking? Not all the time, certainly, for Jesus also advocates fasting (Matthew 6:16-17)—but sometimes, or even often?

Actually, one can make a strong economic case that a Gospel society would be a rich society. People who are devoted to serving their neighbors have good reason to labor, save, and innovate even if they will not keep the results of their labors. The economist F.A. Hayek has emphasized that competition is a "discovery process"—we learn by trying to beat the competition—but charity, too, can be a discovery process—we learn about other people's needs, and our own abilities, when we try to serve them.

Also, the economics of institutions emphasizes that a great deal of inefficiency in society results from "agency problems"—the deviation of the individual from the social interest—and/or "transactions costs"—costly efforts dedicated to aligning individual and social interests. By avoiding agency problems and transactions costs through an ethic of service, the Gospel society might be more productive than a society of self-seeking capitalists.

Jesus is against wealth inasmuch as it is *rival*. Hence he deplores the love of money, for money sets a price on what is *scarce*, so that my having more or better means your having less or worse. When the rich man is tormented in the flames of hell (Luke 16:19-31), it seems clear that he is suffering not so much for his wealth *per se* as for the fact that Lazarus was sitting at his doorstep in abject misery for years and the rich man did nothing to help. Had the rich man provided for Lazarus as generously as for himself, one supposes the rich man would not have been so punished even if his living standard had remained high.

Likewise, it was because the rich young man was unwilling to sell his possessions and give to the poor in order to become His disciple that Jesus spoke the sad words, "It is easier for a camel to pass through the eye of a needle than for a rich man to enter into the kingdom of Heaven" (Matthew 19:24).

Jesus is also against wealth inasmuch as it promotes *complacency*, inasmuch as trust in Mammon displaces trust in God, as another parable about a rich man illustrates:

And [Jesus] said to them, "Take heed and beware of covetousness, for one's life does not consist in the abundance of the things he possesses." Then He spoke a parable to them, saying: "The ground of a certain rich man yielded plentifully. And he thought within himself, saying, 'What shall I do, since I have no room to store my crops?' So he said, 'I will do this: I will pull down my barns and build greater, and there I will store all my crops and my goods. And I will say to my soul, "Soul, you have many goods laid up for many years; take your ease; eat, drink, and be merry".' But God said to him, 'Fool! This night your soul will be required of you; then whose will those things be which you have provided?' So is he who lays up treasure for himself and is not rich towards God." (Luke 12:15-21)

No doubt this rich man would have done better to have distributed his harvest among the poor than to have made plans to support a comfortable retirement with it. But the poor are not mentioned. Rather, it is the rich man's complacency that is condemned. The opposite of this rich man is the disciple of Jesus who thinks not for the morrow and does not worry about what he will eat, drink, or wear, trusting in God to provide for him as for the birds of the air and the lilies of the field.

But Jesus is not against *enjoyment*. As His first miracle, according to the Gospel of John, He changed water into wine at a poor wedding feast in Galilee (John 2:1-10). What is interesting here is not only that He approves of and assists the innocent merrymaking of humble people, but that this miraculous beverage seems to have been to wine what Solomon in all his glory was to raiment, for the master of the feast, unaware of the miracle, reproaches the host, saying: "Every man at the beginning sets out the good wine, and when the guests have well drunk, then the inferior. You have kept the good wine until now!" (In an echo of this miracle, champagne was invented by the Benedictine monk Dom Perignon.)

Though Jesus once fasted for forty days in the wilderness, during His ministry He was the frequent recipient of dinner invitations, in the homes of tax collectors, Pharisees, and pious commoners, to the extent that He was reproached for being "a glutton and a winebibber" (Matthew 7:34), and His ministry was supported financially by certain affluent ladies (Luke 8:1-3). He tells His disciples, too, to accept hospitality: "eat and drink such things as they set before you" (Luke 10:7). And His parables are full of wedding feasts.

The Church calendar reflects Jesus's approval of celebration with an abundance of feast days and celebrations, many more, indeed, than the typical Christian is aware of or has the time or inclination to observe, and the major Christian feasts move even the secular world today to celebrate as, perhaps, it would otherwise not know how to do. A *holy day* for God becomes a *holiday* for men, as G.K. Chesterton said, and we would hardly know what the word *merry* means, were it not companion to the word *Christmas*.

That Jesus was also in favor of *enterprise* is suggested by the frequent favorable use of commercial metaphors in his parables. In the parable of the talents (Matthew 25:14-30), a nobleman who is going on a journey distributes his wealth among his servants and instructs them to do business till he returns. A servant who receives five talents (*talent* is an ancient monetary unit of high value), and another who receives two talents, each double their money, and are rewarded. A third servant who receives one talent buries it in the earth and is punished. In another parable, Jesus teaches:

> The kingdom of heaven is like a merchant seeking beautiful pearls, who, when he had found one pearl of great price, went and sold all that he had and bought it. (Matthew 13:45-46)

Certainly, Christians would misread these parables if they responded by maximizing the return on their investments and then going jewelry shopping. The parables are metaphors for the spiritual life. Yet Jesus seems to have applauded the prudence, energy, alertness, and imagination of the entrepreneurs in His parables, and also, *service*, to their master in the servants who were given the talents, to the love of beauty in the case of the pearl buyer.

There is in all honest entrepreneurship an element of the Golden Rule. Henry Ford made a car that was affordable for the common man because, were he a common man, he would want to be able to afford a car. Sam Walton transformed retail to help people on a budget. An entrepreneur who puts profit before serving the customer, who is willing to earn more than the value he provides, relying on slick advertising and fine print to grow his market and grab revenues, cheats his customers in spirit if not in law.

Most entrepreneurs do not become rich; those who do are exposed to temptations; but they can always sell all they have and give to the poor. Even if they did, their charity might benefit mankind less than their entrepreneurship had done. The enterprises of a Gospel society might be like nonprofits in their public-spiritedness; yet like today's private corporations in their ingenuity and energy.

The great Christian cathedrals may serve as a symbol of what a Gospel society would be like, for the revealed preference of the modern tourist confesses that these palaces of the Immortal King surpass all the palaces of mortal kings; yet they were financed neither by taxes nor by profits but by donations; and their doors were open to the poor.[56]

Finally, would a society that lived by the Gospels be a *free* society? Well, yes.

But we have been assuming a society in which *everyone* lives by the ethics of the Gospels. The trouble with a Gospel society is that it would be

---

[56] This will do for a symbol, though sometimes pilgrims were charged an entrance fee.

absurdly *vulnerable*. One bad man could lay it waste, because it would not resist him. He could not destroy it, perhaps, but he could plunder it and enslave it. And to avoid tempting others to plunder them, some of the most serious Christians have (according to the hagiographical literature) pursued the most radical extremes of poverty and deprivation, living in deserts and caves with fantastically abstemious diets, for as St. Francis said, "if we had possessions, we should need weapons and laws to defend them."

The irony of Christianity

Our study of the ethics of the Gospels and their implications for society raises two questions:

1. Why don't Christians behave the way the Sermon on the Mount seems to tell them to?

2. Why don't Christian societies look like the Gospel society we have envisioned?

Of course these are really one question—if Christians lived by the Gospels, Christian societies would look like the Gospel society—and it is a difficult one. One reason is *sin*, but that is not a full explanation because the set of actions Christians regard as sins and repent of is not the same as the set of actions by which they deviate from the Gospel teachings.

Most Christians lead lives outwardly similar to worldly people, and what they typically repent of is harsh words, white lies, inattention at prayers and the like, not usually their whole worldly lifestyles. The other part of the answer is that *Jesus's teachings are a unity*, each of them shedding light on and reinforcing the others, and taken out of context they may only do harm.

If an angry, lustful man tries to "think not for the morrow," the result may be only that he sleeps with his friend's wife and murders the man who insulted him, when a little forethought would have made him restrain himself. If a timid or greedy man tries to obey "do not resist the wicked man," it may only provide an excuse for him to behave as a coward or a paid collaborator.

Jesus told His disciples that He *deliberately* spoke in parables in order to hide His meaning from the multitude (Matthew 13:13-14), and He warned potential followers:

If anyone comes to Me and does not hate his father and mother, wife and children, brothers and sisters, yes, and his own life also, he cannot be My disciple. And whoever does not bear his cross and come after Me cannot be My disciple. For which of you, intending to build a tower, does not sit down first and count the cost, whether he has enough to finish it, lest, after he has laid the foundation, and is not able to finish it, all who see it begin to mock him, saying, "This man began to build and was not able to finish." (Luke 14:26-30)

The Christian, then, confronts the following difficulty: that he can hardly conceive how to move at once from his accustomed worldly way of life to the Gospel ideal; and that to embrace one Gospel teaching while failing to do the others may make him worse than he was before. Yet there may be a way—there may be many ways—to bridge the gap, or rather, to vary the metaphor, to ascend the mountain.

Think of the Christian as a person trying to climb a mountain whose slopes are full of cliffs and waterfalls and other insurmountable obstacles, yet who knows there is a way up. He may sometimes move horizontally along the mountain's face—the analogy is to a Christian who lives an honest but unremarkable worldly life for a time—while he looks for a path up. And then, suddenly, he finds a way, and begins a dangerous upward climb, risking his neck. *Hagiography*, the literary genre that records the lives of saints as examples for other Christians to emulate, is full of the strange and extreme courses men and women have followed as they sought a way to live the Gospel ideal.

There may be room to practice the Gospels in the context of a bourgeois life that looks externally similar to a worldly life. Consider the following question: What is the difference between a doctor who heals people for money, and a doctor who heals people as an act of service, but has to get some pay for it in order to survive? There may be not only a moral but a practical difference between the two: the servant-doctor might seek out the patients most in need rather than best able to pay, and he may be less likely to misdiagnose patients and prescribe expensive treatments profitable to himself but not really necessary.

But to strangers the difference might be hard to detect. As it can be hard to distinguish the service motive from the profit motive, so the Christian who is "in the world but not of it" may be hard to distinguish from his surroundings, yet be different, nonetheless.

Render unto Caesar

No discussion of Christianity and political freedom is complete without a discussion of Jesus's most famous political remark. Jesus Himself never engaged in any violence, except perhaps when he "drove out" the vendors and money-changers from the temple (Matthew 21:12-13). Yet it is often claimed that Jesus endorsed the legitimacy of (violent) secular authority with the words "give unto Caesar what is Caesar's." This episode deserves a closer look. Matthew narrates it as follows:

> Then the Pharisees went and plotted how they might entangle Him in His talk. And they sent to Him their disciples with the Herodians, saying, "Teacher, we know that You are true and teach the way of God in truth; nor do You care about anyone, for Your do not regard the person of men. Tell us, therefore, what do You think? Is it lawful to pay taxes to Caesar or not?"

> But Jesus perceived their wickedness, and said, "Why do you test Me, you hypocrites? Show Me the tax money." So they brought Him a denarius. And he said to them, "Whose image and inscription is this?"

> They said to Him, "Caesar's."

> And He said to them, "Render therefore to Caesar the things that are Caesar's, and to God the things that are God's."

> When they heard these things, they marveled and went their way. (Matthew 22:15-22)

One interpretation of this Gospel passage is that Jesus says people should pay their taxes. That much is certainly true. We could arrive at the same conclusion by applying "turn the other cheek" to the citizen's relationship to the tax collector, or Jesus's advice that "if anyone wants to sue you and take away your tunic, [you should] let him have your cloak also" (Matthew 6:40). Indeed, in the "give unto Caesar" passage, as in the Sermon on the Mount, Jesus actually advises his disciples to go *beyond* non-resistance, and not only accede to the demands made upon them, but to offer *more*.

For what does the logic of "render... to Caesar the things that are Caesar's" imply? On what grounds does Jesus call the tax money "Caesar's"? On the grounds that it bears Caesar's image and inscription. But *all* the money bears Caesar's image and inscription! So Jesus is telling his audience to give not only their tunic, but their cloak as well; to give not only the tax money, but *all* their money to Caesar. And that advice, of course, is quite consistent with Jesus's other advice not to lay up treasures on earth, nor to have gold or silver or copper in one's money-belt.

By the same token, however, to advise people to pay taxes to Caesar is not the same thing as to recognize Caesar's *right* to tax. Without this distinction, the episode does not make sense. Matthew, Mark, and Luke all make it clear that those who put the question to Jesus are trying to trap Him in His words, as Luke says, "in order to deliver Him to the power and the authority of the governor" (Luke 20:20). But how is the question a trap?

That Jesus would have gotten in political trouble if He had said not to pay taxes to Caesar is obvious enough, but He could easily avoid trouble by saying "Yes, pay taxes to Caesar." And if that is all that He did—which is how Christians sometimes read the passage—what did the Pharisees' agents have to "marvel" at?

The episode can only make sense if one bears in mind that the illegitimacy of the Roman occupation was so axiomatic to first-century Jews that "tax-collectors [for the Roman occupation] and prostitutes" were regularly listed together as epitomizing moral depravity. Had Jesus said no more than "pay taxes to Caesar," He would have discredited Himself. That was why the question was a trap. Later, just before the Crucifixion, when the chief priests declare to Pilate, "We have no king but Caesar" (John 19:15), it is understood that this is the utmost betrayal of the Jewish national vocation as God's people.

What evokes the wonder of the Pharisees' agents is that Jesus manages to endorse paying taxes to Caesar *without* legitimizing the Roman occupation, and while being true to His own teachings and not giving the lie to the elaborate compliments with which the Pharisees prefaced their question. Jesus's answer is perfectly consistent with His being even more opposed to Caesar than His interlocutors are. It would be tendentious but semantically plausible to interpret Jesus's saying as, "the money is tainted with Caesar's image; get rid of it!"[57]

---

[57] It should be borne in mind that to legitimize Caesar would have been as offensive to some Roman patriots at the time as it was to Jewish patriots. Until shortly before the birth of Christ, the Romans had enjoyed a special form of participatory government called the *res publica*, from which the word "republic" is derived. Romans had founded the Republic in 509 B.C. when they overthrew a monarchy, and had taken great national pride in their kingless form of government, under which nearly all of Rome's conquests had been achieved. In the first century B.C., a gradual breakdown of the Republic had occurred, ending in civil war and usurpation of *de facto* despotic power by Julius and Augustus Caesar.

It is worth noting that according to Luke, when the chief priests bring Jesus before Pilate, they say "We found this fellow perverting the nation, and forbidding to pay taxes to Caesar, saying that He Himself is Christ, a King" (Luke 23:2). This charge appears to contradict what Jesus said. Were the chief priests lying, or was this their understanding of Jesus's "render unto Caesar?"

Presumably they were lying, yet Luke does not explicitly say so, and *neither does Jesus*, Who, when Pilate seeks to confirm this charge by asking, "Are you the King of Jews?" says simply, "It is as you say" (Luke 23:3). There is a difference between telling the Jews they should pay taxes to Caesar and telling Caesar the Jews should pay taxes to him, and Jesus refrained from doing the latter.

There is another New Testament passage, from the Epistle of Paul to the Romans, which is sometimes cited in favor of government authority. Paul writes:

> Let every soul be subject to the governing authorities. For there is no authority except from God, and the authorities that exist are appointed by God. Therefore whoever resists the authority resists the ordinance of God, and those who resist will bring judgment on themselves. For rulers are not a terror to good works, but to evil. Do you want to be unafraid of the authority? Do what is good, and you will have praise from the same. For he is God's minister to you for good. But if you do evil, be afraid; for he does not bear the sword in vain; for he is God's minister, an avenger to execute wrath on him who practices evil. Therefore you must be subject, not only because of wrath but also for conscience's sake. For because of this you also pay taxes, for they are God's ministers attending continually to this very thing. Render therefore to all their due: taxes to whom taxes are due, customs to whom customs, fear to whom fear, honor to whom honor. (Romans 13:1-7)

First, we should observe in what sense the above passage is true, and consistent with the Gospels. Paul's advice not to resist authority is one with Jesus's advice "do not resist the wicked man." A ruler is indeed no terror to good works, for the good man "does not fear those who kill the body but cannot kill the soul" (Matthew 10:28) and "he who loses his life for My sake shall find it" (Matthew 10:39).

Paul and other Christian martyrs "had praise from" the Roman authorities, in the sense that their heroic martyrdoms brought them praise from all generations to come. Governing authorities, like floods and fires and earthquakes and plagues, are appointed by God in the sense that they do not happen without His will, even if His purpose in allowing them is sometimes opaque to us.

Admittedly this is not the most direct reading; yet if we read it as a straight-forward legitimation of Roman power, or a *fortiori* of state power generally, is that the passage becomes obviously false. Did Paul have praise from the authorities when, about fifteen years after he wrote the Epistle to the Romans, he was (probably) beheaded under the emperor Nero? Did Jesus have praise from Herod when his soldiers mockingly crowned Him with thorns and flogged Him? Were the commands of Nero, or for that matter of Pontius Pilate, "ordinances of God," like the Ten Commandments?

Some Christians seem to read this passage as if Paul was offering a generic endorsement of all governments. Then they escape the embarrassing implications of this—it would be an endorsement of every ruler from the Emperor Claudius to Adolf Hitler to Joseph Stalin—by applying it only to governments that they like. Perhaps I do not understand them.

Paul seems to have had a more favorable view of Roman power than events later justified; and he had scruples about civil disobedience that the other apostles did not. This may be seen by contrasting three episodes in the Book of Acts in which apostles were miraculously freed from prison.

First, Peter and other apostles are arrested by agents of the high priest, but during the night an angel of the Lord opens the prison doors and tells them to go teach in the temple, where they are found the next day, to the surprise of the high priest (Acts 5:17-26). Second, Peter was arrested by agents of king Herod, but an angel of the Lord appeared and struck off his chains and led him out of the prison, after which, as punishment for their failure to hold Peter, Herod orders the guards killed (Acts 12:1-19). These escapes are acts of civil disobedience, since by law the apostles should have stayed in prison. When Paul is given an opportunity for a similar miraculous escape from prison, he behaves differently:

> At midnight Paul and Silas were praying and singing hymns to God, and the prisoners were listening to them. Suddenly there was a great earthquake, so that the foundations of the prison were shaken; and immediately all the doors were opened and everyone's chains were loosed. And the keeper of the prison, awaking from sleep and seeing the prison doors open, supposing the prisoners had fled, drew his sword and was about to kill himself. But Paul called with a loud voice, saying, "Do yourself no harm, for we are all here." (Acts 16:25-28)

The jailer, impressed, immediately accepts baptism, and then "brought [Paul and Silas] into his house"—so at this point, they apparently leave the jail after all, but only with the permission of the newly-converted jailer—and the next morning they are informed that the magistrates have ordered them to be released. What follows seems to bear witness to a faith in Roman justice on Paul's part that is almost tragi-comic:

> But Paul said to them, "They have beaten us openly, uncondemned Romans, and have thrown us into prison. And now do they put us out secretly? No indeed! Let them come themselves and get us out." And the officers told these words to the magistrates, and they were afraid when they heard that they were Romans. Then they came and pleaded with them and brought them out, and asked them to depart from the city. (Acts 16:37-39)

The same faith in Roman justice seems to explain why Paul sought deliberately to be brought before the emperors in chains. After being wrongly arrested in some disturbances in Jerusalem, he is repeatedly tried and found innocent but not released by Roman magistrates who fear Jewish mobs. At one point, King Agrippa, one of his judges, remarks that "this man could have been freed, had he not appealed to the emperor" (Act 26:32).

It is not entirely clear from Acts whether this was a strategic blunder on Paul's part, or if he truly *wanted* to speak to the emperor, perhaps in hopes of converting him, even of turning the Roman world into a Christian empire. Whatever Paul's motive, the Emperor turned out to be the cowardly madman, Nero, to this day a byword of insane cruelty, who decorated the sides of the road to Rome with crucified Christians. If Paul was unduly sanguine in his endorsement of Roman power, his courageous quest to bring the Gospel to Rome or die in the attempt turned this foible into a glory. But Paul's disappointed hopes (in his earthly sovereign, not his heavenly Sovereign) place Romans 13:1-7 in a tragic and ironic light.

Ecclesiology

From a historical perspective, the main result of Jesus's ministry was the establishment of the Church; but what is a church? If the answer to that question seems obvious, think again.

In the United States there are hundreds of thousands of church congregations. A typical church (congregation) holds a service on Sunday mornings and maybe at other times during the week. The service consists of sermons, readings from the Gospels and other sacred texts, and music, sung by choirs or the congregation or played on instruments, and other rituals, in particular the distribution of bread and wine that represent, or according to some churches *are*, the body and blood of Christ. So far church seems a bit like a theater, putting on a show, and a bit like a school, teaching.

But then consider this: *no one has to pay for it.* Christians are asked to donate, of course, otherwise the churches could not keep operating. A collection plate is circulated, and there may be social pressure to contribute. But in most churches giving is anonymous, and in every church, those who come without paying are admitted, and welcomed. Think for the moment of churches as an "industry" and it becomes clear how odd it is that, in the midst of the capitalist economy, there is an entire industry that stays in business without charging its customers anything, that "gives to the one who asks."

There is another difference between a church and a theater: churches tell their members what to do, even outside the church. Educational establishments also do this, that is, they assign "homework," but homework is directly related to the class. If the homework is done and is good quality, teachers and professors do not care what else students do with their time. But churches impose rules which apply to their members' whole lives.

In this respect, the church resembles a *government*. But it is also unlike a government, because it does not try (in contemporary America) to coerce its members to follow its rules. Usually the church does not even try to verify whether members are following them. It relies entirely on moral suasion and social pressure, and any member is always free to leave. A church is not exactly a business and not exactly a state. It is not exactly private and not exactly public.

The English word *church* is from Greek *kyriakon*, "those belonging to the Lord"; but the New Testament uses the Greek word *ekklesia*, or "assembly," such as ruled democratic Athens. The word is used twice in the Gospels, both times in Matthew. The first follows Peter's confession of the divinity of Christ:

> When Jesus came into the region of Caesarea Philippi, He asked His disciples, saying, "Who do men say that I, the Son of Man, am?" So they said, "Some say John the Baptist, some Elijah, and others Jeremiah or one of the prophets." He said to them, "But who do you say that I am?" Simon Peter answered and said, "You are the Christ, the Son of the living God." Jesus answered and said to him, "Blessed are you, Simon Bar-Jonah, for flesh and blood has not revealed this to you, but My Father who is in heaven. And I also say to you that you are Peter, and on this rock I will build My church, and the gates of Hades shall not prevail

against it. And I will give you the keys to the kingdom of heaven, and whatever you will bind on earth will be bound in heaven, and whatever you loose on earth will be loosed in heaven." (Matthew 16:13-18)

Jesus says that His church will be built on the rock of Peter's confession of faith, that is, on the belief that Jesus is "Christ, the Son of the living God." The prophecy that "the gates of Hades shall not prevail against it" has been strikingly vindicated, as the Church, now two thousand years old, has long since outlived any state that existed at the time. So the church is, first, a community based on shared belief, with a power to make and repeal rules ("bind... and loose"). It is also a community based on mutual moral accountability, as the other mention of the church in the Gospels makes clear:

> "If your brother sins against you, go and tell him his fault between you and him alone. If he hears you, you have gained your brother. But if he will not hear, take with you one or two more, that 'by the mouth of two or three witnesses every word may be established.' And if he refuses to hear them, tell it to the church. But if he refuses even to hear the church, let him be to you like a heathen and a tax collector. Assuredly, I say to you, whatever you bind on earth will be bound in heaven, and whatever you loose on earth will be loosed in heaven." (Matthew 18:15-18)

While the church is here given a sort of judicial function, judging disputes among its members, it is notable that, consistent with the Sermon on the Mount, the punishment for those who will not listen to the church is non-violent and non-coercive: "let him be to you like a heathen and a tax collector," which means, at worst, let him be a social outcast.

The "kingdom of heaven," to which Jesus gives the church the "keys," is illuminated in the Gospels by means of several metaphors. Jesus compares it to a man who sowed good seed in his field, after which an enemy comes and sows weeds, and who tells his servants not to uproots the weeds until harvest lest they also disturb the grain, but at harvest time to burn the weeds and gather the wheat into his barn (Matthew 13:24-30); to a mustard seed which "is the least of all seeds; but when it is grown it is greater than all the herbs and becomes a tree" (Matthew 13:31-32); to a woman leavening bread; to a treasure hidden in a field (Matthew 13:44); to a merchant who sells all he has to buy a precious pearl (Matthew 13:46); and to a net cast into the sea that catches good and bad fish

(Matthew 13:47-49). None of these metaphors repeat one another, but three recurring themes are:

1. The kingdom of heaven is of transcendent value, a "treasure," a "pearl of great price."

2. Good and bad are intermingled in it but will eventually be separated.

3. The kingdom of heaven *grows*, like a field or rising bread, and like a mustard seed will begin very small but then grow very large.

The last of these is a remarkable prophecy, for the church—the kingdom of heaven—did begin very small, with Jesus and his circle of disciples, and then grew to encompass the Roman Empire and even to extend beyond it. The first was clearly persuasive to the monks and martyrs, who gave up everything the world had to offer for the kingdom of heaven's sake. And it was because the kingdom of heaven was more valuable than all earthly wealth and power that the church, which held the keys to it, was sometimes able to command kings.

A kingdom implies a king, and the kingdom of heaven is no exception. Jesus's favorite appellation for Himself, the Son of Man, comes from the following prophecy in the Book of Daniel:

> In my vision at night I looked, and there before me was one like a son of man, coming with the clouds of heaven. He approached the Ancient of Days and was led into His presence. He was given authority, glory, and sovereign power; all peoples, nations and men of every language worshiped Him. His dominion is an everlasting dominion that will not pass away, and His kingdom is one that will never be destroyed. (Daniel 7:13-14)

So the "Son of Man" enjoys "sovereign power," but not in the same sense as secular rulers. Pilate's question to Jesus—"Are you the King of the Jews?"—is recorded in all four Gospels, and Jesus's answer—"It is as you say"—is recorded in three of them, but in the Gospel of John, Jesus explains further:

> My kingdom is not of this world. If My kingdom were of this world, My servants would fight, so that I should not be delivered to the Jews; but now My kingdom is not from here… You rightly say that I am a king. For this cause I was born, and for this cause I have come into the

world, that I should bear witness to the truth. Everyone who is of the truth hears My voice. (John 18:36-37)

So Jesus is king of a *nonviolent* kingdom: His servants will not fight. But He is a king nonetheless; and Christians' appropriation of the language of sovereign power was probably one reason why the Romans persecuted them. "Whoever makes himself a king speaks against Caesar" (John 19:12).

Finally, the church is to be a unity, whose members are of one family—"whoever does the will of My Father in heaven is My brother and sister and mother" (Matthew 12:50)—and even of one organism—"I am the true vine, and My Father is the vinedresser. Every branch that does not bear fruit He takes away; and every branch that bears fruit He prunes, that it may bear more fruit... Abide in Me, and I in you. As the branch cannot bear fruit of itself, unless it abides in the vine, neither can you, unless you abide in Me" (John 15:1-4).

It is called the Bride of Christ, and even (mystically) the *Body* of Christ, that through which Christ works in the world. The "real unity of them all" which Hobbes wanted to create by force and fear, is created in the Church by free choice and mutual love.

Many readers probably feel that I am whitewashing the Church's historical record. To that, one answer is that my main goal here is not to describe the historical Church but to illuminate the concept of the Church, as described in the New Testament. But I think the historical Church has conformed to the New Testament ideal closely enough to make the New Testament idea of the Church historically relevant. That ideal, though imperfectly realized in the historical Church, is yet the key to the *distinctiveness* of the historical Church compared with other human institutions.

The Church has sometimes wielded the sword, but far more often the non-violent power of moral suasion. Christianity has sometimes fomented divisions, but it also has a remarkable power to bring together people of different families and races, classes and professions, tastes and temperaments.

Even the Spanish Inquisition is an exception that proves the rule. Its peculiar horror lies not in the number of its victims—probably a few thousands or tens of thousands in the course of more than three centuries, three or four orders of magnitude less than the victims of Soviet totalitarianism—but in the fact that those who preached the Gospel practiced the exact antithesis of the Gospel; that Christians mimicked Caiaphas, that innocent people were sacrilegiously tortured and murdered *in the name of Christ*.

Without taking into account this hideous *irony*, the unique horror, and the historical importance, of the Inquisition cannot be understood, and there would be no reason to give it more attention than the hundreds or thousands of other occasions on which a few thousand or more were sacrificed to the jealousy of a tyrant or the bloodlust of a conqueror.

It must be remembered, too, that the Spanish Inquisition, though the Catholic Church certainly participated, was established by and run in the interests of the Spanish *state*. It is appropriate to hold the Church to a higher standard than we hold other institutions, because it sets a higher standard for itself, but we should recognize that that is what we are doing. If the Church has consistently, though worse at some times than others, fallen short of its own ideals, it has risen above the standards set by other human institutions often enough for it to be a pattern.

Church, state, and freedom

With the words "render unto Caesar what is Caesar's, and unto God what is God's," Jesus Christ foreshadowed a new feature of human societies: the separation of church and state, some form of which has been a unique feature of Christian civilizations ever since. But the relationship between church and state, between temporal and spiritual power, has never been settled and unproblematic. A stylized division of the history of church-state relations into four phases may be a useful mnemonic.

First was the Age of the Martyrs (30 AD – 312 AD), from the ministry of Jesus Christ to the conversion of Constantine, and afterwards in Persia and other states that did not convert to Christianity. During this time, as discussed in **Chapter 7**, the Church was exposed to intermittent bloody persecution by a state which sought to destroy it.

The next phase, the Age of Christian Empire, began in 312 AD and lasted until the Bolshevik Revolution of 1917, in the east, and in the west until 1077 AD. During this period, which will be further discussed, Christianity was tolerated within what became known as "Christendom," but secular emperors partially co-opted the church hierarchy, giving rise to special hazards of corruption and heresy, and monasticism played an indispensable role in preserving the Church's purity against the temptations involved in collaboration with secular rulers. In 1077 AD, the papacy in Rome launched a revolution against secular interference in Church affairs.

What followed may be called the Age of the Two Swords, with one sword belonging to the Church, one to the state. This period, which did not occur in the east, was extraordinarily creative—it was in these centuries that the unique genius of European civilization first appeared—but the church became increasingly vitiated by a direct and indirect use of violent power contrary to the teachings of the Gospels, culminating in a devastating civil war (the Reformation) within the Church.

Finally, the Age of Religious Toleration may be dated to the arrival of the Pilgrims in Plymouth on the Mayflower in 1620 and the establishment of a new American civilization, whose almost unblemished record of religious toleration from its founding until the present day has inspired a new pattern of church-state relations which is now accepted, in practice and in theory, by almost all Christians worldwide.

The Age of Christian Empire.

When, in or around 312 A.D., a Roman emperor converted to Christianity, and the church faced the new complex problem of accommodating Caesar within the Church. Jesus had warned that "the kingdom of heaven suffers violence, and the violent take it by force" (Matthew 11:12). This was true in the Christian as in the pagan empire, but the violence took subtler forms. First, emperors sometimes embraced heretical forms of Christianity and persecuted orthodox believers.

Second, emperors tried to instrumentalize the church hierarchy, assuming the right to appoint people to ecclesiastical offices and appointing political allies not suitable to the offices, or even altering the whole structure of the hierarchy. For example, Tsar Peter I of Russia suppressed the office of Moscow Patriarch in 1700, replacing it with a more pliable Holy Synod, and in the two centuries that followed, the Orthodox church in Russia thereafter became much too close an ally of a tyrannical and grotesquely inegalitarian state for anyone's good. In the best of times, imperial favor attracted opportunists to the church who diluted its spiritual life. The lives of three saints in the 3rd-4th centuries AD, Anthony, Athanasius, and Ambrose, illustrate the main ways that the church dealt with the dangerous institution of a Christian empire.

St. Athanasius: Reason triumphant (293-373 AD).

As a community of belief, the Church's unity depends on maintaining distinctions between orthodox (accepted as true) belief and heretical (rejected as false) belief. A variety of opinions exists within the church at any given time at least on minor points and is to some extent tolerated, but the Church—any church—has to reject some innovations as negating doctrines too central for compromise.

One such innovation was the Arian heresy, which emerged early in the 4th century and denied the full divinity of Christ. The theological issue was resolved at the Council of Nicea in AD 325, at which one of the most powerful speakers was the young philosopher Athanasius, then a deacon and the secretary of Patriarch Alexander of Alexandria, and the *Nicene Creed*, still used by Orthodox, Catholic, and Protestant churches, was adopted to affirm the orthodox faith as against the Arian heresy. That would have been the end of it but for the intervention of the Roman emperors.

First the emperor Constantine I, then, more strongly, his son and successor Constantius, came under the influence of Arians, for whom the learned and orthodox Athanasius, who succeeded to the Patriarchate of Alexandria in 328, was a principal enemy. In 335, Athanasius was deposed and exiled to Trier, in the remote Rhineland, on the spurious charge of interfering with the grain supply of Egypt. This was the first of four exiles, during all of which Athanasius retained the loyalty of his people, and after all of which he returned to resume his post as Patriarch of Alexandria, where he died, finally, in his bed.

The story of how Athanasius evaded his enemies will be discussed in connection with the life of St. Anthony. But the life of Athanasius illustrates an important fact: *that the Christian emperors were not able to impose their doctrinal views on the church.* Of course, some emperors agreed with the orthodox position, and some did not care; but those who embraced heretical views, though they sometimes enjoyed long and prosperous reigns, and though they could hijack certain church offices, could never ultimately prevail. Athanasius's life symbolizes the *freedom of thought* which the Church triumphantly retained throughout the age of Christian empire. It stands in opposition to the Westphalian/Hobbesian principle of *cuius regio, eius religio*, the principle that the sovereign is judge of what doctrines are fit to be taught to his subjects.

Athanasius makes an interesting contrast to that other ancient philosopher and symbol of free thought, Socrates. They each valued truth more than life. They each won a moral victory, but in different ways. Socrates, who died for the sake of a *question*, became a father-figure to all subsequent philosophers. Athanasius, who survived against all odds for the sake of an *answer*, is venerated today as "the father of orthodoxy." Socrates faced death bravely for the sake of a truth he did not know and insisted on saying, whatever the cost, that no one else knew, either. Athanasius faced death bravely for the sake of the truth he knew and would not allow to be displaced by error. Yet there is a similarity even in this contrast. For Plato's dialogues characteristically end in *perplexity*, as interlocutors fail to answer Socrates' seemingly simple questions. The

Christian creeds, too, confess the limits of cognition, for the Church has always insisted that they express a *mystery*, which no man can fully comprehend and no formulation can capture.

St. Anthony and the monastic commonwealth (251-356 AD). The life story of St. Athanasius is bound up with that of an older, wilder man, called the "father of monasticism"—St. Anthony. Athanasius himself became the hagiographer of Saint Anthony, and wrote, not that Anthony was the first monk—in his youth, according to Athanasius, Anthony visited and emulated others who had adopted a reclusive lifestyle dedicated to worship—but that he was the first to take the monastic way of life into the distant desert. Anthony sought solitude there, but eventually admirers came to him for instruction, and he began to organize them into loose communities, a new pattern of life later regularized by Pachomius, an ex-military man who established a monastery with a thousand monks and nuns.

Jesus seems to have specifically foreshadowed the monastic life when he said: "There are eunuchs who were born thus from their mother's womb, and there are eunuchs who were made thus by men, and there are eunuchs who have made themselves eunuchs for the kingdom of heaven's sake. He who is able to accept it, let him accept it" (Matthew 19:12).

More generally, the Sermon on the Mount lends itself to being read as an exhortation to monasticism, as it is hard to see how a householder and paterfamilias, with a wife to be kept with a certain decent jealousy and children to be defended and provided for, can be as radically meek as the Gospel demands. St. Anthony himself was inspired by Jesus's exhortation "if you want to be perfect, [to] sell all that you have and give to the poor... and come, follow Me" (Matthew 19:21).

The voluntary socialism practiced, seemingly briefly, by the early church at Jerusalem, was later revived in the monasteries, and experience suggests that *celibacy* is a necessary condition for the success of such communes, because sex and children create a powerful human need for privacy and therefore for private property.

The extent to which these monastic communities existed outside the power of the Roman state, a mere generation after their first appearance, was dramatically illustrated by the life of Athanasius, who took shelter in the monasteries when he was wanted by the Arian emperor. Edward Gibbon tells the story, and a long quote from his *Decline and Fall of the Roman Empire* is justified by the importance of the episode in the history of human freedom. Every detail sheds light on this marvelous adventure by which freedom of thought was won, for the Church and ultimately for the human race.

Athanasius had indeed escaped from the most imminent dangers; and the adventures of that extraordinary man deserve and fix our attention. On the memorable night when the church of St. Theonas was invested by the troops of Syrianus, the archbishop, seated on his throne, expected, with calm and intrepid dignity, the approach of death. While the public devotion was interrupted by shouts of rage and cries of terror, he animated his trembling congregation to express their religious confidence by chanting one of the psalms of David which celebrates the triumph of the God of Israel over the haughty and impious tyrant of Egypt. The doors were at length burst open: a cloud of arrows was discharged among the people; the soldiers, with drawn swords, rushed forwards into the sanctuary; and the dreadful gleam of their armour was reflected by the holy luminaries which burnt round the altar. Athanasius still rejected the pious importunity of the monks and presbyters who were attached to his person; and nobly refused to desert his episcopal station till he had dismissed in safety the last of the congregation. The darkness and tumult of the night favoured the retreat of the archbishop; and though he was oppressed by the waves of an agitated multitude, though he was thrown to the ground, and left without sense or motion, he still recovered his undaunted courage, and eluded the eager search of the soldiers, who were instructed by their Arian guides that the head of Athanasius would be the most acceptable present to the emperor. From that moment the primate of Egypt disappeared from the eyes of his enemies, and remained above six years concealed in impenetrable obscurity.

The despotic power of his implacable enemy filled the whole extent of the Roman world and the exasperated monarch had endeavoured, by a very pressing epistle to the Christian princes of Ethiopia, to exclude Athanasius from the most remote and sequestered regions of the earth. Counts, praefects, tribunes, whole armies, were successively employed to pursue a bishop and a fugitive; the vigilance of the civil and military powers was excited by the Imperial edicts; liberal rewards were promised to the man who should produce Athanasius, either alive or dead; and the most severe penalties were denounced against those who should dare to protect the public enemy. But the deserts of Thebais were now peopled by a race of wild, yet submissive fanatics, who preferred the commands of their abbot to the laws of their sovereign. The numerous disciples of Antony and Pachomius received the fugitive primate as their father, admired the patience and humility with which he conformed to their strictest institutions, collected every word which dropped from his lips as the genuine effusions of inspired wisdom; and persuaded themselves that their prayers, their fasts, and their vigils, were less meritorious than the zeal which they expressed, and the dangers which they braved, in the defence of truth and innocence. The monasteries of Egypt were seated in lonely and desolate places, on the summit of mountains, or in the islands of the Nile; and the sacred horn or trumpet of Tabenne was the well-known signal which assembled several thousand robust and determined monks, who, for the most part, had been the peasants of the adjacent country. When their dark retreats were invaded by a military force which it was impossible to resist, they silently stretched out their necks to the executioner; and supported their national character, that tortures could never wrest from an Egyptian the confession of a secret which he was resolved not to disclose. The archbishop of Alexandria, for whose safety they eagerly devoted their lives, was lost among a uniform and well-disciplined multitude; and on the nearer approach of danger, he was swiftly removed, by their officious hands, from one place of concealment to another, till he reached the formidable deserts, which the gloomy and credulous temper of superstition had peopled with daemons and savage monsters. The retirement of Athanasius, which ended only with the life of Constantius, was spent, for the most part, in the society of the monks, who faithfully served him as guards, as secretaries, and as messengers. (Gibbon, *Decline and Fall of the Roman Empire*)

This account makes it clear why Athanasius's fate was different from that of Socrates. It was certainly not that the late Roman Empire was a milder regime than that of democratic Athens—on the contrary! It was because, not from any definite intention but as a side-effect of their flight from temptation and mortification of the flesh, the monks of the Egyptian desert had liberated themselves from the Roman dominion and established a new kind of republic or commonwealth, with its own constitution of obedience to abbots, later codified in monastic rules like those of St. Basil and St. Benedict. The emperor could not command them.

Monasticism was founded on *real* social contracts, in contrast with the partly or wholly imaginary social contracts of the 17th-century philosophers, for men and women accepted the monastic yoke (the institution of "child oblates" who were brought to the monastery by their parents is a partial exception) of their own free will. It was a *nonviolent* republic: "My servants will not fight,"

Athanasius might have said, like Jesus. But its non-violent devices of retreat and secrecy and voluntary discipline were enough to protect truth against power. Athanasius was free, too, from any loyalty to the law as opposed to the *right*. Socrates could have fled, but felt he must not defy the laws of the city to which he owed so much, even when they were unjust. The Christians had no such scruples, for they were loyal to a greater Lawgiver than any state.

For Hobbes, the idea of life without sovereign power was a horror, and modern anthropology tends to confirm that Hobbes' vision of the life of primitive man was truer than the more optimistic ideas about the "state of nature" held later by Locke and Rousseau. Studies of tribes in Amazonia and New Guinea have found that murder is a leading cause of death. But however poor and wild were the monks of the deserts of Egypt, there was a moral difference, to which subsequent history bears witness. Indeed, the best way to refute Hobbes' famous description of the state of nature may be to juxtapose on it the history of monasticism. Hobbes claims that:

> [In the state of nature, or war,] every man is Enemy to every man...
> [so that] men live without other security, than what their own strength,
> and their own invention shall furnish them withal. In such condition,
> there is no place for Industry; because the fruit thereof is uncertain; and
> consequently no culture of the Earth; no Navigation, nor use of the
> commodities that may be imported by Sea; no commodious Building;
> no Instruments of moving, and removing such things as require much
> force; no Knowledge of the face of the Earth; no account of Time; no
> Arts; no Letters; no Society; and which is worst of all, continuall feare,
> and danger of violent death; And the life of man, solitary, poore, nasty,
> brutish, and short. (*Leviathan*, Location 1330)

In complete opposition to this account, the monasteries were an archipelago of peace, order, and creativity amidst the wildernesses of Egypt or the chaos of the Dark Ages. Not only were the monks not in a state of general mutual enmity or war, but it was precisely there that arts and letters were preserved even while secular literacy was vanishing; where the commodious and beautiful buildings were built that survive to this day; where the earth was cultivated with the greatest skill, to the extent that monasteries have been compared to "agricultural colleges"; where the knowledge of geography was preserved and (by missionaries like St. Patrick) extended; where the rigorous daily schedule of services may have motivated the invention and certainly the spread of clocks; and which even engaged extensively in industry and international trade.[58]

All of these achievements took place in the absence of any sovereign power as Hobbes conceived it; and many of them occurred at times when the population lived in "continual fear and danger of violent death." The ability of the monasteries to survive and flourish in anarchic and backward places was crucial in spreading Christianity and literacy and lifting Europe out of the Dark Ages. The Carolingian and Ottonian emperors of France and Germany in the ninth to eleventh centuries relied heavily on the monasteries for scribal services and revenues.

During the age of Christian empire, it became customary for bishops and patriarchs to be drawn from the ranks of the monastics. This was certainly not the practice in the Age of Martyrs, when there were no monks. St. Paul taught that "a bishop must be... the husband of one wife" (1 Timothy 3:2). But in the Age of Christian Empire, the monastic monopoly on ecclesiastical leadership was a critical safeguard for the independence of the Church, for the vast sacrifice involved in the monastic path to episcopal or patriarchal or papal office tended, albeit with many exceptions, to bar the way for the kind of worldlings who curry favor with sovereigns.

But as important as the monks were in the practical arts, in statecraft, and in ecclesiastical leadership, their greatest contribution was probably what it was in St. Athanasius's time: to provide a physical refuge for reason, truth, philosophy, books, scholarship, the life of the mind. In the monasteries human thought had, for the first time, a lasting refuge from the threats, and the corrupting patronage, of secular rulers. And as historian Brian Tierney has persuasively shown, it was monastic scholars like Gratian (12th century, a canon lawyer and monk of the Camaldolese order) who first began to think out clearly the ideas of natural law and natural rights which are the basis of modern freedom (Tierney, 1997).

The crux of the matter is that the monasteries, and thanks to the monasteries the Church, had an institutional and intellectual integrity independent of and indestructible by the state. The Church could think and judge. Natural rights is an idea at once obvious and subversive. It is obvious in the sense that it is a mere inversion of ethical rules like the prohibition of murder. Logically, to

---

[58] Regular devotional reading of the lives of saints inculcates in a devout Catholic or Orthodox Christian an idea of holy flight from the world which is quite incompatible with Hobbes' insistence that any existence except under civil government is miserable. But Protestantism rather than atheism might explain Hobbes' lack of sympathy with the desert fathers of the Church.

say that it is wrong for anyone to murder me is equivalent to saying that I have a right to life.

To say that it is wrong for anyone to steal my things is to say that I have property rights in them. But it is subversive because when my right to life is interpreted as a property of *me*, it applies vis-à-vis *everyone*. It becomes first problematic, then untenable, for anyone to claim a special "sovereign" exemption from the moral law. As such ideas spread among the people, it became harder for rulers to be oppressive, and led to evolutions and revolutions towards freedom.

St. Ambrose: sovereign power made accountable at last (337-397 AD).

In the eventful life of St. Ambrose, bishop of Milan, one episode deserves our particular attention. The incident in question began when the Roman governor of Thessalonica arrested a popular charioteer. This provoked a riot and several Roman officials were murdered. The Emperor Theodosius, the first firmly Catholic (orthodox) Emperor, and apart from this episode a rather beneficent one, responded by sending troops who massacred seven thousand people. After this, Ambrose refused to let the Emperor take communion. He demanded that the Emperor repent, and promulgate a law that a 30-day waiting period must precede executions to prevent similar incidents in future. The humbled Emperor submitted to these demands and after a time was readmitted to the communion of the Church.

Before this episode, Roman emperors had for centuries enjoyed absolute power. Some, like Caligula, Nero, Domitian, Commodus, and Elagabalus were vicious and crazy, committing terrible crimes for no sane reason. Even the moderate emperors grew increasingly brutal as time passed. Constantine had killed his son on a false charge of treason; Constantius had murdered his nephew. At last, at the dawn of the Christian empire, there was someone who could hold a Roman emperor accountable.

In the story of Ambrose and Theodosius is an answer to our reiterated riddle. *Who guards the guards? The Church.* Ambrose made it clear that Theodosius was subject to the same moral law as others, and Theodosius submitted to Ambrose's authority because the Church had something to give him—communion now, salvation (as he believed) later—which he could get in no other way.

For a thousand years thereafter the Church provided the main check on the exercise of power by kings, emperors, and the warlords of the higher nobility in the west. With a geographical sway that extended beyond that of any medieval European state, with its network of constitutionally self-sufficient monastic orders, with its moral authority in the eyes of the people, its ability to produce martyrs when persecuted, and its wealth, the Church could not be destroyed by any medieval king or emperor, even if it could sometimes be made their tool.

The story of St. John Chrysostom, one of the most beloved of the saints of the East, illustrates the relative weakness of the Church vis-à-vis the state in the eastern part of the Roman empire, better known as the Byzantine empire, and later in the Russian empire which emulated the Byzantine model.

John Chrysostom was a saintly preacher (and former hermit) who was appointed patriarch of Constantinople in 398 AD. He refused to be drawn into the luxurious high society of the capital and made an enemy of (among others) the empress Eudoxia, whose extravagance he had denounced. A plot formed against Chrysostom and he was deposed, and died in exile, but soon afterwards, and to the present day, he became revered as a great saint.

The Age of the Two Swords.

I have named the period after 1077 AD after the medieval Catholic doctrine of the "two swords," which in turn was based on an admittedly puzzling passage in the Gospel of Luke, where hours before His crucifixion, Jesus tells His disciples "he who has no sword, let him sell his garment and buy one" (Luke 22:38), to which they say, "Look, here are two swords," and Jesus says "It is enough."

A few verses later, Jesus prays to God, "Father, if it is Your will, take this cup away from Me; nevertheless not My will, but Yours, be done" (Luke 22:42). An angel then appeared to strengthen Him, and He prayed more earnestly until "His sweat became like great drops of blood" (Luke 22:43-44), after which a multitude appeared, led by the traitor Judas Iscariot, to arrest him, and at this point His disciples naturally ask, "Lord, shall we strike with the sword." To this Jesus—seemingly inconsistently with what He said before—says no, "Permit even this" (Luke 22:49).

From this passage, the medieval popes somehow got the idea that the "two swords" represented Church and state, and that the Church could wield the sword, notwithstanding "turn the other cheek" and "the kingdom of heaven suffers violence and the violent take it by force" and many other New Testament teachings.

The Christian empire in the West, unlike that of the East, was instituted by the Church itself in AD 800, when the popes crowned a king of that line, Charlemagne, "Holy Roman Emperor," and for the next two and a half centuries there was a notional Christian empire in the West, as in the East.

Then, in AD 1077, Pope Gregory VII excommunicated the German "Holy Roman" emperor Henry IV in a dispute over "investiture," the right which the emperors and other secular rulers had assumed to appoint bishops. A collapse of imperial power followed, and Henry IV had to go to Italy to beg the pope's forgiveness, famously standing in the snow for three days until the pope relented. It was a stunning display of papal power, but it did not last.

When Henry returned to Germany and regrouped, renounced his concessions, and marched against Gregory at the head of an army, a second excommunication did not have the same effect, and Gregory died in exile. This was the beginning of a long, bitter, though intermittent struggle, at once ideological and military, which lasted until the death of the last emperor of Henry IV's dynasty, Frederick II, in 1250.

One of the asymmetries in this struggle was that the popes, though they enjoyed temporal power over Rome and its vicinity—the Papal States—did not aspire to rule all of Italy, but instead formed alliances with rising towns like Florence and Milan, which emerged in the course of this struggle, first as republics and centers of commerce, then as the scene of the cultural splendors and erudition of the Renaissance.

So it turned out that the rivalry between the "two swords" favored the emergence of political liberty, and with it a flourishing of art and science. A similar church-state struggle in 17th-century England, where the Puritans of the "New Model" Army enabled Parliament to win a civil war against the king, also contributed to the establishment of political liberty in Britain, in particular to the evisceration of royal power in favor of parliamentary sovereignty and representative government.

In each of these cases, however, the victory was Pyrrhic. The popes' victory was made possible by an alliance with the unscrupulous kings of France, whose "prisoners" they became from 1309 to 1378, during which time the papacy was forced to move to the French town of Avignon. And the Puritans were rejected in favor of a Stuart Restoration.

More fundamentally, the use of military power in Christian causes during the Middle Ages and the Reformation caused disillusionment with institutional Christianity, which seemed to have degenerated into a violent fanaticism alien to the spirit of the Gospels. While the Renaissance and Reformation developed within a still Christian worldview, they turned away from medieval tradition towards ancient pagan philosophy and culture (the Renaissance) or towards the early Church (the Reformation). The Enlightenment was largely anti-Christian in continental Europe, though less so in England and hardly at all in America.

Christianity and freedom.

A claim that the Church was the main institution able to check and balance the state in the ancient Roman empire, or in the Middle Ages, or even in 17th-century England, may be plausible. A claim that even today the only ultimate and reliable answer to the question "Who guards the guards?" is *still* the Church will evoke incredulity.

In the Age of Religious Toleration, the church keeps a lower profile—its martyrs do not die in the arenas, it does not place crowns on the heads of emperors, or organize Crusades—but that does not mean that it has less influence. Polls find that over 90% of Americans believe in God and over 80% self-identify as Christian. Some of this Christianity is mere lip service, but that was always true. Stark and Finke (2005) found that church membership in America has steadily *increased* in the past two centuries.

The Puritan Pilgrims of 1620, like St. Anthony, fled into the wilderness in order to escape worldly temptations and worship God, and like St. Anthony, in doing so they set a new pattern for human society which solved old, vexing problems. Martin Luther and Oliver Cromwell both believed in religious toleration but found intractable difficulties in putting it into practice.

In America, religious toleration emerged quickly and was highly stable, for there, from the beginning, the power of the clergy stopped at the church door, or extended beyond it only in a moral sense. The task of selecting leaders and holding them accountable was delegated to the Christian people—to let non-Christian minorities participate later was unproblematic since their impact could hardly be decisive—and a certain naïve majoritarianism in American democracy, as expressed in slogans like "government of the people, by the people, and for the people" as if "the people" is one well-defined entity, has its origins in the idea of the Christian unity of the Church.

Meanwhile the church enjoyed an autonomy and security unprecedented in history. There was, in America, no question of bishops being appointed by kings. This arrangement of mutual noninterference between church and state represents a very plausible reading of the Gospels, and Americans have tended to regard the long European tradition of the Church claiming political power as unaccountably perverse. In doing so, they fail to appreciate that the Church's political power was often defensive, the Church wielding political power to fend off repression or hostile takeover by the state. Paradoxically, in America the *strength* of the church freed it from the need to seek political power.

The American belief in *natural rights*, and that the purpose of government is to protect them, may be traced through Locke to the medieval canon lawyers; but Americans have never been aware of this debt. They have generally regarded natural rights as "self-evident," mere common sense, and that is true enough. But it is *Christian* common sense, and a vibrant and popular Christianity has inoculated Americans against ideas emanating from Europe that would have displaced these ideas.

Americans have mostly ignored Rousseau, Condorcet, Kant, Hegel, Marx, Spencer and Nietzsche, confident that they had little to learn from Europe, and that, on the contrary, Europe had much to learn from them. So it has proved. In the 20th century the great traditions of post-Enlightenment European political thought, right and left, have proved to be historical dead ends; and Western Europe has undergone a comprehensive Americanization, from democracy to blue jeans and rock-n-roll. Even the Vatican now champions American-style religious toleration.

But American Christianity has not been only a conservative force, fending off bad foreign ideas and keeping America true to its heritage of freedom. It has often championed reform, progressively realizing the latent imperatives of America's founding ideals.

Nobel laureate Robert Fogel has argued that American history has followed a pattern by which the evolution of religion leads the evolution of political reform, with four "Great Awakenings" in religion—in 1730-60, 1800-40, 1890-1930, and 1960 to around 1990—leading to four great eras of political reform: the American revolution, the anti-slavery movement and the Civil War, the creation of the welfare state, and the civil rights movement; and finally the tax revolt of the Reagan era and the 1996 welfare reform.

Fogel's periodization could be disputed; but the links he draws between religion and political reform are compelling. Churches enjoy no institutional representation in the American political system, nor do they typically instruct their members how to vote. Yet religion heavily influences voting behavior and other forms of political participation. Today, for example, one of the strongest predictors of voting Republican is church attendance.

In spite of the Republican bias of American Christians, and the anti-immigration bias of the Republican Party, I think there are signs that immigration (that is, *support* for immigration) is emerging as a distinctively Christian political issue. An immigration amnesty in 1986 was championed and signed by a born-again Christian president, Ronald Reagan. Another Christian president, George W. Bush, strove for and nearly succeeded in passing immigration reform in 2006 and 2007, with widespread support from churches.

The Catholic Cardinal Mahoney of Los Angeles compared a repressive anti-immigration law in Arizona to Nazism.[59] Richard Land, president of the generally conservative Southern Baptist Convention's Ethics and Religious Liberty Commission, has advocated comprehensive immigration reform.[60] Polls by Pew show that religious leaders and frequent churchgoers are significantly more pro-immigration than less frequent attenders.[61]

Ultimately, I think the Bible, the New Testament, the Parable of the Good Samaritan, and in particular one detail in the Parable of the Good Samaritan, will force Christians to turn against the world apartheid system of border controls. When the priest and the Levite see the wounded man on the road to Jericho, they do not just fail to help, they *pass by on the other side of the road*—that is, they deliberately create physical distance between themselves and the suffering man in order to avoid incurring the moral responsibility to help him.

But of course, this is exactly what migration restrictions do: they keep the world's poor at a distance, so that we will not feel conscience-stricken and have to help them. But of course it is perfectly clear in the parable that the priest and the Levite only make themselves the more culpable by trying to avoid moral responsibility; and so it is with rich countries that close their borders to poor immigrants. Christians cannot go on failing to see this indefinitely. Time for a Fifth Great Awakening?

The future of church and state

Church-state relations have been transformed several times during the Church's history, and there is no reason that it they cannot be transformed again, particularly as the spread of Christianity to new regions of the world will provide new sources of Christian thought.

In China, where Christians now probably number tens of millions, church-state relations resemble the ancient Roman Empire: Christianity is illegal, and some Christians are subjected to arrest and torture, yet Christianity continues to spread. In South Korea, about 30% of the population is now Christian. In sub-Saharan Africa the number of Christians increased from less than 10 million to more than 300 million in the course of the 20th century. In Africa, the

---

[59] http://articles.latimes.com/2010/apr/20/local/la-me-0420-mahony-immigration-20100420
[60] http://erlc.com/article/statement-by-richard-land-on-truly-comprehensive-immigration-reform/
[61] http://pewresearch.org/pubs/20/attitudes-toward-immigration-in-the-pulpit-and-the-pew

churches' role is more like that of the medieval Church: the church acts as an agent of charity and civilization amidst a subsistence economy, predominantly illiterate or ill-educated, prone to violence and disease.

During the pontificate of John Paul II, the Catholic Church served as an important agent of global democratization. How would church-state relations change if the conviction became widespread among Christians that to "love thy neighbor" meant not collaborating with the enemies who want to deport him?

Epilogue: Patriotism

Oh beautiful for patriot dream
That sees beyond the years
Thine alabaster cities gleam
Undimmed by human tears
   —Katherine Lee Bates, "America the Beautiful," 1913

"Let us be lovers, we'll marry our fortunes together."
"I've got some real estate here in my bag."
So we bought a pack of cigarettes,
And Mrs. Wagner's pies
And walked off to look for America.
   —Paul Simon, "America," 1968

I am grateful to a friend who, in a conversation a few years ago, opened my eyes to the difference between *patriotism and nationalism*. I had regarded the two words as more or less synonyms, only with different connotations. Since then I have come to see them, not only as different, but almost as opposites. I will not claim that the way the words are used in ordinary language corresponds very closely to how I describe these concepts below, but if my definitions are eccentric, I think they are useful in expressing different things with different names.

Nationalism is the prison-gang instinct writ large. I've got your back if you've got mine. A nationalist thinks he owns his nation, or a bit of it. He does not want outsiders to cut in, lest he get a smaller share of the pie. A nationalist asks what his country can do for him. Love and hate are instrumental to group solidarity, and hatred for others is a good substitute for love for one's own. If one loves the next nation as much as one's own, this is a threat. Because nationalism is self-seeking, a nationalist has no particular reason to be scrupulous about the means which his nation uses to achieve its ends.

Patriotism is *love* of one's country. From a patriot's point of view, his feelings of love reflect the fact that his country is *objectively* admirable, a truth which has nothing to do with the accidental circumstance that it happens to be *his* country. He feels it is an honor, even a surprise, that he is part of it, and fear that he will not deserve that honor drives him to try to be a better person. A patriot asks what he can do for his country, because he loves his country and wants to serve it. Patriotism has nothing to do with hating other countries, just as loving the mountains has nothing to do with hating the beach. There is no inconsistency between being an American patriot and an Anglophile or a Russophile.

I do not think it is possible to be a patriot and a nationalist at the same time, any more than it is possible to feel, at one and the same moment, the mean smugness of a bully, and the humble rapture of a person in love.

A patriot desires the good of his country, including its *moral* good, therefore he will desire for it to do right as much as he desires for it to prosper. He may defy the ruling regime in his country for patriotism's sake, if he thinks the ruling regime is leading his country to disgrace or failing to live up to the ideals to which his country is or ought to be committed. And here the two epigrams of this chapter express something important yet elusive.

In Katherine Lee Bates' well-known song, the patriot's "alabaster cities" is not a reality, a description of America as it is. It is a "dream." The patriot sees it afar off, "beyond the years." The patriot keeps this dream in view in spite of the "human tears"—the oppression, the injustice—that may stain the present. In Paul Simon's "America," two free-spirited wanderers set off on a spontaneous, rambling journey "to look for America." Of course we know from the place-names—Saginaw, Michigan; Pittsburgh; the New Jersey Turnpike—that they are already in America literally, yet they are not satisfied with what they see, and believe there must be more to it.

Perhaps they believe, vaguely, in the "alabaster cities" of the "patriot dream." At any rate, they seem not to find it, as the journey tapers off into a boredom of magazines and cigarettes and chit-chat about other passengers on the bus, but the song ends with the anguished epiphany that everyone is "looking for America":

> *Kathy, I'm lost, I said, though I knew she was sleeping*
> *I'm empty and aching and I don't know why*
> *Counting the cars on the New Jersey Turnpike*
> *They've all come to look for America.*

If we are all "looking for America," I want to relate a time when I *found* America. The date was May 1, 2006. There was an immigration protest that marched down 16th St. to Lafayette Park and then to the Washington Mall. It was at Lafayette Park that I joined them. I arrived a little before the marchers, and I saw them coming, in their thousands upon thousands. I remember the way the shadows of the tall buildings fell on that human river. There were people from dozens of nations—the "melting pot"—waving the American flag and wearing it on T-shirts, marching for "liberty and justice for all." There were no doubt native citizens and naturalized citizens and legal immigrants and illegal immigrants, but these difference of legal status were disdained for the moment in favor of what we had in common: we were *human beings*, united by the cause of *freedom*, and, like the Founding Fathers, defying a government to get it.

It was one of the most patriotic moments of my life, and indeed I cannot imagine how anyone can separate the idea of patriotism from the idea of feeling proud and glad that foreigners want to become Americans. And for that moment, the patriot dream, the shining city whose doors are open to everyone with the will and the heart to get here, seemed so close. If you have never felt that patriot dream, you are missing out on something. Join us!

Bibliography

Chesterton, G.K. (1908) *Orthodoxy*.

Coase, Ronald. (1960) "The Problem of Social Cost." *The Journal of Law and Economics*, Vol 3., pp. 1-44.

De Jasay, Anthony. (1996) *Before Resorting to Politics*. Edward Elgar Publishing Company.

Glover, Robert. (2009) "Eyes Wide Shut: The Curious Silence of the Law of Peoples on Immigration and Citizenship Paper presented at the annual meeting of the ISA's 50th ANNUAL CONVENTION "EXPLORING THE PAST, ANTICIPATING THE FUTURE", New York Marriott Marquis, NEW YORK CITY, NY, USA. http://www.allacademic.com/meta/p_mla_apa_research_citation/3/1/0/4/0/p310401_index.html

Habeas Corpus Act of 1679. http://en.wikisource.org/wiki/Habeas_Corpus_Act_of_1679.

Helpman, Elhanan. (1987). "Imperfect competition and international trade: evidence from fourteen countries." *Journal of the Japanese and International Economies Volume 1, Issue 1*, Pages 62-81.

Hobbes, Thomas. *Leviathan*. (1651). http://www.fullbooks.com/Leviathan.html

James, Harold. (2002) *The End of Globalization: Lessons from the Great Depression*. Harvard University Press.

Jefferson, Thomas, and US Congress. (1776) *The Declaration of Independence.*. http://www.earlyamerica.com/earlyamerica/freedom/doi/text.html

King, Martin Luther. (1963). "Letter from Birmingham Jail."http://abacus.bates.edu/admin/offices/dos/mlk/letter.html

King, Martin Luther. (1963) The "I Have a Dream" speech. http://www.usconstitution.net/dream.html

Krugman, Paul. (1979). "Increasing Returns, Monopolistic Competition, and International Trade." *Journal of International Economics.* *Volume 9, Issue 4,* Pages 469-479.

Landsburg, Steven. (1995) *The Armchair Economist.* Free Press.

Lewis, C.S. *Mere Christianity.* (1943). http://lib.ru/LEWISCL/mere_engl.txt

Locke, John. (1689) *Two Treatises of Government.*

Madison, James. *The Federalist #51.* (1788). http://www.constitution.org/fed/federa51.htm

Magna Carta, (1215). http://www.archives.gov/exhibits/featured_documents/magna_carta/translation.html

Mayflower Compact. (1620). http://www.pilgrimhall.org/compact.htm

Plato. *Crito.* (4th century B.C). http://classics.mit.edu/Plato/crito.html

Plato. *The Apology.* (4th century B.C.) http://evans-experientialism.freewebspace.com/plato_apology.htm

Poe, Edgar Allen. "The Cask of Amontillado." (1846). http://poestories.com/read/amontillado

Rowley, Charles K, Thorbecke, Willem and Wagner, Richard E. (1995). *Trade Protection in the United States.* Edward Elgar Publishing.

Rowley, Charles and Nathanael Smith. (2009). "Islam's democracy paradox: Muslims claim to like democracy, so why do they have so little?" *Public Choice,* Vol. 139, Issue 3, pp. 273-299.

Rowley, Charles and Smith, Nathanael (2009). *Economic Contractions in the United States: A Failure of Government.* The Locke Institute in association with the Institute of Economic Affairs.

Smith, Adam. *An Inquiry into the Nature and Causes of the Wealth of Nations.* (1776). http://www.econlib.org/library/Smith/smWN.html

Smith, Steven D. (1998). *The Constitution and the Pride of Reason.* Oxford University Press.

Spencer, Metta. (1998). *Separatism: Democracy and Disintegration.* Maryland.

Stark, Rodney. (2005). *The Victory of Reason.* New York.

Start, Rodney and Roger Finke. (2005). *The Churching of America, 1776-2007: Winners and Losers in Our Religious Economy.* Rutgers University Press.

The Holy Bible.

Thoreau, Henry David. (1849). "Civil Disobedience.".http://thoreau.eserver. org/civil.html

Tierney, Brian. (1997). *The Idea of Natural Rights: Studies on Natural Rights, Natural Law, and Church Law 1150 - 1625* (Emory University Studies in Law and Religion).

US Constitution. http://www.usconstitution.net/const.html

About The Locke Institute

John Locke
(1632-1704)

Officers of The Locke Institute

Founded in 1989, The Locke Institute is an independent, non-partisan, educational and research organization. The Institute is named for John Locke (1632 – 1704), philosopher and political theorist, who based his theory of society on natural law, which required that the ultimate source of political sovereignty was with the individual. Individuals are possessed of inalienable rights, variously described by Locke as "life, health, liberty and possession", or more directly, as "life, liberty and property". It is the function of the state to uphold these rights since individuals would not enter into a political society unless they trusted that the state would protect these very rights that they already hold in the state of nature.

The Locke Institute seeks to engender a greater understanding of the concept of natural rights, its implications for constitutional democracy and for economic organization in modern society. The Institute encourages high-quality research utilizing, in particular, modern theories of property rights, public choice, law-and-economics and the new institutional economics, as a basis for a more profound understanding of important and controversial issues in political economy. To this end, it commissions books, monographs and shorter studies involving substantive scholarship written for a wide audience, organizes major conferences on fundamental topics of political economy, and supports independent research. The Institute maintains a publishing relationship with Edward Elgar Publishing. It also publishes its own monograph series.

In order to maintain its independence, The Locke Institute accepts no government funding. Funding for the Institute is solicited from private foundations, corporations and individuals. In addition, the Institute raises funds from the sale of publications. The Institute is incorporated in the Commonwealth of Virginia, USA, and enjoys non-profit, tax exempt status under Section 501(c)3 of the United States Internal Revenue Code.

Academic Advisory Council of The Locke Institute

Richard A. Epstein (President)
Professor of Law, University of Chicago

Armen Alchian
Emeritus Professor of Economics, University of California at Los Angeles

Michael A. Crew
Professor of Economics, Rutgers University

Antony de Jasay
Janville, Paluel, France

Harold Demsetz
Emeritus Professor of Economics, University of Los Angeles

William M. Landes
Professor of Economics, University of Chicago

Henry G. Manne
Emeritus Dean of the Law School, George Mason University

Professor Sir Alan Peacock
The David Hume Institute, Edinburgh, Scotland

Judge Richard A. Posner
U. S. Court of Appeals for the Seventh Circuit
Senior Lecturer in Law and Economics, University of Chicago

Robert D. Tollison
Professor of Economics, Clemson University

Gordon Tullock
Emeritus Distinguished Professor of Law and Economics, George Mason University

Officers of the Institute are listed above. Please direct all enquiries to the address listed below:

The Locke Institute
5188 Dungannon Road
Fairfax, Virginia 22030
USA
Tel: (703) 934-6934
Fax: (703) 934-6927
Email: crowley@gmu.edu
http://www.thelockeinstitute.org